Jesus:
Life and Times

A clash of kingdoms... and the triumph of mercy

Steve Maltz

malcolm down
PUBLISHING

Acknowledgements

Without my faithful crowdfunders, this book would never have happened, so bless you all! Also thanks to my editors and proofreaders, particularly David Serle, Christine Carlebach and Jackie Stratton, for all the work you put into a very complicated manuscript. Thank you, David Shepherd, for your persistent prodding and prompting when I was running out of steam and also for the huge amount of time you spent on the manuscript. I am also delighted to have Malcolm Down on the team, renewing an acquaintance that started about eighteen years ago, when he was one of the first to take a chance on me. Finally, posthumous thanks to Alfred Edersheim, who provided the heart, soul and the raw material for this undertaking.

Contents

Author's note

Because this book is a retelling of Alfred Edersheim's book, there will be places where I extensively quote from the original. These blocks of text will always be indented and, because they are reproduced exactly as seen, will not always follow modern grammatical conventions!

Where I have a phrase in 'quotation marks' this will be text lifted straight from Edersheim's book.

If further explanation is needed regarding text from Edersheim's book, a footnote is sometimes provided. Otherwise, if you wish to research further, I recommend you purchase or download Edersheim's original book for further analysis.

Any Bible quotes reproduced from Edersheim's book will be from the KJV.

Occasionally Edersheim refers to the Talmud without giving a reference, so it has not always been possible for me to give an exact reference.

My remit is to provide an accurate summarised modern-day version of a nineteenth-century book, although modern commentators may question some of his facts or assumptions. Please bear this in mind.

The text version used in this book is the one at:
http://www.ntslibrary.com/PDF%20Books/The%20Life%20and%20Times%20of%20Jesus%20the%20Messiah.pdf

Prologue

There is a pair of old tomes gathering dust in my study. I bought them in my early days as a new believer, intending to read them cover to cover and then to subsequently impress my Christian friends with the depth of my knowledge of *The Life and Times of Jesus the Messiah*. Yes, that was also the title of those books, volume one and volume two, written by Alfred Edersheim (1825-89), a Jewish believer, around 140 years ago. A must-read for those eager to really get inside the story of the Gospels but, clearly, an impossible read for most of us. Why would that be?

Have you seen the size of these books? Around half a million words, ignoring footnotes and extensive appendices! A dense read, suffused with a nineteenth-century vocabulary, packed with obscure references and paragraph-long sentences, drowning in commas. Frankly unsuitable for most of us modern Christians, more used to Twitter feeds and bite-sized content! Spoon-fed disciples, faced by a hulky trowel and screaming for someone to sift and sieve.

I am that person, I hope. Well, at least I am going to give it a good go! Having written around thirty Christian books over twenty years, my motivation is totally selfish. *I write to understand*. My books have covered topics from the Church to the Bible, Israel, evangelism, apologetics, science, politics, language, philosophy, history… without being an expert or an authority on any of these subjects. My books have educated many, all over the world, but the first person to benefit has always been… me! I have learned to interpret the research of others, particularly theologians and academics, and make them accessible to the average person such as you and me. This has worked well for me in the past, so I have embraced this new challenge – and boy, has it blessed me!

First: Here is some background to this project, taken from *A Brief Biography of Alfred Edersheim* by Eugene J. Mayhew:[1]

---

1. Eugene J. Mayhew, *Michigan Theological Journal*, 1992,3, pp. 168-199.

A Jewish convert to true biblical Christianity. He now stands as one of the foremost Hebrew Christian scholars in the history of the Church ... Millions of Bible teachers, pastors and students have benefited from Edersheim's awesome accomplishments in biblical research. Mentioning his name is often associated with depth and trustworthiness in biblical backgrounds and the study of the life of Jesus Christ. A first-class scholar who was a lecturer at Oxford University. He also spent many years as a pastor of congregations in Scotland and England and served in Jewish evangelism in Romania. Even more than a century since his books were first published, many of them are still reprinted on a regular basis and regarded as standard sources by Bible scholars and theologians. Simply speaking, Alfred Edersheim has become a well-established 'household' name in the world of biblical studies. His magnum opus, The Life and Times of Jesus the Messiah published in 1882, is still unparalleled and unsurpassed and stands as the finest work on the subject after 110 years!

The 1,700-page *The Life and Times of Jesus the Messiah* by Alfred Edersheim[2] is an absolute masterpiece. It is so fascinating in terms of insights, and some of his prose sucks you right in, with evocative descriptions and surprising expressions of the joy of his discoveries. You have always had to dig for these hidden gems, but I have done this for you. In downsizing the book by 80 per cent, I have had to be careful to include the central gospel narrative and filter out the peripheral content which, although having an immense value in its own right, could possibly detract us from our journey. Of course, with 80 per cent of content jettisoned, there is going to be some good stuff left out, but that's not necessarily a bad thing as every chapter includes links to the relevant page in Edersheim's original book. So, you are free to do your own deeper studies, made more

---

2. Originally published in New York by Herrick, 1886.

convenient by easy accessibility to a free online version of the book.[3]

The book is basically a harmony of the Gospels, a (mostly) chronological account from the Nativity stories to the resurrection and its aftermath. It draws from the Jewish background of those first-century times, a subject in which Edersheim was a world authority. To keep the book down to a manageable size, all Bible verses are in reference form, for you to read using your favourite translation. For the most rewarding read, I suggest you look up the verses first before reading the content of the chapter.

I pray that this reimagining of a classic book will bless your reading of it, as it did my writing of it. I hope that your understanding of the Life and Times of Jesus our Messiah will be greatly enriched and that your love for him will reach new heights, as has mine.

Praise God.

---

3. http://www.ntslibrary.com/PDF%20Books/The%20Life%20and%20Times%20of%20 Jesus%20the%20Messiah.pdf (accessed 16.2.22).

Chapter 1: The Lie of the Land

(Book 1: Chapters 1-8)

We begin with what was once believed (perhaps rightly so) to be the centre of the universe, Jerusalem. To the Jews in our story, it was where God could be found, in the only really acceptable place, the Temple. Here, in the innermost sanctuary, which the high priest alone might enter once a year, had stood the ark. Also, from the golden altar rose the cloud of incense, a symbol of Israel's accepted prayers. A seven-branched lampstand shed the perpetual light of the brightness of God's covenant presence. The Bread of the Face (shewbread) was laid on the table week by week, a constant sacrificial meal that Israel offered to God. On the great blood-sprinkled altar of sacrifice smoked the daily and festive burnt offerings. The vast courts of the Temple were thronged with Jews out of every nation under heaven.

The Jews may have been scattered, whether the Greek-leaning Jews in the West or the staunchly Hebrew Jews in the East, and they may have differed in language and thought patterns, but their heartbeats were 'forever Jerusalem'. The Pharisees were of the latter group, close to home and traditionalists to their core. Then there were those who had settled in Babylonia, yet still considered themselves part of Israel. Here were the richest Jews of all, with a synagogue built by King Jeconiah, using stones from the actual Temple. When Jews had returned from Babylon under Ezra and Zerubbabel, most stayed behind, particularly the wealthy ones. They were quite happy to remain in such comfortable exile! They became people of influence, eventually becoming a real thorn in the side of the Roman invaders. They considered themselves the purest of Jews and contributed greatly through tithes despatched westwards to the Jerusalem Temple priesthood. They gradually stopped speaking Hebrew, preferring the Aramaic language, which was used in their holy writings, the Targumim, paraphrases of Hebrew Scripture.

Out of this culture were birthed a great body of Jewish writings, the Mishnah ('the Second Law') and the Midrash ('the investigation'). A Jewish theology evolved into two major divisions, the Halakhah and the Haggadah, concepts that still sit at the very core of Judaism and, if it only knew it, Christianity too. Halakhah ('to go') provided the rules for godly living and practical instructions, whereas Haggadah ('to tell') provided the utterances from the teachers. These teachings formed the core of the 'traditions of the elders' that were to hold them in an iron grip. At the time of Jesus, the key proponent of Haggadah was Eleazar the Mede, a leader among the great centres of study that had sprung up all over Babylon. Halakhah gave us the principles behind the practical teachings of the Torah and the chief proponent at the time of Jesus was Hillel. More of him later.

In the West, it was a different story. The East represented the future of Judaism; the West, in the hands of the Hellenists (Greeks), represented the future of the rest of humankind. Jews here tended to turn their back on religious practices and veer towards secular professions. Greek thinking, with the stress on intellectual pursuits and bodily pleasures, began to hold sway, rather than the study of the Law, both written and oral. Synagogue rather than Temple became their focus and yet, although not quite as 'religious' as those in the East, they were proud enough of their heritage to consider themselves a beacon among the heathens who surrounded them. A glimmer of light is better than no light at all!

But Hellenism provided real dangers for those who treasured the Hebrew Scriptures. It introduced new ways of examining those divine certainties, by introducing an 'intellectual' and 'philosophical' element. This encouraged digging into the text, guided by the intellect and gleaning depths that, in reality, were only shallows. Such was the grip that Greek philosophy had on the minds of those who allowed it. This was frowned upon by traditionalists. When a young rabbi asked his uncle whether he should study Hellenistic thought, since he believed he has already mastered the Torah, the reply – inspired by Joshua 1:8 – was, 'go and search what is the hour which is neither of the day nor the night and in that hour you may study Greek philosophy'.[4]

To ensure that Hellenism didn't completely steal the hearts and souls of these Jews in the West, the Old Testament was translated into Greek, to keep the fires of faith from flickering out. This was the *Septuagint* (LXX). This was the 'Bible' known by Jesus and the apostles. It was far from perfect, though distinct Jewish elements were incorporated. Yet there were also Grecian elements, with allusions to Greek mythology and philosophic ideas.

The centre in the West was Alexandria, a city larger than Rome, with a thriving Jewish population and a huge synagogue, built in the shape of a basilica. Outside the city, in Leontopolis, there was even a temple built, with its own priesthood, though it was never seriously considered as a rival to the Jerusalem Temple and was held in great contempt by the Jews in the East. The spiritual leader of the Western Hellenists in Alexandria was Philo, someone held in great esteem many decades later by some of the Church Fathers, though someone in thrall to Greek philosophy, particularly the works of Plato. He was particularly fond of allegory, where multiple meanings can be attributed to passages of Scripture, which can give rise to dangerous and inaccurate speculation.

His brother, Alexander, was one of the richest Jews there, lending money to kings and nobles and even contributing to the gold and silver that covered the gates of the Jerusalem Temple. This wealth did not go unnoticed by the Egyptians, who were very scathing in their opinion of these Jews. Philo himself said, 'Well might the Jews wish no better for themselves than to be treated like other men!' Superstitions abounded, including the fact that Jews worshipped the head of an ass and were carriers of leprosy. Sabbath times became precarious for the Jewish population, considered just an outlet for idleness. They were truly viewed as strangers in a strange land.

---

4. Talmud, Menachot 99b.

Jews were also living in Rome at that time, working as merchants, bankers, even actors. They were originally given some 'poor quarters' of the city to live in but soon spread, with synagogues springing up over every quarter of the city. They grew in influence and were tolerated, left alone on the Sabbath and even exempted from military service. In general, Jews all over the Roman Empire enjoyed religious liberty, even Roman citizenship. The Jerusalem Temple was held in high respect, with many gifts bestowed on it from Gentiles all over the empire, many of them displayed on the magnificent porch. The very existence of the Court of the Gentiles in the Temple acknowledged a certain degree of privilege to non-Jews, even though there were huge marble tablets there warning Gentiles not to proceed further!

Antioch, the capital of Syria, was said to be a great favourite of the Jews, with a large population of them there. Although there was a great connection between Antioch and Jerusalem, the mindset there was Hellenistic; on one occasion a great rabbi was even unable to procure a single copy of the book of Esther in Hebrew! But, unlike other places in the West, there was growing negativity towards the Jews, with resentfulness over Jewish isolationism, perceived superiority and growing wealth and influence.

There was one thing that united all of these communities, whether in the East or the West: *their love for Jerusalem.* Every Jew faced Jerusalem in their prayers and in the synagogues, all of which sent their Temple tributes annually. Many endeavoured to travel there at the time of the three great pilgrim feasts, despite the costs and inconvenience. Every day devout Jews prayed this: 'Proclaim by Your loud trumpet our deliverance and raise up a banner to gather our dispersed and gather us together from the four ends of the earth. Blessed be You, O Lord! who gathers the outcasts of Your people Israel.' They all yearned to return to their holy city. It was the epitome of holiness in a land considered the holiest place of all. In fact, there was said to be a gradation of sanctity, ten degrees of holiness, from the bare soil of the Holy Land to the Most Holy Place in the Temple.

In the preparation of great drama, the greatest in human history, it is well to set the scene with the cast of actors who will inhabit our dramatic canvas. Hugely influential is the scribe (*sopher*). He seems to be the mouthpiece of the people, always pushing to the front of the action, always deferred to, on account of his learning. He is filled with the water of knowledge, the divine aristocrat, the teacher of the Law. He may stand alongside the Pharisees, the religious caste of traditionalists, but he is not necessarily one of them. Instead, he holds an office as the sage or the learned student. It was said that they should always be absolutely believed, even if they declared that left is right and right is left! They owed their origins to Ezra, the great biblical giant, who created this learned dynasty through the formation of the Great Assembly (the Great Synagogue), which guided the religious progress of the Jews from that time on.

By now the Great Assembly was no more, the 'ecclesiastical' role had now passed to the elders. Alongside them were the two religious parties, the Pharisees and the Sadducees, working within the religious court, the Sanhedrin. The lifeblood of this institution was the 'traditions of the elders', the Halakhah mentioned earlier, the rules for living. Some of them were originally based on Holy Scripture or derived from it according to interpretations of the teachers. Sometimes God's Word was 'lost in translation'.

Halakhah was said to have originated with Noah' son Shem, passed on to Abraham and the other patriarchs. But, of course, this was just legend and therefore unprovable and irrelevant. A further legend has these traditions being given to Moses on Mount Sinai, as *the oral Torah*. This legend is far more persistent and is a central thread of the Talmud, the huge collection of legends and writings preserved over the centuries. The thinking was that Moses intended to have all the Torah written down, but that God refused on account of the future subjection of Israel to the nations, who would take all of the Law from them as their own! This way

Israel would always have something that they could call their own, to differentiate them from the others... *the oral Torah!* The sad thing is that Israel has often placed this oral Torah on a higher plain than God's Holy Scripture, *the written Torah.*

This oral Torah in actual fact drew from the traditions of the elders and the sayings of the scribes or the teachings of the rabbis, all man-made commentary on what was truly divine, the written Torah. These eventually were written down, after the time of Jesus, in the *Mishnah*, which itself became incorporated into the Talmud. To be honest, this huge collection is not so much a systematic theology as a hotchpot of ideas, fancies, truth mixed with superstition, incongruities, embellishments of biblical stories and the lives of rabbis, who are afforded almost God-like status in places.

It must be made clear, as we are about to embark on our wonderful foray into the Gospels, that there is a *total divergence between the Talmud of Rabbinic Judaism and the New Testament of Christianity.* It is the latter that we truly follow, as our story begins...

Chapter 2: Set-up

(Book 2: Chapters 1-2)

The scene is set. Jerusalem is ruled by a despotic Jewish king (Herod), is richly adorned with palaces and monuments and is often crowded with visitors from other lands. It is a city built on four hills, connected by the immense bridge that spans the Valley of the Cheesemongers. There is a deep cleft to the east, between the Mount of Olives and the magnificent Temple, wondrously beautiful and enlarged and rising terrace upon terrace, surrounded by massive walls, a palace, a fortress, a sanctuary of shining marble and glittering gold. There is the 'lower city', the business quarter with its markets and bazaars and the 'upper city', with its palaces. Two worlds in one city.

The Temple was in its forty-sixth year of construction and workmen were still on-site at this time, mixing with a vast cosmopolitan and seething crowd of far-flung Hellenists, country cousins from Galilee with their coarse speech, sophisticated Jerusalemites, white-robed priests and Levites, Temple officials, austere Pharisees with their *talliths* (prayer shawls) and *tefillin* (phylacteries), ironical Sadducees, white-dressed Essenes, the proud 'teachers of the Law' and the quick-witted scribes and, tucked away in the outer court, confused and bemused Gentiles. Some visitors had come to pay vows or bring offerings, others to seek purification, still others to meet friends, or ask questions of the smaller Sanhedrin that met by the gate or the larger one that met in a chamber belonging to the high-priestly family of Annas. In the Court of the Gentiles were the moneychangers changing foreign coins to currency acceptable here, to those selling animals for sacrifice and the noisy beggars, often riddled with disease.

The population has been estimated as close to a quarter of a million, swelled enormously during festival times. Thousands of priests were attached to the Temple, all carrying out their duties according to their schedules. The poorer students and scholars filled the academies of learning and the synagogues numbered in their hundreds, along with even more numerous Jewish schools and Rabbinic *yeshivas*.[5] Edersheim was at his most eloquent in describing the big picture:

> One could have imagined himself almost in another world, a sort of enchanted land, in this Jewish metropolis, and metropolis of Judaism. When the silver trumpets of the Priests woke the city to prayer, or the strain of Levite music swept over it, or the smoke of the sacrifices hung like another Shekhinah[6] over the Temple, against the green background of Olivet; or when in every street, court, and housetop rose the booths at the Feast of Tabernacles, and at night the sheen of the Temple illumination threw long fantastic shadows over the city; or when, at the Passover, tens of thousands crowded up the Mount with their Paschal lambs, and hundreds of thousands sat down to the Paschal supper – it would be almost difficult to believe, that heathenism was so near, that the Roman was virtually, and would soon be really, master of the land, or that a Herod occupied the Jewish throne.

Herod. This recklessly cruel, ever watching tyrant. Now, here was a real stumbling block. This was a travesty, two and a half centuries in the making, beginning in a bad place, with the purchasing of the priesthood by a renegade Jew who took the Greek name 'Jason' and then proceeded to Hellenise the people. This led to the persecutions of Antiochus Epiphanes and the Maccabean uprising, still celebrated annually at Chanukah time, commemorating the rededication of the Temple.

The descendants of the heroic Maccabees were not so heroic. They became both high priests and kings but party strife and worldliness,

---

5. A Jewish educational institution where traditional religious texts are studied together.

6. Shekhinah means the glory of the Lord.

ambition and corruption led to the decay and decadence of the Maccabean house. The country became subject to Rome, through the Governor of Syria. Just before this, a district of Idumaea had been conquered by the Maccabean King Hyrcanus I and its inhabitants had been forced to adopt Judaism. Eventually, one of the sons of this kingdom was to ascend the throne of Israel, Herod the Great. There followed much political manoeuvring in a timeline shared with Anthony and Cleopatra, but also much military carnage, with the slaughtering of families of his rivals and the appointing of an obscure Babylonian to the high priesthood, with a rival drowned in his bath at Herod's command. His own family weren't protected from his madness. He denounced his own sons to the Roman emperor, and they were subsequently strangled in prison, with 300 of their supporters massacred. Five days before the end of his life he also managed to procure the execution of rival, Herod Antipas, his last violent act.

So ended a reign almost unparalleled for reckless cruelty and bloodshed. His people detested him, what with his dubious origins and his deeds of cruelty. He had surrounded himself with foreign councillors and was protected by foreign mercenaries. As long as he lived, no woman's honour was safe and no man's life secure. An army of all-powerful spies spread through Jerusalem and torture would extract any confession from the most innocent. Yet he was true to his Judaism. He built the Temple, ensuring that the sanctuary itself was entrusted to the workmanship of priests only. He never intruded into the Holy Place, neither did he interfere with any functions of the priesthood. He even seemed to have had some support from some rabbis, who felt that he had some sway with the feared Roman rulers.

It was also under his rule that Hillel and Shammai lived and taught in Jerusalem. These two, whom tradition designates as 'the fathers of old', both gave their names to 'schools' whose direction was very different.

Hillel was a fascinating figure. He was the mild and earnest student who came from Babylon to learn in the Academies of Jerusalem, supporting his family on a third of his scanty wages as a day labourer, that he might pay for entrance into the schools. Some saw him as the second Ezra, whose learning placed him at the head of the Sanhedrin and who laid down the principles of Rabbinism and who was the real founder of traditionalism. Some also falsely represent him as one whose principles closely resemble the teaching of Jesus. Instead, we remember that in his extreme old age and near his end he may have presided over that meeting of Sanhedrin which, in answer to Herod's enquiry, pointed to Bethlehem as the birthplace of the Messiah. We think of him also as the grandfather of that Gamaliel at whose feet Saul of Tarsus sat.

And so there were two worlds in Jerusalem, side by side. On the one hand, was Hellenism with its theatre and amphitheatre, foreigners filling the court and crowding the city. On the other hand was the old Jewish world, represented by the schools of Hillel and Shammai and overshadowed by Temple and synagogue. And each was pursuing its course, by the side of the other. If Greek was the language of the court – and indeed must have been understood and spoken by most in the land – the language of the people, spoken also by Christ and his apostles, was a dialect of the ancient Hebrew, Aramaic. As the language of the Temple and the synagogue was Hebrew, the sermons of the rabbis had to be crafted into the common language, to be understood by all.

It was a peculiar mixture of two worlds in Jerusalem; not only of the Grecian and the Jewish but of piety and frivolity also. The devotion of the people and the liberality of the rich were unbounded. Fortunes were lavished on the support of Jewish learning, the promotion of piety, or the advance of the national cause. Thousands of payments for offerings and the costly gifts in the Temple bore evidence of this. These Jerusalemites were so polished, so witty, so pleasant in the way they dealt with each other. Their very language was different. There was a Jerusalem dialect, quicker, shorter, 'lighter' and their hospitality, especially at festive seasons, was boundless. No one considered their house their own, and no stranger or pilgrim was neglected.

And thus was this City of God, over which destruction had been prophesied by prophets of old. Also would be the hour of Jerusalem's uprising, when it would welcome its Messiah. Oh, when would he come? In the feverish excitement of expectancy, they were only too ready to listen to the voice of any pretender, however coarse and clumsy. Yet he was at hand – even now coming, only quite other than the Messiah of their dreams.

> He came to that which was his own, but his own did not receive him. Yet to all who did receive him, to those who believed in his name, he gave the right to become children of God ...
> (John 1:11-12)

The scene was well and truly set.

Chapter 3: First Contact

(Book 2: Chapter 3)

Just imagine this. You are one of fifty priests (out of a pool of around 20,000) on duty that day at the Temple. The first lot was drawn. This was for inspection duties of the courts by torchlight in the early hours. Then the next lot covered the lighting of a fresh flame in the dying embers of the altar. Then there were those privileged ones selected to take part in the daily sacrifice ceremony, to trim the golden lampstand and make ready the altar of incense within the Holy Place. Then to bring out the spotless lamb, to water it from a golden bowl and then to lay it on the north side of the altar, with its face to the west. Then, a priest, standing on the east side of the altar, with the solemn duty of sprinkling sacrificial blood from a golden bowl.

You have still not been chosen. Another lot, for the offering of the incense, symbolising Israel's accepted prayers. This was the highest duty. Who will be chosen for this highest act? It was a once-in-a-lifetime honour. All eyes suddenly fell on you, a man well into your sixties. Your name is Zacharias (Zechariah).

You are well known, twice-blessed, in fact, being both a priest and married to a daughter of a priest. You lived in the hill country just south of Jerusalem, rather than in the priest centres in Jerusalem and Jericho. Your selection for this task is to bring great honour to your family and, as a man known for his righteousness, this is well-deserved. Yet there is a sorrow about you and your wife, Elizabeth. You are childless and her child-bearing days are surely behind her; the flower of hope has closed its fragrant cup.

But all is briefly forgotten as you think of the task in hand. You now need to choose two special friends or relatives to assist you: one to clear up the detritus from the day before, the other to spread out the live coals on the golden altar. The ceremony now begins and beautiful music summons the priests, Levites and the people.

You wait for the right moment as you stand alone within the Holy Place, bearing the golden censer. It arrives, it is time to act, to spread the incense on the altar, as near as possible to the Holy of Holies. Everyone else has withdrawn and are lying prostrate in silence. All eyes are on the fragrant cloud of praise and prayer that rises up as the incense kindles. You stoop down in reverence... but are stopped in your tracks.

On the south side of the altar stands the angel Gabriel. This is unprecedented; this has never happened before, especially to such a lowly priest as yourself. You are troubled and fearful: *could anything good come out of this*? Your hesitancy manifests in your doubt-laden response to Gabriel's message of impending fatherhood. You wish you had bitten your tongue, but Gabriel does it for you by striking you dumb! There is going to come a much-prayed-for child, Jochanan (John), meaning 'the Lord is gracious'. The child will be great before the Lord, a Nazarite, as Samson and Samuel of old had been. He will wholly belong to God, and for this lifelong work he would be filled with the Holy Spirit, from the moment life woke within him.

You had asked for a sign and, ironically, received the sign of dumbness: both a sign and, because of your faltering faith, a punishment! But it is a sign to Elizabeth and your waiting family, a sign that would last the full term of the pregnancy to come. You stand at the top of the steps by the Court of the Priests to lead in the priestly benediction, as was customary. Of course, you are silent and your sign becomes a sign for all of the people. They know that something significant has just happened not just for you but... *for all of Israel*!

When the words of the angel were known by all, the truly significant aspect was the coming of Elijah as the forerunner of the Messiah. According to Jewish tradition, he was to appear personally and not merely in spirit and power. Yet nowhere was it written that he was 'to make ready a people prepared for the Lord'. This was new.

MATTHEW 1:18-25; LUKE 1:26-80

(Book 2: Chapter 4-5)

The focus now moves from this insignificant priest to a humble, unassuming family in Galilee; simple 'country folk', with their awkward speech. If the rabbis had been writing the script for what was about to come, the cast of characters would be very different and far more important! As it stood, the Messianic announcements came to a simple virgin girl from Nazareth and from the womb and mouth of Elizabeth, her relative, rather than the result of a learned investigation by priests or rabbis. The world is being turned upside down; nothing is going to go according to acceptable plans and procedures. It is all going to be entirely new and strange. Edersheim describes it thus:

> The design of the Gospels was manifestly not to furnish a biography of Jesus the Messiah, but, in organic connection with the Old Testament, to tell the history of the long-promised establishment of the Kingdom of God upon the earth.

The drama switches to Nazareth in Galilee. This region was far from poor. It was cultivated to the utmost and thickly covered with populous towns and villages, the centre of every known industry and the busy road of the world's commerce. We must not think of Nazareth as a lonely village. The great caravan route which led from Acco by the sea to Damascus divided as it split into three roads. One of them, the ancient *Via Maris* led through Nazareth. Men of all nations would appear in its streets bringing strange thoughts, associations and hopes connected with the great outside world. But, on the other hand, Nazareth was also one of the great centres of Jewish Temple life, housing priests when not on duty in Jerusalem.

Judaism, as practised in Galilee, had a greater simplicity and freedom than the tradition-strangled areas in the south. Home life would be all the purer and weddings were simpler than in Judea. Money was less of an issue and widows were better looked after, being allowed to stay in their husband's house.

At the time of their betrothal, although both were of the royal lineage of King David, Joseph and Mary were extremely poor. We notice this not because of his profession as a carpenter, but from the offering at the presentation of Jesus in the Temple. Accordingly, their betrothal must have been of the simplest and the dowry settled as the smallest possible. From that moment Mary was the betrothed wife of Joseph; their relationship was as sacred as if they had already been wedded. Any breach of it would be treated as adultery, neither could the marriage be dissolved except by regular divorce. Yet months might intervene between the betrothal and marriage.

Five months of Elizabeth's confinement had passed, when a strange messenger brought first tidings to Mary, her kinswoman, in far-off Galilee. It was not in the solemn grandeur of the Temple, between the golden altar of incense and the seven-branched lampstand that the angel Gabriel now appeared, but in the privacy of a humble home at Nazareth. The greatest honour bestowed on man was to come amid circumstances of deepest human lowliness. *How typical of our heavenly Father!*

Teenage virgin Mary seemed to have dealt with the angelic visitation far better than her priestly relative. She was 'highly favoured' and her natural humility chimed well with the message. As with Zacharias, she was told the name to give to the child, a name – Yeshua (salvation) – that was going to define his ministry and purpose. Her response was not of trembling doubt, asking for a 'sign', but rather to enquire for further guidance. The angel then explained how she would be favoured, how the Holy Spirit will make his home with her.

Mary had a bit of explaining to do on returning home after her three-month visit with Elizabeth. What conversations these women must have had together! How different it would be trying to convey these events to Joseph on her return! For, however deep his trust in his sweetheart, only a direct divine communication could have chased all questioning from his heart and given him that assurance which was needed in the grand scheme of things. His mind would have been in turmoil. Divorce? *But we haven't even consummated the marriage yet!* He would have had to give her a letter of divorce in the presence of two witnesses. *What a mess!* He needed assurance and it arrived… in a dream.

The fact that such an announcement came to him in a dream was a good thing. 'A good dream' was one of the three things popularly regarded as marks of God's favour, and so general was the belief in their significance that there was a popular saying: 'If anyone sleeps seven days without dreaming, call him wicked.' Thus, divinely set at rest, Joseph could no longer hesitate. He was now on the team.

History was being played out and the script had already been written. The promise of a virgin-born son as a sign of the firmness of God's covenant of old with David and his house;[7] the now unfolded meaning of the former symbolic name Immanuel (God with us); even the unbelief of Ahaz[8] (in not listening to God's promises), with its counterpart in the questioning of Joseph.

We end this chapter with the same man who opened it, Zacharias, with his song at the birth of his son, John. It was unbelief that had struck him dumb and the answer of faith restored speech to him. The first evidence of his dumbness had been that his tongue refused to speak the benediction to the people and the first evidence of his restored power was that he spoke the benediction of God in a rapturous burst of praise and thanksgiving.

The sign of the unbelieving priest standing before the awestruck people, vainly trying to make himself understood by signs, was most fitting. Most fitting also that, when 'they made signs' to him, the believing father should burst in their hearing into a prophetic hymn. But far and wide, as the news spread throughout the hill-country of Judea, fear fell on all, the fear also of a nameless hope. The silence of a long-clouded day had been broken and the light, which had suddenly flickered into life, laid itself on their hearts in expectancy. '"What then is this child going to be?" For the Lord's hand was with him.'

---

7. Isaiah 7:14.
8. Isaiah 7:11-12.

Chapter 4: Birth and Aftermath

MATTHEW 1:25; LUKE 2:1-20
(Book 2: Chapter 6)

Both the Old Testament and Rabbinic teaching pointed to Bethlehem as the birthplace of the Messiah. Yet nothing could have been less expected; a counting of the people, a census taken at the bidding of a pagan emperor and executed by the hated Herod. If the whole story was a fabrication, surely they would have come up with something more heroic and triumphant!

If the census had been performed in the 'Roman' manner, there would have been no cross-country trek on a donkey; they would have simply been registered in the place of their birth, which would have been Nazareth. But Herod had insisted on the 'Jewish' manner, where registration was needed at the place of their tribal lineage. For both Joseph and Mary, this would have been to the city of David, their common ancestor, Bethlehem.

The way had been long and weary, at least three days' journey, whatever route had been taken from Galilee. Most likely it would be the usual route that avoided the area of the hated Samaritans, along the eastern banks of the Jordan and by the fords of Jericho. A sense of rest and peace must have crept over the travellers when at last they reached the rich fields that surrounded the ancient 'House of Bread' (Bethlehem), at the foot of the great castle which Herod had built for himself.

The little town of Bethlehem was crowded with those who had come from all the outlying districts to register their names. Every house would have been fully occupied. The inn was filled up and the only available space was where ordinarily the cattle were stabled. Being poor, this would not have been as great an imposition to Joseph and Mary as we imagine it to be. At least there would have been seclusion and privacy from the noisy, chattering crowds. The whole scenario is one of humility and is a most fitting starting place for the unfolding divine narrative. Again, if the story had been fabricated, it does not fit in with Jewish expectations at that time, that would have had him born in a palace, in royal splendour!

A passage in the Mishnah leads to the conclusion that the flocks which pastured there were destined for Temple sacrifices and, accordingly, that the shepherds, who watched over them, were not ordinary shepherds, but of a more edgy nature. They needed to be of strong stuff for what they witnessed that night: heaven and earth seemed to mingle, as suddenly an angel stood before their dazzled eyes, while the outpouring glory of the Lord seemed to enwrap them, as in a mantle of light.

The angelic message was that the long-promised Saviour, Messiah, Lord, was born in the City of David and that they might go and see and recognise him by the humbleness of the circumstances surrounding his Nativity. But first, the heavenly host sang as they had only once before to Isaiah when heaven's high Temple had opened and the glory of God swept its courts, almost breaking down the trembling posts that bore its boundary gates.[9] The same glory heralded the announcement of the kingdom coming; now that of the King who has come.

LUKE 2:21-38

(Book 2: Chapter 7)

Mary seems an enigma, but is she? Her role as a mother is a timeless one, but not all mothers are called to nurture humankind's Messiah! Strange that she should have 'pondered ... in her heart' the shepherds' account; stranger that afterwards, she should have wondered at his lingering in the Temple among Israel's teachers;[10] strangest of all that, at the very first of his miracles (at Cana[11]), she seemed so detached from the action. There is a peculiar dynamic here. Jesus could not, in any true sense, have been subject to his parents, once they had fully understood his divine mission.

---

9. Isaiah 6:1-4.

10. Luke 2:42.

11. John 2:1-12.

He was still his mother's child as he 'grew in wisdom and stature, and in favour with God and man' (Luke 2:52). The mystery of the incarnation would have been needless and fruitless had his humanity not been subject to all its right and ordinary conditions. And also we can understand why the mystery of his divinity had to be kept from everyone until the time was right. Had it been otherwise, the thought of his divinity would have so dominated as to deflect from the lessons learned about his humanity while he was growing up. God was truly running this show.

As a Jewish woman and mother, Mary had to fulfil all the requirements of the Law, for both herself and her child. The first of these was circumcision, representing the covenant between God and Abraham and his seed. The ceremony took place on the eighth day when the child received the name 'Yeshua' (Jesus). Also, the firstborn son of every household was to be 'redeemed' of the priest at the price of five shekels. The earliest time for this was thirty-one days after birth; neither father nor mother must be of the tribe of Levi and the child must be free from all such bodily blemishes as would have disqualified him for the priesthood.

It was a thing much dreaded, that the child should die before his redemption. Mothers who were within convenient distance of the Temple would naturally attend personally in the Temple and in such cases, when practicable, the redemption of the firstborn and the purification of his mother would be combined. Such was undoubtedly the case here, as they were still in the vicinity.

In the Temple, Jesus was formally presented to the priest, accompanied by two short 'benedictions' and money changed hands. The sin offering was, in all cases, a turtledove or a young pigeon, followed by a burnt offering of the same, rather than the lamb that they would have presented if they hadn't been so poor. While at the Temple they had an encounter with Simeon, said by legend to be the son of the great Hillel and the father of Gamaliel. Here was a man who combined the three characteristics of Old Testament piety: justice, fear of God and, above all, longing expectancy for the Messiah, 'the consolation of Israel'.

The other encounter was with the widow Anna (*channah*), of the tribe of Asher, a tribe with a tradition of beautiful marriageable women. She may have been fair to view when she was younger, but she was also a woman of virtue, one given to prayer and fasting, but not of the self-righteous, self-satisfied kind which was prevalent. For her the synagogue was not enough, the Temple was the focus of her devotion. Her earnest longing was for the time of promised 'redemption'.

MATTHEW 2:1-18
(Book 2: Chapter 8)

The story of the visitation by the Magi is a curious one. The very term 'Magi', used by many commentators, has negative and positive connotations. It can imply the magical arts but it can also be possibly referring to the Eastern priest-sages, whose researches seem to have embraced much deep knowledge, though often tinged with superstition. It is to these latter that the Magi spoken of here must have belonged. At the period in question, the Jewish diaspora among the Medes and Persians would have given them knowledge of the great hope of Israel.

Would these Eastern Magi connect a celestial phenomenon with the birth of a Jewish king, unless they had access to Jewish knowledge regarding the birth of the Messiah King? They came to Jerusalem to find out more and in their simplicity of heart sought out the official head of the nation, Herod, who, true to his innate paranoia, saw the whole thing as a threat. The subsequent conduct of Herod shows that the Magi must have told him that their earliest observation of the celestial phenomenon had taken place two years before they arrived in Jerusalem.

Regarding this celestial phenomenon, where did this idea come from regarding the birth of the Messiah? We can be clear that God would not have spoken through the superstitions and errors of astrology (though it didn't stop some rabbis from delving). Also, Jewish expectation would not have been of a few Magi guided by a star to his home; it was not a narrative that would appeal to them. So, what about Scripture? Balaam's prophecy in Numbers 24:17 was too vague; Isaiah's prophecy of those 'bearing gold and incense' in Isaiah 60:6 doesn't work in a contextual sense, as it refers to Jerusalem.

Thus, there is no historical basis for this story, either in the Old Testament or in Jewish tradition. So, again we ask, what rational explanation can be given of its origin, since its invention would never have occurred to any contemporary Jew? There may be a possible answer from the realm of astronomy, though. Here is the thinking...

There was a celestial phenomenon that occurred two years earlier. It was the conjunction of Jupiter and Saturn in the constellation of Pisces, something that had also happened three years before the birth of Moses (according to legend). This has been attested by experts[12] and would have presented the most brilliant and unmissable spectacle in the night sky. It would have given the impression of a new star in the sky, possibly the 'star of the Magi'. This has also been noticed in the astronomical tables of the Chinese.[13] The jury is out.

The sad conclusion of this story is, of course, the slaughter of the infants living in Bethlehem and its vicinity by Herod. This was not the mass slaughter of legend, probably no more than around twenty of them, according to the population of Bethlehem at that time. But the deed was nonetheless atrocious, and these infants may justly be regarded as martyrs – even the first witnesses for Christ.

---

12. Johannes Kepler, *De Stella Nova* (Prague: Paul Sessius, 1605).

13. Alexander von Humboldt, *Cosmos* (Baltimore, MD: John Hopkins University Press, 1997), Vol. I, p. 92.

Chapter 5: Childhood

The tyrant Herod was dying… horribly. He knew that his time was almost up and had installed himself back in his palace under the palm trees of Jericho. Yet he was still capable of evil deeds and had two popular and honoured rabbis burnt alive, simply for attempting to pull down the immense golden eagle which hung over the great gate of the Temple.

Feeling his death approaching, Herod summoned the noblest of Israel and shut them up in the Hippodrome, with orders to his sister to have them slain immediately upon his death, in the grim hope that the joy of the people would thus be changed into mourning. Soon he was dead. He had reigned for thirty-seven years. The rule for which he had so long plotted, striven and stained himself with untold crimes, passed from his descendants. A century more, and the whole dynasty of Herod had been swept away.

It was time for Joseph and Mary to return. The first intention of Joseph seems to have been to settle in Bethlehem, but he changed his mind when he found out that Herod's son Archelaus was now in charge. He was truly his father's son and had stated his intentions by silencing a rebellion (caused by the execution of those two rabbis) by the slaughtering of more than 3,000, within the precincts of the Temple, no less! It was time to keep a low profile, so the Holy Family settled in Nazareth.

Of the following years, during which Jesus passed from infancy to childhood, from childhood to youth and from youth to manhood, the Gospels are quite silent. Remember, the intention was to present a history of the Saviour, not a biography of Jesus of Nazareth. We are only furnished with the facts necessary for our salvation. Also, we are aware that one of his names was *Notsri* (of Nazareth).

This is in line with the whole language of the prophets. The Jews had no fewer than eight names by which the Messiah was to be called. The most prominent among them was that of *Tsemach*, or 'Branch'. This is also conveyed by the term *Netser* (also Branch) in such passages as Isaiah 11:1, which was likewise applied to the Messiah. Jesus would, as *Notsri*, be therefore identified with the office of Messiah purely by the 'accident' of his residence and the linguistic connection between the two terms.

But we can go further. We can see Christ as this divinely placed 'Branch', small and despised, from the root of Jesse but destined to grow. The Nazarene from lowly Nazareth was to fulfil the prophecies from old. A greater contrast could scarcely be imagined than between the scholastic studies of the Judeans and the active pursuits of the Galileans. It was a common saying: 'If a person wishes to be rich, let him go north; if he wants to be wise, let him come south.' The very neighbourhood of the Gentile world, the contact with the great commercial centres close by and the constant intercourse with foreigners who passed through Galilee along one of the world's great highways would highlight these contrasts.

Galilee was to Judaism 'the Court of the Gentiles', a place outside the acceptable religious establishment, whereas the Rabbinic Schools of Judea were the 'Holy of Holies' by comparison. Unlike the Judeans, Galileans weren't too keen on Rabbinic study. Their lives were very different. As Edersheim remarks:

The smiling landscapes were gloriously grand, free, fresh, and bracing. A more beautiful country could scarcely be imagined. Corn grew in abundance; the wine, though not so plentiful as the oil, was rich and generous. Proverbially, all fruit grew in perfection and altogether the cost of living was about one-fifth that in Judea. Assuredly, Galilee was not the home of Rabbinism, but instead a place of generous spirits, of warm, impulsive hearts, of intense nationalism, of simple manners, and of earnest piety.

Jesus spent by far the longest part of his life upon earth with such people, as he grew up among them as one of them: 'And the child grew and became strong; he was filled with wisdom, and the grace of God was on him.' Having entered life as the divine infant, he began it as the human child, subject to all the stresses and strains of growing up, through the designated stages; the new-born babe (*Yeled*), the suckling (*Yoneq*), the hungry suckling (*Olel*), the weaned child (*Gamul*), the child clinging to its mother (*Taph*), the child shaking himself free (*Elem*) and the ripened one (*Bachur*)!

Education begins in the home, and homes in Israel were places of nurture, influence and example, as well as teaching. What really marked out Jewish fathers was what they felt towards their children and with what reverence, affection and care the latter repaid what they had received. The relationship of father to son mirrored that of God towards Israel. The tender care of a mother is that of the watchfulness and pity of the Lord over his people.

From the first days of their existence, a religious atmosphere surrounded the child of Jewish parents. Admitted to the number of God's chosen people by the deeply significant rite of circumcision, they were then separated unto God, whether or not they accepted the privileges and obligations implied in this dedication. They were bound to the Torah (Law), to the *Chuppah* (the marriage canopy) and to good works; in other words, that they might live 'godly, soberly, and righteously in this present world'. The mother's role was significant; the preparation and execution of the Sabbath meal, as well as the observances, including the placing of the *Mezuzah* on the doorpost, with God's name on the outside of the little folded parchment, which was reverently touched by each who came or went and then the fingers kissed that had come in contact with the Holy Name.

Long before he could go to school, or even synagogue, the Jewish boy would be brought up in an atmosphere of private and united prayers, the weekly Sabbath celebrations and the festival seasons. In mid-winter, there was Chanukah, the festival of lights in each home. In most houses, the first night only one candle was lit, the next two, and so on to the eighth day; and the child would learn that this was symbolic and commemorative of the dedication of the Temple, its cleansing and the restoration of its services by the lionhearted Judas the Maccabee.

In early spring, there was the joyful time of Purim, the Feast of Esther and of Israel's deliverance through her, with its bonhomie and boisterous enjoyments. The Passover might call the rest of the family to Jerusalem; then, after the Feast of Weeks (*Shavuot*), came bright summer. But its golden harvest and its rich fruits would remind them of the early dedication of the first and best to the Lord and of those solemn processions in which it was carried up to Jerusalem.

As autumn seared the leaves, the Feast of the New Year (*Rosh Hashanah*) spoke of the casting up of humanity's accounts in the great Book of Judgement and the fixing of destiny for good or for evil. Then followed the Fast of the Day of Atonement (*Yom Kippur*), the most solemn time of all; and, last of all, in the week of the Feast of Tabernacles (*Succot*), there were the strange leafy booths in which they lived, keeping their harvest-thanksgiving and praying and longing for the better harvest of a renewed world.

It was no idle boast that the Jews were trained to recognise God as their Father and as the Maker of the world from earliest youth and that they learned the laws, to have them engraved upon the soul. But while the earliest religious teaching would, of necessity, come from the lips of the mother, it was the father who was responsible for teaching the Torah. This was a solemn, spiritual duty, carried out as if they had personally received the Law on Mount Sinai. Directly the child learned to speak, his religious instruction was to begin, including passages from the Bible, short prayers and select sayings of the sages.

Special attention was given to the cultivation of the memory, since forgetfulness might prove as fatal in its consequences as ignorance or neglect of the Law. A young child would have been taught what might be called his birthday text – some verse of Scripture beginning, or ending with, or at least containing, the same letters as his Hebrew name.

The earliest hymns taught would be the Psalms for the days of the week, or festive Psalms, such as the *Hallel* (Psalm 136), or those connected with the festive pilgrimages to Jerusalem. Regular lessons started in the fifth or sixth year when every boy was sent to school. The teachers would teach them the Law, according to their capacity, with great patience and strictness tempered by kindness but, above all, with the object to keep them from vice and show sin in its repulsiveness and to train them in gentleness, truthfulness and to do this without showing partiality or undue severity, or loosening of discipline. Even at an early age, teaching had a moral purpose for these Jewish schoolboys.

Up to ten years of age, the Hebrew Bible exclusively was the textbook; from ten to fifteen, the Mishnah, or traditional law; after that age, the student should enter into those theological discussions which occupied time and attention in the higher Academies of the Rabbis. The study of the Bible commenced with that of the book of Leviticus, followed by the rest of the Torah, then the Prophets, followed by the Writings.

This was how Jesus' early days were filled. From his intimate familiarity with Holy Scripture in its every detail, we may assume that his humble home possessed a copy of the Bible as it was. In this way, '... the child grew and became strong; he was filled with wisdom, and the grace of God was on him.'

LUKE 2:41-52
(Book 2: Chapter 10)

The silence is broken by his first visit to the Temple. Jesus was twelve years of age, not yet a 'Son of the Commandment' (*Bar Mitzvah*) and so not yet obliged to attend the feasts in Jerusalem. But it was Passover time and he had tagged along with his parents. The land was at relative peace at that time; even the Zealots were calm. Annas ruled in the Temple as high priest when they arrived and Jesus glimpsed the Holy Temple, possibly for the first time since he was a baby. It would have been on at least the third day of the festival when we find Jesus sitting among the teachers. The first two days were the compulsory days and Joseph and Mary would have fulfilled their religious obligations by now and would have returned to their temporary residence.

The Talmud tells us that the members of the Sanhedrin, who on ordinary days sat as a Court of Appeal, were inclined to teach on Sabbaths and feast days at 'the terrace'[14] of the Temple. This is the most likely scenario where we find the boy Jesus among the audience that surrounded these teachers. He would not be setting a precedent, as Jewish tradition gives other instances of precocious and advanced students making a nuisance of themselves (in the view of the rabbis!). But perhaps a precedent was set by the effect he had upon the teachers as all who heard him were 'amazed' at his insight and discerning answers. So, what could they have been talking about? Perhaps they may have been discussing the Passover itself in the light of his future role as 'the Lamb of God, who takes away the sin of the world' (John 1:29)? And what of his reaction to his parents, once they had been reunited? It seems that something had now been awakened in him. He realised that he had been in his 'Father's house' going about his 'Father's business'.[15]

What happened next was telling. Whatever had been awakened in him was not going to his head but, instead, we see his quiet, immediate, unquestioning return to Nazareth with his parents and his willing submission to them while there.

What about the rest of his childhood and young adulthood? He probably followed his father's trade as a carpenter. Having a trade was positively encouraged, even considered a religious duty, as long as it didn't interfere with Torah studies. We know next to nothing about his father and know a bit more about his brothers, James and Jude and his

---

14. Talmud, Sanhedrin 88b.
15. Luke 2:49 footnote in NIV.

probable cousin Simon (the Zealot) from their actions in later life. Jesus was a diligent studier of the Word. Edersheim observed it thus:

> He saw much to show the hollowness, self-seeking, pride and literalism which a mere external observance of the Law fostered. The Law of Moses in all its bearings, the utterances of the prophets – Isaiah, Jeremiah, Ezekiel, Daniel, Hosea, Micah, Zechariah, Malachi – and the hopes and consolations of the Psalms, were all to him literally true and cast their light upon the building which Moses had reared. It was all one, a grand unity, not an aggregation of different parts, but the unfolding of a living organism.

Chapter 6: The Call

MATTHEW 3:1-12; MARK 1:2-8; LUKE 3:1-18
(Book 2: Chapter 11)

There is something mysterious, even mystical, in the almost absolute silence in the thirty years between Jesus' birth and his first call to duty. The story now switches to Zacharias' son, John, as he explodes onto the scene like his Old Testament precursor, Elijah. Both suddenly appeared to threaten terrible judgement, but also to open possibilities for good. John came suddenly out of the Judean wilderness, as Elijah from the wilds of Gilead. John bore the same strange ascetic appearance as his predecessor. The message of John was the counterpart of that of Elijah. Thus, the history of John the Baptist was the fulfilment of that of Elijah in 'the fullness of time'.[16]

Roman society was ripe for judgement. Philosophy and religion had nothing to offer; they had been tried and found wanting. Tacitus declared human life one great farce and expressed his conviction that the Roman world lay under some terrible curse. All around was despair, conscious need and an unconscious longing. Can greater contrast be imagined than the proclamation of a coming kingdom of God amid such a world?

Pilate has just entered the scene; history was ready to unfold. The ancient kingdom of Herod was now divided into four parts; Judea in the south being under the direct administration of Rome, two other tetrarchies under the rule of Herod's sons (Herod Antipas and Philip), while the small principality of Abilene was governed by Lysanias, though little is known about him.

Herod Antipas reigned over Galilee, the main focus for the ministry of Jesus and of John the Baptist. Like his brother Archelaus, Herod Antipas was an absolute nightmare, with no religious feelings at all and under

---

16. See Matthew 17:11-13.

absolute control of his wife, which would determine his final downfall. He was covetous, avaricious and as cunning as a fox, all common qualities to those in similar positions throughout the eastern end of the empire.

This was the political backdrop when John enters the scene from the wilderness of Judea. Roman society was a mess, Israel's condition was not much better and it was surprising that no attempt had been made by the people to right themselves through an armed uprising. In these circumstances, the cry that the 'kingdom of heaven has come near' and the call to prepare for it must have awakened echoes throughout the land.

John's outward appearance and methodology corresponded to the character and object of his mission, that of Elijah, whose mission he was now to fulfil. Concerning this 'kingdom of heaven', which was the great message of John and the great work of Jesus himself, it is the whole Old Testament summarised and the whole New Testament realised. The idea of it did not lie hidden in the Old to be opened up in the New Testament, but this rule of heaven and Kingship of God was the very substance of the Old Testament; the object of the calling and mission of Israel, the meaning of the Torah and the need to follow it.

This was the distinctive call of Israel, alone among all of the nations of the time. How imperfectly Israel understood this kingdom. In truth, the men of that period possessed only the term itself; what explained its meaning, filled and fulfilled it, came once more from heaven. According to the Rabbinic views of the time, the terms 'kingdom', 'kingdom of heaven' and 'kingdom of God' were equivalent. In fact, the word 'heaven' was very often used instead of 'God' to avoid speaking the sacred name. This probably accounts for the exclusive use of the expression 'kingdom of heaven' in Matthew's Gospel, the most 'Jewish' of the four accounts, where it appears more than thirty times.

John preached on the importance of repentance. How seriously did they listen to him? Did they really understand and fear the final consequences of resisting the coming 'kingdom'? Did they follow this call in both hearts and minds? Or else did they imagine that, according to the popular understanding of the time, the vials of wrath were to be poured out only on the Gentiles, while they, as Abraham's children, were sure of escape? In the words of the Talmud, 'the night' (Isaiah 21:12) was 'only to the nations of the world, but the morning to Israel'.[17]

For there was one thing the Jews were certain of, that all Israel had a part in the world to come and this specifically because of their connection with Abraham. 'The merits of the Fathers' is one of the commonest phrases in the mouth of the rabbis. Abraham was represented as sitting at the gate of Gehenna, to deliver any Israelite who otherwise might have been consigned to its terrors. They were in terrible error and John warned them that God was able to raise up children unto Abraham from those stones that strewed the riverbank!

Since he was urging repentance, it was only natural that the hearers wondered whether John himself was the Messiah. It was said: 'If Israel repented but one day, the Son of David would immediately come.' But here John pointed them to the difference between himself and his work and the person and mission of the Messiah. John's mission was in *preparation*, the Messiah's mission was that of *final decision*. After this came the harvest.

MATTHEW 3:13-17; MARK 1:7-11; LUKE 3:21-23; JOHN 1:32-34
(Book 2: Chapter 12)

John's message of repentance awakened echoes throughout the land and brought hearers from city, village and hamlet. For once, every distinction was irrelevant. Pharisee and Sadducee, the outcast taxman and semi-pagan soldier met here on common ground. Their bond of union was the common 'hope of Israel', the only hope that remained, that of 'the kingdom'. The long winter of disappointment had not destroyed, nor the storms of suffering swept away what had struck its roots so deep in the soil of Israel's heart.

17. Talmud, Jer. Taan. 64a.

That kingdom had been the last word of the Old Testament. To the Jew of the day, the central part of their worship revolved around the sacrificial system. Yet they would know that their Scriptures looked beyond their offerings, that 'The blood of goats and bulls and the ashes of a heifer sprinkled on those who are ceremonially unclean' (Hebrews 9:13) were only 'a shadow of the good things that are coming' (Hebrews 10:1), of 'the new covenant [which] is established on better promises' (Hebrews 8:6).

The shadow was about to give way to reality as Jesus now appears in our story. Although there seems not to have been any personal contact between Jesus and John, despite being cousins, each must have heard and known of the other. Yet, when the two met there was an unspoken familiarity. With John, it was deepest, reverent humility. He knew of him and now he saw him; that look of quiet dignity, of the majesty in the only unfallen, sinless man. At that moment there was instant meaning to that express command of God which had sent him from his solitude to preach and baptise and proclaim the kingdom.

A question often asked is, why did Jesus go to be baptised? Reasons given include that of his personal sinfulness, of his coming as the representative of a guilty race, or as the bearer of the sins of others, or of acting in solidarity with his people, or of his surrendering himself to death for humanity, of his purpose to do honour to the baptism of John, or thus as a token of his Messiahship, or to bind himself to the observance of the Law, or in this manner to commence his Messianic work, or to consecrate himself solemnly to it or, lastly, to receive the spiritual qualification for it. *Perhaps the truth is a lot simpler?*

We must not seek for any ulterior motive in the coming of Jesus to this baptism. He had no ulterior motive of any kind; it was an act of simple submissive obedience on the part of the perfect One, and this submissive obedience may have had no motive beyond itself. It asks no reasons, it cherishes no ulterior purpose. And so it was the fulfilment of 'all righteousness'. Our difficulty can be in thinking simply of his humanity or in just emphasising his divinity. But the Gospels always present him as the God-Man, in an inseparable mystical union of the two natures.

The baptism of Christ was the last act of his private life and, emerging from its waters in prayer, his one outstanding thought would be, 'I must be about my Father's business.' A present, visible demonstration from heaven was to be given. We can understand how what he knew of Jesus must have overwhelmed John with the sense of Christ's transcendence and led him to hesitate over baptising One 'the straps of whose sandals' he was not worthy to untie.

Jesus stepped out of the baptismal waters 'praying'. As the prayer of Jesus winged heavenwards, the Holy Spirit descended on him. The voice from heaven proclaimed, 'You are my Son, whom I love; with you I am well pleased' – the ratification of the great Davidic promise of Psalm 2 and the beginning of Jesus' Messianic work.

Nowhere in Rabbinic writings do we find any hint of a baptism of the Messiah, nor of a descent upon him of the Spirit in the form of a dove. This is repugnant to Jewish thinking. Therefore, it rings true, deflecting from any possible contrivance, where events match expectations. Yet it goes further, perhaps troublingly so, as, although the Gospel text is explicit, there is no support in the Old Testament of the idea of the Holy Spirit in the form of a dove, but rather that the dove symbolises Israel (Song of Songs 1:15) and that Jesus is seen as the perfect Israelite.

MATTHEW 4:1-11; MARK 1:12-13; LUKE 4:1-13
(Book 3: Chapter 1)

As to what follows next there can be no greater contrast. And yet, what followed the baptism was entirely necessary, as regarding the ministry of Jesus. He was eventually going to enter a world of sin and, for the kingdom of heaven to be established, it was going to be necessary to defeat the representative, founder and holder of the opposite power, 'the prince of this world' (John 12:31; 14:30; 16:11). The patriarchs had set the example. So had Moses and all the heroes of faith in Israel. *Spiritual trials must precede spiritual elevation.*

We can see parallels between Moses and Elijah. Firstly, we can see them marking the three stages in the history of the Covenant. Moses was its giver, Elijah its restorer, the Messiah its renewer and perfecter. But there's a difference. Moses failed after his forty days' fast when in indignation he cast the tablets of the Law from him;[18] Elijah failed before his forty days' fast;[19] Jesus was attacked for forty days and endured the trial. Moses was angry against Israel; Elijah despaired of Israel; *Jesus overcame for Israel.* When Moses and Elijah failed, it was not only as individuals but as giving or restoring the Covenant. When Jesus conquered, it was not only as the perfect man but also as the Messiah. His temptation and victory have therefore a two-fold aspect: the general human and the Messianic, and these two are closely connected.

We can now also draw the conclusion that, in whatever Jesus overcame, we can overcome. Each victory which he has gained secures its fruits for us who are his disciples. We walk in his footprints.

Picture this scene. He is in the wilderness. He is weary with the contest, faint with hunger, alone in that desolate place. His voice falls on no sympathetic ear, no voice reaches him but that of the tempter. Nothing is bracing or strengthening in this featureless, barren, stony wilderness, only the picture of desolation, hopelessness, despair. He must, he *will* absolutely submit to the will of God. But can this be the will of God? One word of power and the scene would be changed. Let him despair of everyone, of everything – he can do it.

By his will, the Son of God, as the tempter suggests, can change the stones into bread. He can do miracles, but this would really have been to change the idea of Old Testament miracle into the pagan conception of magic, which was absolute power inherent in an individual, without moral purpose. The moral purpose here was absolute submission to the will of God. This was to be the watchword of his ministry on earth. As our story unfolds, the moral purpose will remain central.

The Spirit had driven him into that wilderness. His circumstances were God-appointed and Jesus absolutely submitted to that will of God

---

18. Exodus 32:19.
19. 1 Kings 19:3.

by continuing in his present circumstances. To have set himself free from what they implied would have been despair of God and rebellion. He does more than not succumb. He conquers. He emerges on the other side triumphant, with this expression of his assured conviction of the sufficiency of God.

They had all been overcome, these three temptations against submission to the will of God, yet all his life long there were echoes of them: of the first, in the suggestion of his brethren to show himself; of the second, in the popular attempt to make him a king;[20] of the third in the question of Pilate: 'Are you the king of the Jews?' (John 18:33).

Edersheim provides a poetic epitaph to these events:

Foiled, defeated, the Enemy has spread his dark pinions towards that far-off world of his, and covered it with their shadow. The sun no longer glows with melting heat; the mists have gathered on the edge of the horizon and enwrapped the scene which has faded from view. And in the cool and shade that followed have the Angels come and ministered to his wants, both bodily and mental. He has refused to assert power; he has not yielded to despair; he would not fight and conquer alone in his own strength; and he has received power and refreshment, and heaven's company unnumbered in their ministry of worship. He would not yield to Jewish dream; he did not pass from despair to presumption; and lo, after the contest, with no reward as its object, all is his. He would not have Satan's vassals as his legions, and all heaven's hosts are at his command. It had been victory; it is now shout of triumphant praise. He whom God had anointed by his Spirit had conquered by the Spirit; he whom heaven's voice had proclaimed God's beloved Son, in whom he was well pleased, had proved such and done his good pleasure.

---

20. John 7:3-5; John 6:15.

The enemy 'left him' – yet only 'until an opportune time'. But this first contest and victory of Jesus decided all others to the last. By showing absolute obedience, absolute submission to the will of God, he provides us with a model and an example of the kingdom of God.

Chapter 7: Beginnings

JOHN 1:15-51
(Book 3: Chapter 2-3)

Our focus shifts to John the Baptist and, particularly, the question about his identification with Elijah. The answer lies in understanding the difference between Old Testament times and Gospel times. When it was stated that 'the spirit and power of Elijah' (Luke 1:17) could 'restore all things' (Matthew 17:11), we need to consider this in an Old Testament mindset, with the accent on outward deeds and by outward means. But 'the spirit and power' of the Elijah of the New Testament, which was to accomplish *inward* restoration through the reality of the kingdom of God, could only accomplish that object if 'they received it'.[21] So, John was not really Elijah to Israel but represented him in his mission to call people to repentance.

This question was posed by a 'deputation' sent from Jerusalem. This would have been from the Sanhedrin, with the Pharisees (*Perushim* – separated ones) taking the leading role. History has shown us that the Pharisees of this time were not held in too high esteem by some rabbis. The Talmud talks of seven kinds of Pharisees, being quite insulting to six of them and also speaks of 'a plague of Phariseeism' in one or two places. Nevertheless, they were closer to God's Word than the liberal and worldly Sadducees, who rejected the traditionalism of the Pharisees and also had contrary views on the afterlife, angels and the concept of predestination; in fact, they rejected all three!

The day after Jesus had left the wilderness, John saw him and remarked, 'Look, the Lamb of God, who takes away the sin of the world!' (John 1:29) he was considering the servant of the Lord from Isaiah 53, but also the Passover lamb and the daily sacrifice. All three ideas are expressed

---

21. See Matthew 11:14.

in this single exclamation. It is from the teacher Hillel that much of the symbolism is expanded, the importance of this sacrifice regarding the forgiveness of sin. The Hebrew word for lambs is *kebhasim* and this is derived from *kabhas*, 'to wash', from where we make the connection, 'because they wash away the sins of Israel'.[22]

We next find Jesus in the Galilee area with the calling of his first disciples, followed by the events at Cana, with the wedding, in John 2. The circumstances suggest the wedding of a virgin, rather than a widow and tradition demanded that this would be on a Wednesday (or perhaps the Tuesday night). This serves to cement events into reality, with Jesus returning from the wilderness on a Friday, followed by John's remarks. Then, on the Sabbath he met the two disciples, returning to Galilee on the Sunday – *the beginning of his active ministry* – followed by the wedding at Cana three days later.

Returning to that Sabbath, John the Baptist stood with Andrew and one other (probably the Gospel writer, John). They had come to be taught by him, but not for long. The call to follow Jesus was compelling. It needed no direction of John the Baptist, no call from Jesus. But as they went in modest silence, in the dawn of their rising faith, scarcely conscious of the what and the why, they referred to him as 'Rabbi' – 'my teacher'. His response, 'Come … and … see' is among the most common Rabbinic formulae. Andrew then recruited his brother, Simon, to the cause.

Then it was Sunday morning. He was preparing to return to Galilee. It was probably a distance of about twenty miles from here to Cana. By the way, two other disciples – Nathanael ('God-given' – later known as Bartholomew) and Philip – were to be added. He now had five disciples (possibly six, if John had recruited his brother James by then).

JOHN 2:1-12

(Book 3: Chapter 4)

Jesus' conversation with Nathanael was in fact his first sermon and here

---

22. Isaiah 1:18.

he made use of a significant expression concerning himself, 'Son of Man' (John 1:51). Nathanael had referred to his divinity, the 'Son of God' in verse 49 and so here Jesus reminds them too of his humanity. Both were equally important in understanding his mission to come. A Christ, God, King, and not primarily the 'Son of Man,' would not have been the Christ of prophecy, nor the Christ of humanity, nor the Christ of salvation, nor yet the Christ of sympathy, help and example.

This idea of the 'Son of Man' in its full and prophetic meaning provides a telling background to the miracle at the marriage of Cana. We are now entering into the ministry of the 'Son of Man' as he freely mingles with humanity, sharing its joys and engagements, entering into family life at this wedding ceremony, then by transforming the water into wine showing himself *also* to be the 'Son of God'.

On the evening of the actual marriage, the bride was led from her paternal home to that of her husband. Edersheim describes the scene most vividly:

> First came the merry sounds of music, then they distributed wine and oil and nuts among the children. Next, the bride, covered with the bridal veil. Her long hair flowing, surrounded by her companions and led by 'the friends of the bridegroom' and 'the children of the bride-chamber.' All around were in festive array, some carried torches, or lamps on poles, those nearest had myrtle branches and chaplets of flowers. Everyone rose to salute the procession or join it and it was deemed almost a religious duty to break into praise of the beauty, the modesty, or the virtues of the bride.

Arriving at her new home, she was led to her husband. The bride and bridegroom were crowned with garlands, then a formal legal instrument, called the *Kethubah*, was signed, which declared that the bridegroom now had the responsibility to honour, keep and care for her. Then, after the prescribed washing of hands and benediction, the marriage supper began, the cup filled and the solemn prayer of bridal benediction spoken over it. It might be more than one day until at last 'the friends of the bridegroom'[23] led the bridal pair to the bridal chamber and bed.

So Jesus arrives at this wedding. He is now about to embark on his 'Father's business' and what passed at the marriage feast marks the beginning of this period. We stand at the threshold, over which we pass from the old to the new. *The Messiah is about to declare himself.*

Outside the reception room were six stone pots of wine, most likely holding eleven to sixteen gallons each. At some point, Mary informed her son that the wine had been used up early, surely a major embarrassment for the hosts. Although Mary knew that a new period in his life had opened, was she really expecting such a miracle? What she had learned in those thirty years of bringing him up was to have absolute confidence in him, but what she also had to learn was that his submissiveness to family life was just a phase and things had now changed. Her words indicated that perhaps she was ready to let him flow into his destiny.

This was a true miracle; 'the conscious water saw its God, and blushed'. This, his *first miracle*, was intended as a sign pointing to the deeper and higher that was to be revealed and of the manifestation of his Glory. Perhaps we now see the deeper purpose in this? 'And his disciples believed in him.'

Although St Augustine spiritualises this as an allegory, this only trivialises our view of the miracle. For it is a miracle and will ever remain so; power with a moral purpose. And we believe it because this 'sign' is the first of all those miracles in which the miracle of miracles gave 'a sign' and showed 'his glory': the glory of his person, the glory of his purpose and the glory of his work.

---

23. See Luke 5:34.

JOHN 2:13-25

(Book 3: Chapter 5)

Straight away he led his family and disciples to Capernaum[24] (*Kephar Nachum*), to become his base of operations. The synagogue stood by the shores of Lake Galilee, built of white limestone on a dark basalt foundation. North of it, up the gentle slopes, stretched the town. East and south was the lake, in an almost continuous succession of lovely small bays, of which more than seventeen could be counted within six miles, and in one of which nestled Capernaum. After a few days, they left for Jerusalem, as it was Passover time.

It was time to confront the moneychangers (*Shulchanim*). What was their function? They had an official purpose which came out of the necessity for all Jews and proselytes (women, slaves and minors excepted) to pay the annual Temple tribute of half a shekel, equal to a common Galilean shekel (two denars).

The priests claimed exemption through a 'loophole' based on Leviticus 6:23, concerning the burning of any offering of a priest. This Temple tribute had to be paid in exact half shekels of the sanctuary, or ordinary Galilean shekels, which meant that foreign coinage had to be converted to this currency. Hence the need for the moneychangers, who were paid commission on each transaction.

It all amounted to a tidy profit for these traders, particularly as the Temple coinage was needed for other transactions, such as the purchasing of the sacrificial animals. Some brought their sacrifices with them (in fact, there were four shops on the Mount of Olives where pigeons were sold to pilgrims). It's not difficult to see how these activities could lead to corruption and how utterly the Temple would be profaned by this. From Jewish writings, we hear about some improper transactions, even the taking advantage of the poor people who came to offer their sacrifices, with greedy price hikes.

---

24. John 2:12.

All of this, whether the moneychanging, selling of doves and the market for sheep and oxen, was a terrible desecration. It was also liable to gross abuses. But was there about the time of Jesus anything to make it especially obnoxious and unpopular? The official priesthood had always derived considerable profit from it. What became of the profits of the moneychangers? The Jerusalem Talmud gives no less than five different answers, showing that there was no fixed rule as to the distribution of these profits. Although four of these answers point to their use for the public service, the reality is that they took huge chunks of it for themselves, though they had to pay a considerable rental to the leading Temple officials. The profits from the sale of meat and drink offerings went to the Temple treasury.

Corruption went as high as the high priest, Annas, whose greedy family owned much of the Temple market and were growing rich on the proceeds. The Talmud records a curse delivered by a prominent rabbi on this family, and they were to receive their comeuppance many years later (three years before the destruction of Jerusalem) when they were finally done away with.

Now we can better understand Jesus' actions and his later open denunciation of the Temple market as 'a den of robbers' (Luke 19:46). For such a holy place, at such a holy time, this was quite unseemly and also, with the weighing of the coins, deductions for loss of weight, arguing, disputing and bargaining, no wonder Jesus reacted in the way that he did. He was simply about his Father's business and would return to this theme later on in his ministry when he revisited the Temple courts.

So who there in the Temple courts would have heard of Jesus? The zeal of his early disciples must have spread to others and the many Galilean pilgrims who were present would certainly tell others as they returned to their homes. Some would follow him and watch what he did. As he dealt with those who were defiling the Temple, there was not a hand lifted, not a word spoken to arrest him as he drove both the sheep and the oxen out of the Temple; not a word said, nor a hand raised, as he scattered the changers' money, and overthrew their tables. His presence awed them, his words awakened even their consciences; they knew only too well how true his denunciations were. It was a scene worth witnessing, a protest and an act which, even among less emotional people, would have gained him respect and admiration.

When the Temple officials gathered the courage to come forward and engage with Jesus, they acted cunningly, appealing to those around them. They asked for a 'sign' to prove his authority to do what he did. *The game had started.* This was the first round in the sparring match between Jesus and those in authority. This first action of Jesus determined their mutual positions and their first step against him would lead eventually to the last, in his condemnation to the cross. He knew this already; his answer hinted as much. He had then, as afterwards, only one 'sign' to give: 'Destroy this temple, and I will raise it again in three days.' They misunderstood, viewing the 'Temple' merely as a building, of which they fully knew the architecture, manner and time of construction, but of whose spiritual character they had no knowledge nor thought.

Chapter 8: Born Again

JOHN 3:1-21
(Book 3: Chapter 6)

Other Jewish teachers claimed the power of doing miracles and were popularly credited with them. But what an obvious contrast between theirs and the 'signs' which Jesus did! For example, the 'miracle' of the creation of a calf by two rabbis every Sabbath eve for their Sabbath meal! One observer who recognised Jesus' authenticity was Nicodemus (*Naqdimon*), one of the Pharisees and a member of the Jerusalem Sanhedrin. We can scarcely realise the difficulties which he had to overcome to lead him to acknowledge a Galilean, untrained in the schools, as a teacher come from God and to consult him on, perhaps, the most delicate and important point in Jewish theology. It is highly likely that John, the Gospel writer, was there to take notes, reporting on the important teachings here from the mouth of the Messiah.

Jesus took him straight to the point. 'Very truly I tell you, no one can see the kingdom of God unless they are born again.' It is true that persons in certain circumstances – the bridegroom on his marriage, the chief of the Academy on his promotion, the king on his enthronement – were likened to *those newly born*. The expression, therefore, was not only common but quite fluid. Of course, in the first place, it was only a simile and never meant to convey a real regeneration, of *actually* being born again as a child. As far as proselytes were concerned, it meant that having entered into a new relation to God, they also entered into a new relationship to humanity; just as if they had at that moment been newly born, his natural family was no longer his nearest of kin. He *was a new man*. Then, secondly, it implied a new condition with all his sins forgiven and now belonging to the past.

It was a huge jump for Nicodemus to understand this new teaching of Jesus, and yet how all-important to him was that teaching. He would understand having a new relationship towards God and fellow human beings, and even the forgiveness of sins, but he would have had no conception of a moral renovation, a *spiritual birth*, a way into the kingdom of God. What Nicodemus had seen of Jesus had shaken his existing views. And so it is with us also, when, like Nicodemus, we first arrive at the conviction that Jesus is the teacher come from God.

Jesus ever has but one thing to say: 'Very truly I tell you, no one can see the kingdom of God unless they are born again.' The kingdom is something *other*. We may better ourselves through self-development, self-improvement, self-restraint, submission to a grand idea or a higher law and morality, *but to see the kingdom of God transcends everything*. It is not a mere improvement, but rather the submission of heart, mind and life to him as our divine King. To see it needs the birth from above.

Accordingly, all this originally sounded quite strange and unintelligible to Nicodemus. There was now only one gate by which someone could pass into the kingdom of God, for that which was of the flesh could ever be only fleshly. Nicodemus now understood in some measure what entrance into the kingdom meant but, because it ran counter to the Judaism of the day, it was something unimagined in Jewish theology.

How did this all square with the teacher, Moses, whom Jewish tradition respected above all? There was one symbol that was never adequately explained by tradition. Even after being fed by the manna in the wilderness, they still had not believed but murmured and rebelled and this was followed by the judgement of the 'venemous snakes' (Numbers 21:6). Then, when they repented by gazing at the bronze snake, their faith was to set them free.[25] Before this symbol, as has been said, tradition has stood dumb. A bronze serpent giving them life? The true meaning of this act was that Israel lifted up their eyes, not merely to the serpent, but rather to their Father in heaven and his mercy. The true interpretation is what Jesus taught; if the uplifted serpent, as a mere symbol, brought life to all who gazed on it, then shall the uplifted Son of Man give true life

---

25. Read Numbers 21:4-9.

to everyone that believes, looking up in him to the giving and forgiving love of God, which his Son came to bring. This highest teaching is all that Nicodemus or, indeed, the whole Church, could require or be able to know. Jesus explained to him and to us the how of the new birth. It is necessary to 'believe' as the important first step. For whosoever believes in him should not perish but have everlasting life.

Chapter 9: First Stirrings

—⁓—

JOHN 4:1-42

(Book 3: Chapter 7-8)

Samaria was on the shorter road between Galilee and Judea, though Judeans preferred a long detour to avoid it. Why should that be? Samaritans were considered hostile and impure, but not by Jesus. Of course! He had no problems passing through that region. They were truly a multinational people; some would be descendants of the ten tribes, whether mixed or unmixed with Gentiles, including fugitives from Assyria. The southern Judeans considered them impure foreigners. Impure they certainly were, in terms of their idolatry. They exercised a form of Judaism that consisted of a mixture of their former superstitions with Jewish doctrines and rites. They had their own capital in Shechem and even built a rival temple on Mount Gerizim.

Jews and Samaritans were natural enemies. On all public occasions, the Samaritans exercised hostility towards the Jews and took every opportunity to insult them. At various times they had sold Jews into slavery, attempted to desecrate the Jerusalem Temple and killed pilgrims on their road to Jerusalem. The Jews retaliated by treating the Samaritans with every mark of contempt.

We stand on the way from Shiloh and if we do a wide sweep we can see more than seven miles northwards, up to the twin heights of Gerizim and Ebal, which enclose the Valley of Shechem. Following the straight olive-shaded road from the south, to where a spur of Gerizim, jutting south-east, forms the Vale of Shechem, we stand by that Well of Jacob in Sychar, where Jesus has an encounter. Jacob had originally bought the land and sunk a well there, later giving it to his son Joseph. This was also the scene of Israel's first rebellion against God's order,[26] against the Davidic line and the Temple.

---

26. 2 Chronicles 10.

Here several ancient Roman roads met and parted, the south road leading to Jerusalem. Jesus would have rested on the low parapet which enclosed the well, while his disciples went to buy the necessary provisions in the neighbouring Sychar. It was the evening of a day in early summer. Possibly John remained with the Master, to record the encounter with the poor Samaritan woman who came, not for any religious purpose but simply to draw water.

Even if he had not spoken, the woman would have recognised the Jew by his appearance and dress if, as seems likely, he wore the fringes on the border of his garment. Also, his speech would, by its pronunciation (mostly the use of vowels), place his nationality beyond doubt. But it was more than that. He was what Israel was intended to have become to humankind; he was God's gift to humankind. As always, *the seen* is to Christ the emblem of the unseen and spiritual. It was with the ignorant woman of Sychar, as it had been with the learned 'Israel's teacher' (John 3:10). As Nicodemus had seen, and yet not seen, so also with this woman. Jesus was unable to draw from the deep well but he was himself the living water.

She was astounded that he, a Jew, would even speak to her, let alone unravel details about her that no mortal could have even guessed. When Jesus so unexpectedly laid open to her a past which he could only supernaturally have known, the conviction at once arose in her that he was a prophet. But, since they acknowledged no other prophet after Moses, for a Samaritan, to be a prophet meant that *he was the Messiah*. All her life she had heard that Gerizim was the mount of worship, the holy hill which the waters of the flood had never covered, and that the Jews were in deadly error. But here was an undoubted prophet, and he a Jew, no less! Were they then in error about the right place of worship, and what was she to think, and to do?

The Lord answers her questions by leading her far beyond all controversy, to the very goal of all his teaching. How he speaks to the simple in heart! As he spoke, she grasped the glorious picture which was set before her. She saw the coming of the kingdom of the Messiah. "'I know that Messiah" (called Christ) "is coming. When he comes, he will explain everything to us.'" It was then that, according to the need of that simple woman, he told her plainly that he was the Messiah. So true is it, that 'babes' can receive what often must remain long hidden 'from the wise and prudent' (KJV). It was the crowning lesson of that day. Nothing more could be said, nothing more need be said.

When the disciples had returned from Sychar, they were appalled that Jesus should be talking to a woman; it ran counter to all that they thought of the way a rabbi conducted himself. Yet, in their reverence for him, they dared not ask any questions. Meanwhile, the woman had hurried to tell others of this man who knew so much about her. We can readily assume that others gathered around her to learn of the indisputable fact of his superhuman knowledge. And many became believers in this Jesus.

MATTHEW 4:12; MARK 1:14; LUKE 4:14-15
(Book 3: Chapter 9)

The brief 'revival' in Samaria was, as Jesus had indicated to his disciples, the beginning of something bigger. It formed the introduction to his ministry in Galilee, which might be summed up by the words 'in the power of the Spirit', with which he describes his return to Galilee. He takes up the message of John the Baptist, only with a wider sweep, not just announcing the kingdom of heaven, but now calling those who heard him to believe the gospel which he brought them.

It was probably early summertime and it all started very quietly when the disciples had returned to their homes, while Jesus taught in various synagogues in Galilee. He has returned to the region a different man, a man on a mission. He had moved on from being 'the carpenter's son' (Matthew 13:55), particularly after what many had witnessed at his visit to Jerusalem. Accordingly, they were now prepared to receive him with a little more reverence. We next hear of him on his second visit to Cana.

JOHN 4:43-54

This was the home of Nathanael, where Jesus was most welcome. It was here that the second recorded miracle of his Galilean ministry was performed. It was going to have a great effect upon the whole district, even as far as Nazareth. It was the healing of the son of Herod Antipas' official.

In the Talmud, various cases are recorded in which those seriously ill, even at the point of death, were restored by the prayers of celebrated rabbis. One instance is especially illustrative. When the son of Gamaliel was dangerously ill, he sent two of his disciples to one Chanina ben Dosa for prayers for the restoration of his son. Chanina is said to have gone up to his upper chamber to pray. On his return, he assured the messengers that the young man was restored. The messengers noted down the hour and on their arrival at the house of Gamaliel found that at that very hour 'the fever left him, and he asked for water'. Of course, this may be a legend, as a response to Jesus' exploits in the New Testament.

What Jesus intended to show with this miracle was that he, who was life personified, could restore life at a distance as easily as by his presence; by the word of his power as readily as by a personal touch. Jesus was in Cana, the poor lad was in Capernaum, twenty-five miles away. This is a lesson of the deepest importance for all of us, regarding the person of Christ. Through this, we come to know the meaning and the blessedness of believing in Jesus. This was not only the Messiah of the Jews but the Saviour of the world.

Edersheim sums this up in his usual lyrical manner:

And so are we ever led faithfully and effectually, yet gently, by his benefits, upwards from the lower stage of belief by what we see him do, to that higher faith which is absolute and unseeing trust, springing from an experimental knowledge of what he is.

Chapter 10: The Synagogue

—∾—

LUKE 4:16
(Book 3: Chapter 10)

After a short stay in Cana, we follow Jesus to Nazareth, the city of his childhood. It has only been a few months since he left there, but much had happened since! He would hear the familiar double blast of the trumpet from the roof of the synagogue minister's house, proclaiming the advent of the holy day. Once more it sounded through the still summer air, to tell all that work must be laid aside. Then a third time it was heard, to mark the beginning of the Sabbath. Jesus returned to that place where, as a child, a youth, a man, he had so often worshipped in humility, sitting not up there among the elders and the honoured, but far back with the hoi-polloi.

Familiar faces were around him, familiar words fell on his ear. And now he was again among them, suddenly a stranger among his own countrymen; this time, to be looked at, listened to, tested, tried, used or cast aside, as the case may be. It was the first time, so far as we know, that he taught in this synagogue, and this was his boyhood synagogue in Nazareth.

Synagogues became the cradle of the Church. They originated during the Babylonian captivity, when it was realised that, deprived of the Temple, there needed to be places and opportunities for common worship on Sabbaths and feast days. After the return to the Land, such 'meeting houses' continued and thrived. Here those who were ignorant even of the language of the Old Testament would have the Scriptures read and explained to them, as well as a common place for prayer. Thus, the regular synagogue service developed, first on Sabbaths and on the feast or fast days, then on ordinary days, at the same hours as the worship in the Jerusalem Temple. The services on Mondays and Thursdays were special, these being the ordinary market days when the country people came into the towns and would be able to bring any case that might require legal decision before the local Sanhedrin, which met in the synagogue.

Synagogues were scattered over the whole country, and in Jerusalem and some other large cities there were not only several synagogues, but these were arranged according to nationalities and even crafts. Contrary to common thought, synagogues did not face the east; this was condemned on the grounds of the false worship mentioned in Ezekiel 8:16. The prevailing direction was towards the west, as in the Temple. In general, however, it was considered that since the Shekhinah – God's glorious presence – was everywhere, the direction was not of paramount importance.

We are now in the Nazareth synagogue. The officials are all assembled. There is the *Chazzan*, or minister, who must be not only irreproachable, but his family too would be beyond reproach. Humility, modesty, knowledge of the Scriptures, distinctness and correctness in pronunciation, simplicity and neatness in dress are expected qualities, reminiscent of those insisted on by Paul in the choice of deacons and elders.[27]

Let us now follow the worship on that Sabbath in Nazareth. On his entrance into the synagogue, the chief ruler would request Jesus to act for that Sabbath as the *Sheliach Tsibbur*, the leader of the service. For according to the Mishnah, the person who read the portion from the Prophets in the synagogue was also expected to conduct the devotions, at least in greater part. If this rule was enforced at that time, then Jesus would ascend the *Bima* (podium) and standing at the lectern, begin the service in prayer.

After this followed the *Shema*, from the word 'shema' or 'hear,' with which it begins. It consisted of three passages from the Torah, followed by this prayer:

True it is that You are Yahweh, our God, and the God of our fathers, our King, and the King of our fathers, our Saviour, and the Saviour

---

27. 1 Timothy 3:1-13.

of our fathers, our Creator, the Rock of our Salvation, our Help
and our Deliverer. Your Name is from everlasting, and there is no
God beside You. A new song did they that were delivered sing to
Your Name by the seashore; together did all praise and own You
King, and say, Yahweh shall reign, world without end! Blessed be
the God who saves Israel.[28]

This prayer finished, there followed certain eulogies or benedictions.
There were eighteen of them, later nineteen. Then we get to the primary
object of the synagogue service. The minister approached the ark and
brought out a roll of the Law. It was taken from its case and unwound.
The time had now come for the reading of portions from the Law and
the Prophets. On the Sabbath, at least seven people were called upon
successively to read portions from the Law, none of them consisting of
less than three verses. The *Methurgeman*, or interpreter, stood by the
side of the reader and translated into Aramaic, the common tongue. Yet
he was not allowed to read out this translation, as it might popularly be
regarded as authoritative Scripture, which it wasn't!

MATTHEW 4:13-17; MARK 1:14-15; LUKE 4:15-32
(Book 3: Chapter 11)

The visit to Nazareth was in many respects decisive. Jesus' townsfolk had
no doubt heard of his exploits in Cana and Capernaum, so there would
have been a high degree of expectancy.

Jesus commenced the first part of the service and then read out those
eulogies which were appropriate. And now, one by one, priest, Levite and,
in succession, five Israelites had read from the Law. There is no reason to
disturb the almost traditional idea that Jesus himself read the concluding
portion from the Prophets, the Haphtarah. The whole narrative seems
to imply this. Similarly, it is most likely that the Haphtarah for that day

---

28. Talmud, Ber. Ii. 2.

was taken from the prophecies of Isaiah and that it included the passage quoted in the Gospel account.

When unrolling, and holding the scroll, much more than the sixty-first chapter of Isaiah must have been within range of his eyes. On the other hand, it is quite certain that the verses quoted by Luke could not have formed the whole Haphtarah. According to the traditional rule, the Haphtarah ordinarily consisted of not less than twenty-one verses though, if the passage was to be 'explained', or a sermon to follow, that number might be shortened to seven, five or even three verses.

Now the passage quoted by Luke consists really of only one verse (Isaiah 61:1), together with a clause from Isaiah 58:6 and the first clause of Isaiah 61:2. This could scarcely have formed the whole Haphtarah, just a small part of it. Jesus would have read the Haphtarah and the text of his sermon in Hebrew and then translated it into Aramaic, the common tongue.

It was, indeed, divine wisdom, *the Spirit of the Lord upon him*, which directed Jesus in the choice of such a text for his first Messianic sermon. It struck the keynote for the whole of his Galilean ministry. Isaiah 61:1-2 was regarded as one of the three passages in which mention of the Holy Spirit is connected to the promised redemption.

What followed was the Pethichah, the introductory text to his sermon. This was totally unexpected for the assembly. 'Today this scripture is fulfilled in your hearing.' The focus was this: Scripture is about to be fulfilled by the One who was now addressing them, in the gospel which he bears to the poor, the release which he announces to the captives, the healing which he offers to those whom sin had blinded, and the freedom he brings to them who were bruised. These were bold statements to make; bold... but true!

A new age had just been heralded. This was so unspeakably in contrast to any preaching from rabbis that had been heard in that synagogue. Edersheim observes:

Indeed, one can scarcely conceive the impression which the Words of Christ must have produced, when promise and fulfilment, hope and reality, mingled and wants of the heart, hitherto unrealised, were awakened, only to be more than satisfied. There was a breathless silence. On one point all were agreed: that they were marvellous words of grace, which had proceeded out of his mouth.

But then the penny dropped. This was the son of Joseph, their village carpenter![29] The atmosphere turned from admiration and expectation to something very different. It prompted a response from him: 'No prophet is accepted in his home town.' They could not bear his presence any longer, not even on that holy Sabbath. They thrust him out from the synagogue and the city itself, not before trying to topple him over the nearby cliff. 'He came to that which was his own, but his own did not receive him' (John 1:11). Cast out of his own city, Jesus pursued his solitary way towards Capernaum.

Capernaum would be his new home. Here he would preach in the synagogue, built by his first Gentile convert, a centurion. Here also was the home of his earliest and closest disciples, the brothers Simon and Andrew and of James and John, the sons of Zebedee. Here he spent the summer, mostly alone, as he built up his ministry in Galilee.

---

29. Matthew 13:54-56.

Chapter 11: Healing and the Sabbath

JOHN 5
(Book 3: Chapter 12)

Autumn came and Jesus travelled from Galilee to 'an unknown feast' in Jerusalem, possibly Rosh Hashanah, the Feast of Trumpets. It appears that he was alone. So where did John get his report on what happened there? The language of the report indicates that Jesus himself recounted it later to his special friend. And what did happen there? The healing at Bethesda.

It was a pool enclosed within five porches by the sheep market, presumably close to the sheep gate, that opened from the busy northern suburb of markets, bazaars and workshops, eastwards upon the road which led over the Mount of Olives and Bethany to Jericho. In the five porches surrounding this pool lay 'a great number of disabled people' in anxious hope of a miraculous cure.

It was thought that an angel descended into the water, causing it to bubble up, and that only he who first stepped into the pool would be cured. This, of course, was not good news to the many who weren't cured! This bubbling up of the water was due not to supernatural but to physical causes, it being a common phenomenon with springs. It seems that Jesus preferred to be here among the suffering multitude than in the pomp of the Temple and among the priests and authorities.

The contrast was clear to all except the actual priests and authorities themselves. Their lives smacked of indifference to the masses, while around them were those who suffered, stretching lame hands into emptiness and wailing out their mistaken hopes into the eternal silence. While the religious leaders were discussing the niceties of what constituted labour on a Sabbath, multitudes of their people were left to perish in their ignorance. On the one hand, a suffering multitude with false expectancies and, on the other hand, the neighbouring self-seeking Temple priests and teachers, who neither understood, heard, nor would have cared for such a cry.

That was the Sabbath of the Pharisees, but not the Sabbath of Jesus, who was quite happy to heal on that day. He selected the most wretched among them all, this 'impotent' (KJV) man, for thirty-eight years a hopeless sufferer, without helper or friend. He healed him as a direct act, no need for any stirring of the waters by an angel!

This didn't go unnoticed. This wretched man was healed without going anywhere near the healing waters! Jesus didn't just teach. He *acted* and this must have sent warning messages to the religious authorities, with their impotent wranglings. Also, it was the holy Sabbath. Unheard of! He, who had made him whole, had told the man to take up his bed and walk, something forbidden on the Sabbath! Here was simple trust, unquestioning obedience to the unseen, unknown but real saviour.

They met again later on at the Temple. What Jesus told him completed the inward healing. As he trusted and obeyed Jesus in the outward cure, so also did he do so inwardly and morally. From the external to the internal, through the temporal to the spiritual and eternal, which is so characteristic of the kingdom of heaven. The healed man now knew to whom he owed faith, gratitude and trust of obedience; and the consequences of this knowledge must have been immeasurable. It would make him a disciple in the truest sense. The man healed by Christ stands in a unique position so that if he were to go back to sin, he would be condemning himself to an uncertain future.

Why would the healed man tell the authorities that it was Jesus? It was only natural that he should do so. This is why Jesus made himself known in the clearest and most obvious way he could, in the Temple area. This was his second declaration in that place. The first time was when he purged his Father's House of the moneylenders. And now, once more in that house, it was his same understanding about God as his Father, and his life as the business of his Father, which answered any anger from others about his 'breach of the Sabbath'.

The Father's Sabbath was *his* Sabbath. The Father's work and his work were the same. He was the Son of the Father. And in this he also taught what the Jewish leaders had never understood, the true meaning of the Sabbath, by emphasising that which was the fundamental thought of the Sabbath – 'the LORD blessed the Sabbath day and made it holy' (Exodus 20:11). He had raised another question, that of his equality with God, and for this he was taken to task.

And so ended that day in Jerusalem. And this is all that we need to know of his stay at the Unknown Feast. With this inward separation and the gathering of hostile parties closes the first and begins the second stage of Jesus' ministry.

Chapter 12: Fishers of Men

—*᠊᠊᠊*—

MATTHEW 4:18-22; MARK 1:16-20; LUKE 5:1-11
(Book 3: Chapter 13)

As Jesus returned to Galilee, it would have been a relief to escape from the stifling spiritual atmosphere of Jerusalem; from the self-seeking, intellectual, heartless collection of rabbis, whose first active persecution Jesus had just encountered in Jerusalem, to the honest, simple, earnest, impulsive Galileans.

His return to Capernaum could not have remained hidden. Close by, on either side of the city, the country was studded with villages and towns, a busy, thriving, happy multitude. During that bright summer he had walked along that lake and by its shore and in the various synagogues preached his gospel. And they had been 'astonished at his doctrine: for his word was with power' (KJV). For the first time, they had heard what they felt to be 'the Word of God' and they had learned to love its sound. What wonder that, immediately on his return, 'the people pressed upon him to hear [it]' (KJV).

Now let us consider fishermen and the scene that next confronts Jesus in our story. It was a busy scene for, among the many industries by the Lake of Galilee, that of fishing was not only the most generally pursued, but perhaps the most lucrative. Tradition had it that since the days of Joshua, and by one of his ten ordinances, fishing in the lake, though under certain necessary restrictions, was free to all. And as fish was among the favourite foods, whether on weekdays or especially at the Sabbath meal, many must have been employed in connection with this trade.

Those engaged in that trade, like Zebedee and his sons, were often men of means and standing, including some rabbis. We can picture it, on that bright autumn morning, the busy scene by the lake, with the fishermen cleaning and mending their nets, perhaps not noticing the gathering crowd. It was Jesus' first walk by the lake on the morning after his return from Judea. They would probably not have known of his presence until he spoke to them. The lives of four of them were about to change. It was time for a commitment to permanent discipleship. The expression 'Follow me' would be readily understood, as implying a call to become the permanent disciple of a teacher. Similarly, it was not only the practice of the rabbis but also regarded as one of the most sacred duties for a master to gather around him a circle of disciples.

Thus, neither Peter and Andrew, nor the sons of Zebedee, could have misunderstood the call of Christ, or even regarded it as strange. Much had changed since their initial call after Jesus had returned from his wilderness temptations. Since then, Jesus had suffered the first persecutions from the religious authorities and proved that he meant business. Now they were giving up their professions to follow him. These four disciples were the first to follow Jesus and would now enjoy the closest relationship with the Master as his mission unfolds.

On that memorable return from his temptation in the wilderness, they had learned to know him as the Messiah and they followed him, but now the Messianic activity of Jesus had passed into another stage and that call would not come as a surprise to their minds or hearts. This now was something totally different from a call to any other discipleship. It was not to learn more of doctrine, but to begin, and to become, something quite new. The disciples of the rabbis, even those of John the Baptist, followed in order to learn; in this case, they were to become 'fishers of men' (KJV). This was a major call on their lives and demanded a special commitment.

What had passed between Jesus and, first the sons of Jonah and then those of Zebedee, happened very quickly. But already the people were pressing around the Master, hungry for the Word. Simon Peter's boat became his pulpit; he had consecrated it by consecrating its owner. When Christ is in the boat and bids us let down the net, there must be a 'great multitude of fishes' (KJV). And all this in this symbolic miracle. Already the net was breaking, when they beckoned to their partners in the other boat that they should come and help them. But what did it all mean to

Simon Peter? He had been called to full discipleship and he had obeyed the call. He had been in his boat beside the Saviour and heard what he had spoken and it had gone to his heart. And now this miracle which he had witnessed! Finding such a quantity of fish on one spot on the Lake of Galilee was not strange, the miracle was in knowing where this spot was! Jesus could see through the intervening waters, right down to the bottom of that sea; he could see through him, to the very bottom of Peter's heart. This is what he meant when 'he fell down at Jesus' knees, saying, Depart from me; for I am a sinful man, O Lord' (KJV). And this is why Jesus comforted him: 'Don't be afraid; from now on you will fish for people.'

Chapter 13: Galilee Healings

MATTHEW 8:14-17; MARK 1:21-34; LUKE 4:33-41

(Book 3: Chapter 14)

It was the first Sabbath after his return from Jerusalem and the calling of his disciples. He was now being watched from afar. It seems that the authorities of Jerusalem had sent people to track his steps in Galilee. But all seemed calm and undisturbed. It is morning and Jesus goes to the synagogue at Capernaum. He goes to teach there and among the hearers was someone in deep trouble.

Jewish ideas at that time of demonic activity were vague as to the means proposed for their removal. These may be broadly classified as: magical means for the prevention of such influences (such as the avoidance of certain places, times, numbers, or circumstances, amulets etc.) or magical means for the cure of diseases and direct exorcism (either by certain outward means or else by formulae of incantation). While the Gospel accounts aren't clear as to the views of Jesus or of the Gospel writers regarding the exact character of the phenomenon, they do give details as to how the demonised were set free. This was always the same. It consisted neither in magical means nor formulae of exorcism, but always in the word of power which Jesus spoke, or entrusted to his disciples and which the demons always obeyed.

In the synagogue at Capernaum on that Sabbath morning, what Jesus had spoken produced an immediate effect on the demonised, though one which would have surprised all. The very presence of the Christ meant the destruction of this work of the devil. The two couldn't live together! One stronger than the demon had entered the building. It was the Holy One of God, in whose presence the powers of destruction cannot be silent, but must speak and accept their ineffectiveness and ultimate doom. There was no battle; victory was secured by virtue of who Jesus was. He had come not only to destroy the works of the devil but *to set the prisoners free.*

He gagged the confessions of the demon. It was not by such voices that he would have his Messiahship ever proclaimed! Such testimony was both unfitting and dangerous. Jesus was perhaps the only person in history to control his own narrative! Those who witnessed this turned to their neighbour and asked, 'What is this? A new teaching – and with authority! He even gives orders to impure spirits and they obey him.'

From the synagogue, we follow him and his disciples to Peter's home, to his mother-in-law, prostrate with a burning fever. The Talmud gives this disease the name 'Eshatha Tsemirta' and prescribes for it a magical remedy involving an iron knife and a thornbush! Bending over the sufferer, Jesus 'rebuked the fever' (Luke 4:39) as he had done to the demon earlier, then lifting her by the hand, she rose up. Healed, to 'minister' to them, as the first deaconess in Church history! And what a Sabbath meal it must have been, after that scene in the synagogue and after that healing in the house, when Jesus was the guest, they who had witnessed it all sat and ate together.

It was evening. The sun was setting and the Sabbath was over. All that day word had spread about what had been done in the synagogue. It had also been whispered what had taken place in the house of their neighbour, Simon. One conviction had been clear to them all, that he spoke with authority; with authority and power he commanded even the unclean spirits and they obeyed. No scene is more characteristic of the Christ than that on this autumn evening at Capernaum. Let Edersheim explain:

On that evening no one in Capernaum thought of business, pleasure or rest. There must have been many homes of sorrow, care and sickness there and in the populous neighbourhood around. To them, to all, had the door of hope now been opened. Truly, a new sun had risen on them, with healing in his wings. No disease too desperate, when even the demons accepted the authority of his rebuke. From all parts, they bring them; mothers, widows, wives, fathers, children, husbands. The whole city throngs, a hushed, solemnised, overawed multitude, expectant, waiting at the door of Simon's dwelling. There they laid them, along the street up to the marketplace, on their beds or brought them, with pleas and hopes. What a symbol of this world's misery, need, and hope; what a symbol, also, of what the Christ really is as the great consoler! Never, surely, was he more truly the Christ than when, in the stillness of that evening, under the starlit sky, he went through that suffering throng, laying his hands in the blessing of healing on every one of them and casting out many devils.

So ended that Sabbath in Capernaum, a Sabbath of healing, joy and true rest (though perhaps not for Jesus himself!). But far and wide, into every place of the country around, throughout all the region of Galilee, spread the tidings, and with them the fame of him whom demons must obey, though they dare not pronounce him the Son of God. And on people's ears fell his name with the sweet softness of infinite promise, 'like rain upon the mown grass, as showers that water the earth' (Psalm 72:6, KJV).

MATTHEW 4:23; MARK 1:35-39; LUKE 4:42-44
(Book 3: Chapter 15)

What an exhausting day that must have been for him. Yet, the following day, Jesus woke up very early, between three and six o'clock in the morning. It was not until some time afterwards that the disciples went out looking for him. After such a day, and with the prospect of starting his second journey through Galilee – this time in far different circumstances – he knew that he had to gird himself in prayer. Thus also would they learn that he was not merely a worker of miracles, but that he, whose word demons obeyed, lived a life not of outward but of inward power, in fellowship with his Father and who soaked his work with prayer. But as yet, it seemed difficult for them to realise this.

They all wanted a repeat performance in Capernaum, more of what they experienced the day before. But this was the very reason why he had withdrawn here. He had come, not to attract the crowds and be proclaimed a king, but to preach the kingdom of God. He was not to be the expected hero of Jewish legend but someone very different!

This second journey through Galilee, which the three Gospels connect with the stay at Capernaum, marks a turning point in the working of the Christ. As already stated, the occurrences at the Unknown Feast in Jerusalem formed a new point of departure. Jesus had fully presented his claims to the religious authorities and they had been fully rejected by the scribes and the others. As a result, he separated himself from that 'untoward generation' (Acts 2:40, KJV) and thus began his systematic persecution by the authorities when his movements were tracked and watched.

MATTHEW 8:2-4; MARK 1:40-45; LUKE 5:12-16

Significantly, his work began where that of the rabbis ended. Whatever remedies – medical, magical, or sympathetic – Rabbinic writings may indicate for various kinds of disease, leprosy is not included in the catalogue. They left aside what even the Old Testament marked as spiritual death, by insisting that those so stricken avoid all contact with the living and even to take the appearance of mourners. There was simply no hope offered for them! As the leper passed by, his clothes rent, his hair dishevelled and the lower part of his face and his upper lip covered, it was as one going to death who reads his own burial service, while the mournful words, 'Unclean! Unclean!' which he uttered proclaimed that his was both a living and a spiritual death.

Again, the Old Testament and even Jewish traditions saw leprosy primarily as a moral, spiritual issue rather than a sanitary issue. The isolation they suffered from the world, stopping them from entering any walled city, could not have been merely prompted by the wish to prevent infection.

Although the sacrificial ritual for the cleansed leper implies at least the possibility of a cure, it is in every instance traced to the direct agency of God. The possibility of any cure through a human agency was never contemplated by the Jews. Rabbinic Law teaches us how to recognise true leprosy from its symptoms. Anyone might make the medical inspection, although only a descendant of Aaron could formally pronounce clean or unclean. Once declared leprous, the sufferer was soon made to feel the utter heartlessness of Rabbinism.

To banish him outside walled towns may have been a necessity which, perhaps, required to be enforced by the threatened penalty of forty stripes save one. Similarly, lepers were to be the first to enter and last to leave a synagogue and that they should occupy a separate compartment (*Mechitsah*), ten palms high and 6ft wide.

The Old Testament mentioned eleven principal kinds of defilement. In the elaborate code of defilements in Jewish tradition, leprosy was not only one of 'the fathers of uncleanness' but, next to defilement from the dead, stood foremost among them. Not merely actual contact with the leper, but even his entrance defiled a home and everything in it, to the beams of the roof. The rabbis loved to trace disease to moral causes. 'No death without sin, and no pain without transgression' and 'The sick is not healed, till all his sins are forgiven him'. These are much-repeated sayings.

We can now in some measure appreciate the contrast between Jesus and his contemporaries in attitudes towards the leper. There was no Old Testament precedent for the healing of the leper in the Gospel accounts, not in the case of Moses, nor even in that of Elisha, and there was no Jewish expectancy of it. But to have heard him teach, to have seen or known him as healing all manner of disease, must have carried to the heart the conviction of his absolute power. Surely nothing is beyond this power?

The leper approached him, something he would have never dared to do to a rabbi. 'Lord, if you are willing, you can make me clean.' This is not a prayer, but simple faith in his power and an absolute commitment to him of his helpless, hopeless need. And Jesus, touched with compassion, responded.

It is not quite so easy at first sight to understand why Jesus should instruct the leper to tell no one of this amazing miracle. The kingdom of God was not to be promoted through ostentation and bluster (as it tends to be these days), but as we study the character of Jesus, we see that the opposite is true. Yet the nature of this miracle was such that word was going to get out in one way or another! But what it now meant was that he could no more enter the cities, but remained outside, where people came to him from every quarter.

In the meantime, the ex-leper had to present himself to the priest and conform to the ritual requirements of the Mosaic Law as they examine this claim of this impossible healing! This was, in fact, going to be a testimony to them. There were to be consequences, of course, for Jesus. The open rupture between Jesus and the Jewish authorities, which had commenced at the Unknown Feast at Jerusalem, was to lead now to active hostility. The synagogues of Galilee are no longer the quiet scenes of his teaching and miracles; his word and deeds no longer pass unchallenged. Now he has to deal with the presence and hostile watchfulness of the scribes and Pharisees, who for the first time appear on the scene of his ministry. It is through their influence that the Galileans, so accepting of him before, were being subtly poisoned against him.

Now we find him accused of blasphemy and now it became sinful for Jesus to extend mercy on the Sabbath to him whose hand was withered, and people began to question why he was consorting with 'publicans and sinners' (Matthew 9:10, KJV). The religious 'spin doctors' were plying their trade to some success. 'Fake news' was around even in those days!

MATTHEW 9:1-8; MARK 2:1-12; LUKE 5:17-26
(Book 3: Chapter 16)

We know that the Gospels only report events of importance to the narrative of his life and times so it is interesting to note that, in the second journey of Jesus through Galilee, no other special event is recorded than the healing of the leper. This was a key event in the battle Jesus had with the religious authorities. For the rabbis stood powerless in the face of the living death of leprosy, so they had no word of forgiveness to speak to the conscience burdened with sin and no word of welcome to the sinner. But this was the inmost meaning of the two events which the Gospels places next to the healing of the leper; the forgiveness of sins in the case of the paralytic and the welcome to the chief of sinners in the call of Levi-Matthew.

The unspoken charge of the scribes was that, by forgiving sins, Jesus blasphemed by making himself equal with God.[30] The healing of the paralytic was to show the scribes that he had 'authority' for the forgiving of sins, something which the Jews rightly regarded as the divine prerogative. The words which Jesus spoke to the paralytic, 'Get up, take your mat and go home' are to the very letter the same that he used when he healed the man at the Pool of Bethesda. After this encounter in Jerusalem, the authorities had sent representatives to watch, oppose and, if possible, entrap Jesus. Now that he was claiming authority to act as he did in forgiving the sins of the paralytic, their dossier was beginning to fill up alarmingly!

It was probably wintertime by now. The home in question was probably his temporary home. The general impression is that this audience was rather in a state of indecision than of sympathy with Jesus. It included 'Pharisees and doctors of the law' (KJV) who had come on purpose from the towns of Galilee, from Judea and from Jerusalem. Their influence must have been felt by the people. Although irresistibly attracted by Jesus, an element of curiosity, if not of doubt, would mingle with their feelings as they looked at their leaders, who were still generally respected. Dare they embrace this 'miracle worker' or did fear of the authorities trump everything?

Jesus is speaking the Word, standing in the covered gallery that ran round the courtyard of such houses and opened into the various apartments. Perhaps he was standing within the entrance of the guest-chamber, while the scribes were sitting within that apartment, or beside

---

30. John 5:18.

him in the gallery. The court before him is thronged with people, spilling out into the street.

All are listening, enthralled by his words, when all of a sudden some men appear carrying a paralytic on his pallet. But with a courtyard crowded out into the street, to catch Jesus' attention would have been a tall order. In the hearts of those who bore the paralysed, was the belief that Jesus could and that he would heal. They must have heard it from others; they must have witnessed it themselves in other instances. And as for the paralytic himself, he would have the fear, born out of tradition, that his sins may hinder his healing! This was indeed a most anxious man. And so their minds were made up. If they could not approach Jesus in the traditional manner, they had to find another way. One can imagine Jesus pausing and the breathless surprise of the crowd as an opening through the tiles appeared, and slowly a pallet was let down before them.

It must have been a marvellous sight. This energy and determination of faith exceeded anything that had been witnessed before. Jesus saw it and he spoke. This open outburst of faith shone out the more brightly, from its contrast with the clouds of unbelief within the breast of those scribes who had come to watch and ensnare Jesus.

As yet no one had spoken, for the silence of expectancy had fallen on them all. Could he, and, if he could, would he help – and what would he do? Jesus knew that there was not only faith but also fear in the heart of that man. Hence the first words which he spoke to him were: 'Be of good cheer' (KJV). Remember, he was speaking to one who had been taught that suffering was a consequence of sin. Jesus spoke forgiveness to his soul; there was a higher need for the word which brought forgiveness, before that which gave healing.

He first spoke forgiveness, then he proved he had the authority to do so by healing the man! Had the two been inverted, there would have been evidence of his power, but not of his divine personality, nor of his having authority to forgive sins; and this, not the doing of miracles, was the object of his teaching and mission, of which the miracles were only secondary evidence. Putting it in simpler terms, he first told them who he was, then he proved it by his actions! If the healing had failed, so would his claims about himself! It would have been far safer for him to reverse these actions, but since when has Jesus ever been safe?

The scribes were appalled. 'He blasphemes!' From their point of view, they were right, for God alone can forgive sins and that power has never been given to a person. But was he a mere man, like even the most honoured of God's servants? Man, indeed; but the 'Son of Man' in the emphatic and well-understood sense of being the representative man, who was to bring a new life to humanity; the Second Man, the 'last Adam' (1 Corinthians 15:45), the Lord from heaven.

Chapter 14: The Apostles

(Book 3: Chapter 17)

There are two main differences between Christianity and all other religious systems, including Rabbinic Judaism. All others offer no hope to the sinner until, through some means, he *ceases* to be a sinner. Only then will he be welcome to God. By contrast, Jesus first welcomes them to God and so makes them a forgiven sinner. The one demands and the other imparts life. And so Jesus came not to 'call the righteous, but sinners', not to repentance, as is implied in Matthew 9:13, Mark 2:17 and particularly Luke 5:32, but to himself, to the kingdom. *And this is the beginning of repentance.*

But, as the rabbis were powerless regarding the forgiveness of sins, so they accordingly had no word of welcome or help for the sinner. The very term 'Pharisee' or 'separated one' implied the exclusion of sinners and reeked of self-righteousness. The contempt for those 'others' arose from the thought that as 'the Law' was the glory and privilege of Israel, ignorance of it was inexcusable. It was a principle that 'the ignorant cannot be pious'. The yoke of the 'kingdom of God', as they saw it, was the calling of every 'true Israelite'. To them, it lay in external, not internal conformity to the Law of God, 'in meat and drink', not in 'righteousness, peace and joy in the Holy Spirit' (Romans 14:17). They had got it all so wrong!

As regards to repentance, the teaching of Jesus is in absolute and fundamental opposition to that of the rabbis. According to Jesus Christ, when we have done all we can, we are not to feel condemned in any way. According to the rabbis, as Paul puts it, 'righteousness comes by the Law'[31] and, when it is lost, the Law alone can restore life whereas, according to Christian teaching, it only brings death.

Thus there was, at the very foundation of religious life, an absolute chasm between Jesus and his contemporaries. In one respect, the view

---

31. Implied in Romans 4:13.

of the rabbis was in some measure derived from the Old Testament, though by an external and, therefore, false interpretation of its teaching. In the Old Testament, also, 'repentance' was Teshubhah, meaning 'return' while, in the New Testament, it is 'change of mind'. In point of fact, the full meaning of repentance as Teshubhah for the rabbis is only realised when a person has returned to the observance of the Law. Then, 'sins of commission' are looked upon as if they had been unintentional. In truth, the rabbis knew nothing of forgiveness of sin as something free and unconditional.

So, in terms of the need for repentance, the vital difference between the rabbis and the gospel lies in this: that whereas Jesus Christ freely invited all sinners, whatever their past, assuring them of welcome and grace, the last word of the rabbis is only despair and a kind of pessimism. For it is repeatedly declared in the case of certain sins that even if a person genuinely and truly repented, they must expect immediately to die. Indeed, their death would be the evidence that their repentance was genuine since, though such a sinner might turn from their evil, it would be impossible for them, if they lived, to lay hold of the good, and to do it. Where was the possibility of hope in that?

MATTHEW 9:9-13; MARK 2:13-17; LUKE 5:27-32

It is in the light of the above that the call of Levi-Matthew must be read. We are probably by now in the early springtime when Jesus 'went forth again by the sea side' (KJV). Matthew must have frequently heard him as he taught by the seashore. For this would be the best place for this purpose, as it would be close to the landing place for the many boats that used the lake, as well as close to the highway up to Damascus, the Upper Galilean road. Maximum footfall, as modern marketeers would declare!

Matthew's profession was one held in low esteem by the rabbis (as well as just about everyone else!). It was said that repentance was especially difficult for tax-gatherers and custom-house officers. The Talmud distinguishes between two classes of 'publicans': the tax-gatherer and the

Mokhes, the custom-house official. The latter, which included Matthew in its ranks, was especially hated. There was tax and duty upon all imports and exports, on all that was bought and sold. If it moved (or didn't move), they would find a way to tax it from 2½ to 12½ per cent! The very word 'Mokhes' seems, in its root meaning, to be associated with the idea of oppression and injustice. He was literally an oppressor.

So, here were Jesus and Matthew, the hated and 'irredeemable' Mokhes. But Jesus wasn't like the other rabbis; there was not this great and almost impassable gap between him and Matthew. Matthew had seen and heard him in the synagogue and knew that he was different, so unlike the other rabbis who told him that, for him, repentance was next to impossible. And so Matthew sat before his custom house and hoped. Perhaps he may have witnessed the call of the first disciples; he certainly must have known the fishermen and shipowners of Capernaum. And now it appeared as if Jesus had been brought still nearer to Matthew, and when Jesus fixed on him that look of love which searched the inmost depth of the soul and made him the true 'fisher of men', it needed not a moment's thought or consideration.

'Follow me' and the past seemed all swallowed up in the present heaven of bliss. He said not a word, for his soul was in the speechless surprise of unexpected love and grace; but he rose up, left the custom house and followed him.

Jesus answered the Pharisees. And he not only silenced them but, by doing so, demonstrated his very purpose and mission. 'It is not the healthy who need a doctor, but those who are ill.' He pointed them towards what their own Scriptures meant, their misinterpretation of the doctrine of sacrifice, their ignorance of the fundamental principle of the spiritual meaning of the Law rather than the letter of the Law. 'I will have mercy, and not sacrifice' (KJV). They knew no mercy that was not sacrifice; he knew no sacrifice, real and acceptable to God, that was not mercy. And this also is a fundamental principle of the Old Testament, as spiritually understood. 'I have not come to call the righteous, but sinners.' This marks the standpoint of Jesus and points to his true kingdom.

MATTHEW 10:2-4; MARK 3:13-19; LUKE 6:12-19

The call of Matthew accompanied the call of the other disciples (who were also designated *apostles*), starting with Peter and Andrew, James and John, Philip and Bartholomew (or Bar Telamyon, generally supposed the same as Nathanael). Thomas, who is called Didymus (which means 'twin'), is closely connected with Matthew. James is expressly named as the son of Alphaeus or Clopas. This we know to have been also the name of Matthew's father. James, Judas and Simon seem to have been brothers. Judas is designated as Lebbaeus, from the Hebrew *lebh*, a heart, and is also named Thaddaeus, a term derived from *Thodah*, from 'praise'. In that case, both Lebbaeus and Thaddaeus would point to the heartiness and the thanksgiving of the apostle and hence to his character. Luke simply designates him as Judas of James, which means that he was the brother (less probably, the son) of James. Thus his real name would have been Judas Lebbaeus, and his surname Thaddaeus.

Closely connected with these two we have in all the Gospels, Simon, surnamed Zelotes or Cananaean (not Canaanite), both terms indicating his original connection with the Galilean Zealot party, the 'Zealots for the Law'. He seems to be the son of Clopas, and brother of James, and of Judas Lebbaeus. These three were, in a sense, cousins of Jesus, since, according to Hegesippus,[32] Clopas was the brother of Joseph, while the sons of Zebedee were real cousins, their mother, Salome, being a sister of Mary. Lastly, we have Judas Iscariot, or Ish Kerioth, 'a man of Kerioth', a town in Judah. Thus the betrayer alone would be of Judean origin, the others all of Galilean; and this may throw not a little light on his later actions.

It is clear that the apostolic groupings in the Gospels are ranged into three groups and we may remark how closely connected they were. And

---

32. Christian writer of the early Church period.

yet, as we remember the history of their calling, we remind ourselves that Jesus' decision came after a night of solitary prayer on the mountainside. Then, at early dawn he 'called his disciples ... and chose twelve of them, whom he also designated apostles', 'that they should be with him, and that he might send them forth to preach, And to have power to heal sicknesses, and to cast out devils' (KJV).

Chapter 15: The Sermon on the Mount

MATTHEW 5 – 7
(Book 3: Chapter 18)

Before the calling of the Twelve as his ambassadors and representatives, Jesus probably spent a night of lonely prayer on one of those mountain ranges which stretch to the north of Capernaum. But as dawn broke, the eager multitude waited for him on the plateau beneath. He now approached them with words of comfort and power of healing. As they pressed around him for that touch, he drew back again to the mountain and through the clear air of the bright spring day spoke what has ever since been known as the 'Sermon on the Mount' from the place where he sat.

Once we have drunk from the wellspring of Jesus' teaching there is really no going back to the broken cisterns of the rabbis. It is unlikely that the Sermon on the Mount was really spoken by Jesus on just this one occasion. We can gather this from the plan and structure of Matthew's Gospel account. There is one characteristic of the Sermon on the Mount which, indeed, throws light on the curious chronological recording of events, such as placing it before the calling of the apostles. And that is the connection to the Law of Moses, through the divine revelation in the Ten Commandments from Mount Sinai.

We would regard the 'Sermon' as presenting the fullest picture of the ideal man of God, of the inward and outward manifestation of discipleship. We might discern four main aspects here. First, the right relationship between people and God, true righteousness rather than the prevailing Jewish views of merit and of reward. Secondly, we would mark the same contrast as regards sin and temptation. Thirdly, we would note it as regards salvation and, lastly, as regards what may be termed moral theology and the like.

And all of this serves to show the contrast between New Testament humility, as opposed to Rabbinic pride; New Testament perfection, in terms of the new life offered, as opposed to Rabbinic 'perfection', an attempt by external or internal means to strive for God. This brings us to a general outline of the Sermon on the Mount.

It is not the 'New Testament' Torah or set of laws. Its great subject is neither righteousness, nor yet any 'New' law, but the kingdom of God. It is not a new doctrine, nor yet does it address itself to any outward observances. This marks a difference in principle from all other teachings. Jesus came to found a kingdom, not a school; to institute a fellowship, not to propound a system.

To the first disciples, all doctrinal teaching sprang out of fellowship with him. They saw him and therefore believed; they believed and therefore learned the truths connected with him and springing out of him. The Sermon on the Mount differs from all contemporary Jewish teaching, so therefore it is impossible to compare it with any other system of morality. The difference here is one not of degree, but of standpoint.

The words of Jesus indeed mark the foundation of true morality. Now, every moral system is a road by which, through self-denial, discipline and effort, people seek to reach the goal. Instead, Jesus begins with this goal and places his disciples at once in the position to which all other teachers point as the endpoint! Others work up to the goal of becoming the 'children of the kingdom'; he makes people 'children of the kingdom' freely by his grace. What the others labour for, he gives. They begin by demanding. He begins by giving because he brings good tidings of forgiveness and mercy. Accordingly, in the real sense, there is neither a new law nor a moral system here, but the entrance into a new life: 'Be perfect, therefore, as your heavenly Father is perfect.' It has *always* been there; Jesus just reminds us of the way to think and to act and to embrace what has been freely given to us.

But if the Sermon on the Mount is not a new system of morality, it follows that the promises attached to the Beatitudes must not be regarded as the reward or result of the spiritual state with which they are respectively connected. It is not because a person is 'poor in spirit' that theirs is the kingdom of heaven, in the sense of growing into it, neither is the kingdom the reward of being 'poor in spirit'. It is simply a description of life in the kingdom of heaven, a place where the 'poor in spirit' can feel a sense of belonging.

The connecting link is in each case Jesus himself, because he stands between our present and our future and 'has opened the Kingdom of heaven to all believers.' Thus, the promise represents the gift of grace by Jesus in the new kingdom, as adapted to each case. It is Christ, then, as the King, who is here flinging open the gates of his kingdom.

In the first part of the Sermon on the Mount, the kingdom of God is described generally, first positively and then negatively, marking especially how its righteousness goes deeper than the mere letter of the Old Testament Law.

It opens with the Ten Beatitudes, which are the New Testament counterpart to the Ten Commandments. These present to us, not the observance of the Law written on stone, but the realisation of that Law which, by the Spirit, is written on the fleshly tablets of the heart. These Ten Commandments in the Old Covenant were preceded by a prologue. The Ten Beatitudes have, characteristically, not a prologue but an epilogue. This closes the first section, of which the object was to present the kingdom of God.

This epilogue, in verses 17 to 20 of Matthew 5, forms a grand climax and transition to the criticism of the Old Testament Law in its merely literal application, as the scribes and Pharisees tended to do. The second part is contained in Chapter 6 of Matthew. In this, the criticism of the Law is carried deeper, emphasising that there is more to it than mere observance of the outward commandments.

The kingdom of God addresses motivations. What are the reasons for giving charitably? What constitutes riches, and where should they be sought? This is indicated in verses 19 to 21. Regarding prayer, what really matters are our motivations and reasons for it. It is to lay our inner person wholly open to the light of God in genuine, earnest simplicity, to be quite shone through by him. And what prompts real fasting? A right view of the relation in which the body with its wants stands to God, the physical to the spiritual.

It is the spirit of prayer that must rule in all three areas; the self-dedication to God, the seeking first after the kingdom of God and his righteousness, that person, self and life may be baptised in it. Such are the real charities, the real prayers, the real fasts of the kingdom of God.

If we have understood the meaning of the two first parts of the Sermon on the Mount, we cannot be at a loss to understand its third part, as outlined in Chapter 7 of Matthew. First, the kingdom of God cannot be limited. Secondly, it cannot be extended by external means, but rather it comes to us from God. Thirdly, it is not preached when it is merely thought of as an external kingdom. Lastly, it is very real, and true and good in its effects. And this kingdom, as received by each of us, is like a solid house on a solid foundation, which nothing can shake or destroy.

The infinite contrast between the kingdom as presented by Jesus, with Jewish contemporary teaching, is the more striking, that it was clothed in words with which all his hearers were familiar. No part of the New Testament has had a larger array of parallels in Rabbinic thought than the Sermon on the Mount. Many of these Rabbinic quotations are, however, entirely inappropriate, the similarity lying in an expression or a form of words. Occasionally, the misleading error goes even further and that is quoted in an illustration of Jesus' sayings which implies quite the opposite. There is no room here for a detailed analysis, but a few examples will sufficiently illustrate our meaning.

To begin with the first Beatitude, to the 'poor in spirit', since theirs is the kingdom of heaven – this early Jewish saying marks not the optimism, but the pessimism of life. 'Ever be more and more lowly in spirit, since the expectancy of man is to become the food of worms.' A contrast to Jesus' promise of grace to the 'poor in spirit'!

What of the promise of 'the kingdom of heaven'? What did the rabbis understand as the kingdom to all people, Gentiles as well as Jews, who were 'poor in spirit'? What fellowship of spirit can there be between Jewish teaching and the first Beatitude? It is the same sad self-righteousness that underlies the other Rabbinic parallels to the Beatitudes, pointing to the negative rather than the positive.

So, when the rabbis talk of how blessed are the mourners, they put stress on the mourning rather than the blessing. No Rabbinic parallel can be found to the third Beatitude or to the fourth one, to 'those who hunger and thirst for righteousness'. Rabbinism would have quite a different idea of 'righteousness', considered as 'good works' and chiefly as charitable giving. They speak of a quality of mercy that is supposed not only to bring reward but to also atone for sins.

The Beatitude concerned with peacemaking has many analogies for the rabbis but they would never have connected the designation of 'children of God' with any but Israel. A similar remark applies to the use of the expression 'kingdom of heaven' in the next Beatitude. One by one, as we place the sayings of the rabbis by the side of those of Jesus in this Sermon on the Mount, we notice opposite understandings, whether as regards righteousness, sin, repentance, faith, the kingdom, charity, prayer, or fasting.

Only two points may be specially selected because they are so frequently brought forward by writers as proof that the sayings of Jesus did not rise above those of the chief Talmudic authorities. The first of these refers to the well-known words of our Lord, 'So in everything, do to others what you would have them do to you, for this sums up the Law and the Prophets.' This is compared to the following Rabbinic parallel, in which the gentleness of Hillel is contrasted with the opposite disposition of Shammai. The latter is said to have harshly repelled an intending proselyte, who wished to be taught the whole Law while standing on one foot, while Hillel received him with this saying: 'What is hateful to you, do not to another. This is the whole Law, all else is only its explanation.'

Yet there is a vast difference between this negative command or the prohibition to do to others what is hateful to ourselves, and the positive direction to do to others as we would have them do to us. The first does not rise above the standpoint of the Law, being as yet far from that love which would lavish on others the good we desire. The second, from the mouth of Jesus, embodies the nearest approach to the absolute love of which human nature is capable, focusing on our conduct to others.

The second instance that is worth recounting is the supposed similarity between petitions in the Lord's Prayer and Rabbinic prayers. Both the spirit and the manner of prayer are presented by the rabbis so externally and with such details as to make it quite different from prayer as our Lord taught his disciples. It is scarcely necessary to point to the self-righteousness which is the most painful characteristic of Rabbinism.

But there are points of view that may be gained from Rabbinic writings. Helpful to the understanding of the Sermon on the Mount, although not of its spirit. Thus, when we read that not 'one jot or ... tittle' (KJV) shall pass from the Law, it is painfully interesting to find in the Talmud the following quotation and mistranslation of Matthew 5:17: 'I have come not to diminish from the Law of Moses, nor yet have I come to add to the Law of Moses.' But the Talmud here significantly omits the addition made by Jesus, on which all depends: 'till all be fulfilled' (KJV).

Jewish tradition mentions this very letter *yod* (jot) as irremovable, adding that if all in the world were gathered together to abolish the least letter in the Law, they would not succeed. Not a letter could be removed from the Law – a saying illustrated by this curiosity, that the *yod* which was taken by God out of the name of Sarah (Sarai), was added to that of Hoshea, making him Joshua (Jehoshua). Similarly, the guilt of changing those little hooks ('tittles') which make the distinction between some Hebrew letters is declared so great that, if such were done, *the world would be destroyed*.

The above comparisons of Rabbinic sayings with those of our Lord lay no claim to completeness. They will, though, help to explain the impression left on the hearers of Jesus. But what must have filled them with wonder and awe was that he who so taught also claimed to be the God-appointed final Judge of all, whose fate would be decided not merely by professed discipleship, but by their real relationship with him (Matthew 7:21-23).

'The people were astonished at his doctrine: For he taught them as one having authority, and not as the scribes.'

Chapter 16: A Healing and a Raising

MATTHEW 8:5-15; LUKE 7:1-10

(Book 3: Chapter 19)

We are once again in Capernaum. It is remarkable how much in the life and ministry of Jesus centres around that little fishing town. Here was the home of that believing court official whose child Jesus had healed. Here also was the household of Peter and here the paralytic had found forgiveness of his sins and health of his body. Here Matthew had heard and followed the call of Jesus and here the good centurion had in stillness learned to love Israel and serve Israel's King and built that splendid synagogue, which had been consecrated by the presence and teaching of Jesus.

And now, from the Mount of Beatitudes, Jesus returned again to his temporary home at Capernaum. Not that he received much rest, for many in the multitude had followed him. Soon came the summons of the pagan centurion and the healing of his servant, which both Matthew and Luke record.

Yet there are minor differences in these two accounts. This is due to the peculiar standpoint of their narratives. If we keep in view the historical objective of Matthew as primarily addressing himself to Jewish readers, while Luke wrote more especially for Gentile readers, we arrive, at least, at one remarkable outcome of the variations in their narratives. Strange to say, the Jewish Gospel gives the pro-Gentile, the Gentile narrative the pro-Jewish, presentation of the event!

Thus, the Matthew account shows the direct dealing with the pagan centurion on the part of Jesus, while in the Luke account the dealing with the heathen is indirect, focusing on the intervention of Jews and on the grounds of the centurion's spiritual sympathy with Israel.

But the fundamental truth in both accounts is the same. It is not that the Gentiles are preferred before Israel. Their faith is only put on an equality with that of believing Israel. It is not Israel but Israel's fleshly claims and unbelief that are rejected; and Gentile faith occupies not a new position outside the promises made to Israel but shares with Abraham, Isaac and Jacob the fulfilment of the promise made to their faith. Thus, we have here the widest Jewish universalism, the true interpretation of Israel's hope.

The cure was the result of the centurion's faith and of that of his servant. The pagan centurion is a real historical person. He was captain of the troop quartered in Capernaum and in the service of Herod Antipas. He was simply one who had learned to love Israel and to reverence Israel's God, so much so that he had built that synagogue. There might have been something to incline him towards this love in his early upbringing, perhaps in Caesarea, or in his family relationships, perhaps in that obedient servant.

There is a heartfelt appeal for his sick, seemingly dying servant. Again, the centurion in the fullest sense believes in the power of Jesus to heal, in the same manner as he knows his own commands as an officer would be implicitly obeyed. His question was not whether Jesus *could* heal his servant, but rather *would* he heal him. He was on firm ground here; Jesus never disappointed acts of pure faith. The fact that Jesus contrasted the faith of this Gentile with that of Israel indicates that his heart was in the right place. His self-acknowledged 'unfitness' betrayed the real 'fitness' of this good soldier for membership with the true Israel, and his deep-felt 'unworthiness' the real 'worthiness' for the kingdom and its blessings.

There is a good reason for the inclusion of this story in the New Testament. It was that the blessings of the kingdom are not connected with our outward deeds or inward thoughts but are rather granted by the King to that simple faith in him, regardless of your ethnic origins.

The words of Jesus to the believing centurion were in total contrast to Jewish teaching. They were certain that the Gentiles could not possibly share in the feast of the Messiah of Israel. To use Rabbinic terms, Gentiles were 'children of Gehinnom' but Israel 'children of the kingdom', 'children of the upper chamber' and 'of the world to come'. In fact, in their view, God had first sat down on His throne as King when the hymn of deliverance (Exodus 15:1) was raised by Israel – the people who took upon itself that yoke of the Law which all other nations of the world had rejected. What a shock it must have been when he turned their cherished beliefs on their heads!

And so the story of the believing centurion is another application of the Sermon on the Mount. Negatively, it differentiated the kingdom from Israel; while, positively, it placed the hope of Israel and fellowship with its promises within reach of both Jew and Gentile.

Edersheim states the truth plainly:

> He who taught such new and strange truth could never be called a mere reformer of Judaism. There cannot be 'reform' where all the fundamental principles are different. Surely he was the Son of God, the Messiah of men, who, in such surrounding, could so speak to Jew and Gentile of God and his Kingdom.

LUKE 7:11-17
(Book 3: Chapter 20)

It was early springtime in Galilee. Yesterday, it was the sorrow of the pagan centurion which touched the heart of the supreme commander of life and death. Soon afterwards it is the same sorrow of a Jewish mother which touches the heart of the Son of Mary. In that presence, grief and death cannot continue and the touch of death could not make him unclean. It was a journey of more than twenty-five miles from Capernaum to Nain, where he met the funeral procession.

We have a widow and her dead son. We have Jewish thoughts of death and after death, with so little consolation that even the most pious rabbi would be uncertain of his future. And then we have the wretched thoughts of a mother losing a child. In passionate grief the mother has rent her upper garment, the last sad prayers have been offered for the dead, the body has been laid on the ground, hair and nails have been cut and the body washed, anointed and wrapped in the best the widow could procure. She would sit on the floor, neither eat meat nor drink wine. She would eat little food and be unable to pray. She would be in the house of a neighbour, or in another room, or at least with her back to the dead.

Along the road from Endor streamed the great multitude who were following Jesus. Here they met, life and death. The connecting link between them was the deep sorrow of the widowed mother. Jesus touched the bier, perhaps the very wicker basket in which the dead youth lay. He dreaded not the greatest of all defilements, that of contact with the dead, which Rabbinism, in its elaboration of the letter of the Law, had surrounded with endless terrors. One word of sovereign command, 'And he that was dead sat up, and began to speak.'

It wasn't just Jesus' sympathy with intense suffering and bereavement, there was more, what Edersheim calls a 'moral motive', a manifestation of his kingdom. The mother had not called out to him. The simplicity and absence of details, the calmness and majesty on the part of Jesus, all so different from how legend would have coloured the scene. Once more, the miracle is described as having taken place, not in the seclusion of a chamber, nor before a few interested witnesses, but in sight of the great multitude which had followed Jesus.

This meeting of the two processions outside the gate of Nain was accidental, yet not in the conventional sense. The arrival of Jesus at that place and time, coinciding with that of the funeral procession from Nain was either accidental or designed. Both happened in the natural course of natural events, but both were divinely planned. The fear of the divine presence fell on those who saw this miracle at Nain and over their souls swept the hymn of divine praise.

Chapter 17: Condemnation!

LUKE 7:36-50
(Book 3: Chapter 21)

The next recorded event in Jesus' journey through Galilee followed almost immediately. This concerns the much-forgiven woman who had much sinned. A rabbi would have reacted very differently to this woman; however gentle and kind he was, he would have taken precisely the opposite direction from that taken by Jesus.

It was in the house of a Pharisee. Antagonism towards Jesus had not grown to levels we will later see, so there is a degree of mutual respect here. Interestingly, the woman is unnamed and perhaps morbid curiosity has associated her history with the name of Mary Magdalene (despite the scripture not mentioning her name).

Some have mistakenly confused this story with the much later anointing of Jesus at Bethany,[33] because of their similarities; in both cases, there was a 'Simon' (perhaps the commonest of Jewish names) and a woman who anointed Jesus. *But they were two separate events.*

Simon the Pharisee's invitation to Jesus does not necessarily indicate that he was onboard with his teachings, including the story of the forgiven debtor spoken here. The question in Simon's mind was, whether he was more than 'teacher' perhaps even a 'prophet'. Cue, the entry of the woman...

We must bear in mind the prejudice then against any conversation with women to realise the gall of this woman in seeking access to the rabbi Jesus, whom so many, including this woman, believed was the Prophet sent from God.

She had brought with her an alabastron (flask) of perfume. This 'flask', not necessarily of glass, but possibly of silver or gold, though probably

---

33. John 12:1-8.

alabaster, was used both to sweeten the breath and perfume the person. The Pharisee would not have been impressed with Jesus over this. After all, if this strange, wandering, popular man, with his strange, novel ways and words were a prophet, he would have known who the woman was, and he should never have allowed her to approach. What Jesus taught next is not, as generally supposed, a parable but an illustration.

To teach Simon, Jesus entered into the Pharisee's own modes of reasoning. Of two debtors, one of whom owned ten times as much as the other, who would best love the creditor, who had freely forgiven them? A rabbi would, according to his Jewish notions, say that he would love most to whom most had been forgiven. This was Jewish theology, the so much for so much.

On Simon's own reasoning, then. He received little, but *she* received much, *because of her 'many sins'*. Undoubtedly, her faith had saved her. What she had heard from his lips, what she knew of him, she had believed. She had believed in the 'good tidings' of peace (see Luke 2:10, KJV) which he had brought, in the love of God and it had saved her. And it was because she was forgiven that she anointed his feet with the outpouring of her heart and, quickly wiping away the flood with her hair, continued kissing and anointing them. He spoke to her and once more with the tenderest delicacy. 'Your sins are forgiven … Your faith has saved you'. This was in contrast with Simon the Pharisee, who showed little love towards him.

LUKE 8:1-3

(Book 3: Chapter 22)

However interesting and important it is to follow the steps of Jesus through Galilee, the task of recording it all chronologically seems rather tricky. And, of course, that wasn't the purpose of the Gospel writers. Their point of view was that of the internal, rather than the external narrative. And so we find events, teachings and parables grouped together by theme and purpose.

Nevertheless, we now find Jesus returning to Capernaum from his missionary journey, accompanied not only by the Twelve but also by loving, grateful women, who ministered to him. Among them, three are specially named.

Mary, called Magdalene, had received body and soul healing from him. Her designation as 'Magdalene' was probably derived from her native city, Magdala, celebrated for its dyes and wools. Also in the party was Joanna (*Yochani*), 'the wife of Chuza Herod's steward' (KJV). The other is Susanna, the 'lily.' The names of the other loving women are not written down, except in the 'Lamb's book of life' (Revelation 21:27).

MATTHEW 9:35[34]

It was on this return journey to Capernaum that the two blind men had their sight restored. It was then, also, that the healing of the demonised dumb man took place. Even these circumstances show that a new stage in the Messianic drama had begun. It is characterised by a fuller unfolding of his teaching and working and, consequently, by more fully developed opposition from the Pharisees. For the two went together.

That new stage had opened on his return from the Unknown Feast in Jerusalem when the 'religious' leaders started following him. It first actively appeared at the healing of the paralytic in Capernaum when, for the first time, we heard the tut-tutting of the scribes and, for the first time also, the distinct declaration about the forgiveness of sins on the part of Jesus.

The same two-fold element appeared in the call of Matthew and the disdain by the Pharisees at Jesus' subsequent eating and drinking with 'sinners'. It was in further development of this separation from the old and now hostile element, that the twelve apostles were next appointed and that distinctive teaching of Jesus addressed to the people in the Sermon on the Mount, which was alike a vindication and an appeal.

---

34. Although the main story of these healings are elsewhere, Matthew 9:35 is a blanket verse covering these and other healings that occurred at this time.

On the subsequent journey through Galilee, the hostile party does not seem to have actually joined Jesus' band, but their growing and now outspoken opposition is increasingly heard, as we saw in the episode with Simon the Pharisee.

MATTHEW 9:32-34; MARK 3:22; MATTHEW 12:22-29,46-50

But the raising of the dead at Nain put them on full alert and news of this reached the leaders at Jerusalem. There seems just sufficient time between this and the healing of the demonised dumb man for them to witness this significant event. They were 'the scribes which came down from Jerusalem' (KJV). Whatever view the leaders at Jerusalem may have taken of the raising at Nain, it could no longer be denied that Jesus was a miracle worker. The rabbis had seen miracles before, even the expelling of demons, but performing the miracle for them was not enough. By whose authority was the miracle performed? By what power, or in what name, did he do these deeds?

Through what power did Jesus do these works? They agreed that it was through that of Satan, or the chief of the demons. They regarded Jesus as not only temporarily, but *permanently*, possessed by a demon. And this demon was, according to them, none other than 'Beelzebub the prince of the devils' (KJV). Thus, in their view, it was really Satan who acted in and through him and Jesus, instead of being recognised as the Son of God, was regarded as an incarnation of Satan.

All this was because his kingdom was precisely the opposite of what they regarded as the kingdom of God. As we have already seen, this was the foundation of their conduct towards the person of Christ.

Their guilt lay in treating the Holy Spirit as if he was of the devil. This was because 'they were of their father the devil, and knew not, nor understood, nor yet loved the light, their deeds being evil'.[35]

And now we can also understand the growth in their active opposition to Jesus. Once they had decided that the miracles of Jesus were due to the

---

35. See John 8:44.

power of Satan and that he was the representative of the Evil One, their course of action was clear. And so was his. From this point on, his attitude to them would be to denounce them. This hostile Judaism of theirs will now be under the judgement of condemnation. This is why he later wept over the Jerusalem that knew not the day of its 'visitation' (KJV).

As 'the multitudes marvelled' saying 'It was never so seen in Israel' (KJV), the Pharisees, without being able to deny the facts, had concluded that the casting out of the demon from the dumb man and all similar works, were done 'through the ruler of the demons'.[36] This probably explains the visit of his mother and brothers. They feared for his safety, with the Pharisees stirring up such opposition against him.

It may seem here that Jesus was disrespectful of his family. There must have been a higher meaning in his words, that would be better understood after his resurrection. It was now important to realise that earthly relationships, even to those nearest and dearest, would bow to their spiritual relationship. We must never forget that Jesus became like us, entering into earthly relationships solely for the sake of the higher spiritual relationships which he was going to bring. Thus, it was not that Jesus was disrespecting his mother, but that it was all about his mission; not for one moment would he neglect the will of his Father as a result of the attentions of his earthly mother. He is not condemning the mother, but rather he places the Father first and this is ever the right relationship in the kingdom of heaven!

---

36. See Mark 3:22.

Chapter 18: Parables

(Book 3: Chapter 23)

We are once more with Jesus and his disciples by the Lake of Galilee. It is later in winter, perhaps a few weeks before Passover. Jesus had left the house with his disciples and so many people had come to hear him that he had to address them from a boat.

Now he 'told them many things in parables', the first of three such occasions. It was a time, as we saw earlier, of early opposition by the Pharisees that was based on his supposed demonic connections. This first series of parables were spoken to demonstrate the elementary truths concerning the planting of the kingdom of God, its development, reality, and value.

There is an internal connection between the parables and the various stages of the life of Jesus. One thing is common to all of them and forms a point of connection between them. They are all sparked off by some lack of response on the part of the hearers, even when the hearers are professing disciples.

This seems indicated in the reason given to his disciples for his use of such teaching; that to them it was 'given to know the mystery of the kingdom of God' but to the others, 'all these things are done in parables' (KJV).

Let's examine the word 'parable'. The verb from which it is derived means 'to project' and the term itself concerns the placing of one thing by the side of another. Perhaps no other mode of teaching was so common among the Jews as that by parables. Usually, they were almost entirely illustrations of what had been said or taught while, in the case of Jesus, they served as the foundation for his teaching. In them, the light of earth was cast heavenwards and that of heaven earthwards. With Jesus, they were to convey spiritual teaching in a form adapted to the standpoint of the hearers.

This may be illustrated by the later parable of the woman looking for her lost coin (Luke 15:8-10), for which there is an almost literal Jewish parallel. In the Jewish parable, the moral is that a man ought to take much greater pains in the study of the Torah than in the search for a coin, since the former promises an eternal reward, while the found coin is just a bit of cash in the pocket! Jesus' version is far more satisfactory.

His parable is intended to highlight the compassion of the Saviour in seeking the lost, and the joy of heaven in their recovery, rather than the merit of study or of works.

In Jewish writings, a parable (*mimshal*) is introduced by some such formula like this: 'I will tell you a parable' or 'to what is the thing like?' Jewish writers esteem parables as devices to place the meaning of the Law within range of the comprehension of all persons. The 'wise king' had introduced this method, the usefulness of which is illustrated by the parable of a great palace which had many doors so that people lost their way until one came who fastened a ball of thread at the chief entrance when all could readily find their way in and out. Even this will illustrate what has been said of the difference between Rabbinic parables and those employed by our Lord.

In the Gospels, illustrations and even proverbial sayings, such as 'Physician, heal thyself' (Luke 4:23, KJV) or that about the blind leading the blind[37] are designated 'parables'. But the term must be here restricted to special conditions. The first of these is, that all parables bear reference to well-known scenes, such as those of daily life or to events.

Such pictures, familiar to the popular mind, are in the parable connected with corresponding spiritual realities. Yet, here also, there is that which distinguishes the parable from the mere illustration. The latter conveys no more than that which was to be illustrated; while the parable

---

37. Matthew 15:14.

conveys this and a great deal beyond it to those who can follow up its shadows to the light by which they have been cast.

In truth, parables are the outlined shadows, as the light of heavenly things falls on well-known scenes, which correspond to and have their higher counterpart in spiritual realities.

So, we have a scene from nature or from life serving as a basis for exhibiting the corresponding spiritual reality. In these first series, the fact that Jesus spoke to the people in parables and only in parables is strongly marked. It appears, therefore, to have been the first time that this mode of popular teaching was used by him. Accordingly, the disciples not only expressed their astonishment but asked him why.

He answers by making a distinction between those to whom it is given to know the mysteries of the kingdom (the disciples) and those to whom all things were done in parables (everyone else). Here we see three parables directed just to his disciples, the rest having already been dismissed. Jesus also explains his methodology – that speaking in parables to the people was to complete that hardening which had been caused by their voluntary rejection of what they had heard.

The key factor was not so much the content of the parables but the different standpoint of the two classes of hearers towards the kingdom of God. This explanation removes what otherwise would be a serious difficulty. For it seems impossible to believe that Jesus had adopted a special mode of teaching to conceal the truth, which might have saved those who heard him. The hardening lay not in this method of teaching but in the state of spiritual deadness that they had found themselves in, despite clear teachings that they had already heard. They were already hardened before they even heard the parable, so they had already decided their own fate.

We are now in some measure able to understand why Jesus, at this point, for the first time adopted teaching through parables.

The reason is this: all of his former teachings had been plain. In them, he had set forth by word and exhibited by fact (in miracles), the kingdom of

God that he had come to open to all believers. The hearers had separated themselves into two parties; those who understood this, his professing disciples and those being swayed by the insistence of the Pharisees of the 'satanic' origin of Jesus' teaching. Things had become more serious and the presentation of the kingdom of God must now be for decision.

These two parties were far apart, leading the one to a clearer understanding of the mysteries of the kingdom, while the other would now regard these mysteries as wholly unintelligible, unbelievable and to be rejected. This is they who had already hardened themselves!

And the grounds for this lay in the respective positions of these two parties towards the kingdom. 'Whoever has will be given more, and they will have an abundance. Whoever does not have, even what they have will be taken from them.'

Let us now examine this first group of parables. Here we see a pattern; the parables spoken to the people, then the reason and explanation given to the disciples. And, finally, another series of parables spoken to the disciples.

On that bright spring morning, when Jesus spoke to the multitude that crowded the shore, he gave them these four parables: concerning he who sowed, concerning the wheat and the tares, concerning the mustard seed and concerning the leaven. All of these parables refer, as is expressly stated, to the kingdom of God; that is, not to any special phase or characteristic of it, but to the kingdom itself.

The first parable is that of him who sowed. The sower has gone forth to sow the good seed. According to Jewish authorities, there was two-fold sowing with the seed either cast by hand or using cattle. In the latter case, a sack with holes was filled with corn and laid on the back of the animal, so that, as it moved onwards, the seed was thickly scattered, on a beaten roadway, on stony places but thinly covered with soil, or where the thorns had not been cleared away, or undergrowth from the thorn-hedge crept into the field, as well as on good ground. The result in each case need not here be repeated. But what meaning would all this convey to the Jewish hearers of Jesus?

How could this sowing and growing be like the kingdom of God? Certainly *not* in the sense in which they expected it. To us, as explained by the Lord, all this seems plain. But to them, there could be no possibility of understanding, but every possibility for misunderstanding it unless, indeed, they stood in right relationship to the 'kingdom of God'. They needed to believe that Jesus was the divine sower and his Word the seed of the kingdom. If this were admitted, they had at least the right premises for understanding this mystery of the kingdom. It was as if the parables were a test to see where one stood concerning Jesus and the kingdom of God. You either didn't get it and were lost (though hopefully only temporarily!), or you got it and were given a deeper understanding.

According to the Jewish view, the Messiah was to appear by a display of power to establish the kingdom. But this was the very idea of the kingdom with which Satan had tempted Jesus at the outset of his ministry. In opposition to it was this mystery of the kingdom, reached through the reception of the seed of the word and personified by Jesus' moral purpose in all that he did. That reception would depend on the nature of the soil, that is, on the mind and heart of the hearers. The kingdom of God was within;[38] it came not by a display of power.

The 'mystery' deepens in the next parable concerning the tares sown among the wheat. According to the common view, these tares represent what is botanically known as the 'bearded Darnel' (*Lolium temulentum*), a poisonous rye grass, very common in the East, 'entirely like wheat until the ear appears'. But the parable makes more sense if we bear in mind that, according to ancient Jewish ideas, the tares were not from a different seed, but only a degenerate kind of wheat. According to the testimony of travellers, most strenuous efforts are always made in the East to weed out the tares. This parable was, of all others, perhaps the strangest and most unintelligible to Jewish ears. Hence, the disciples especially asked for an

---

38. Luke 17:21, KJV.

explanation here. This was also perhaps the most important for them to understand.

As the subsequent experience of the Church has shown, efforts have been made to create purer wheat by gathering out the tares while they grow together. All such have proved failures, because the field is the wide 'world,' because the tares have been sown into the midst of the wheat and by the enemy. For the wheat must be gathered in the heavenly storehouse and the tares bound in bundles to be burned. Then the harvesters shall be the angels of Christ, the gathered tares 'all the stumbling-blocks and those who do the lawlessness' and their burning the casting of them 'into the lake of fire.'[39]

These first parables were intended to present the mysteries of the kingdom as illustrated by the sowing, growing and mixing of the seed. The final two parables set forth another equally mysterious characteristic of the kingdom; that of its development and power, as contrasted with its small and weak beginnings. The parable of the mustard seed demonstrated the relationship between the kingdom and the outside world. The parable of the leaven was concerned with the kingdom and the world within us. The first exhibits the extensiveness, the other the intensiveness, of its power; in both cases at first hidden, almost imperceptible and then... boom!

Once more we say it, that such parables must have been utterly unintelligible to all who did not see the kingdom in the humble, despised Nazarene and in his teaching. But to those whose eyes, ears and hearts had been opened, they would carry most needed instruction and most precious comfort and assurance. Accordingly, we do not find that the disciples either asked or received an interpretation of these parables. They already had sufficient understanding to get it!

The very idea of parables is not about strict scientific accuracy, but about conjuring up popular pictures. It is characteristic of them to present vivid sketches that appeal to the popular mind. Those addressed were

39. See Matthew 13:41-43.

not to weigh every detail, either logically or scientifically, but at once to recognise the aptness of the illustration as presented to the popular mind. Thus, as regards the first of these two parables, the seed of the mustard plant is seen as the smallest of seeds. In fact, the expression, 'small as a mustard seed' had become a popular proverb and was used, not only by Jesus but frequently by the rabbis, to indicate the smallest amount. Such growth of the mustard seed was also a fact well known at the time and this is the first and main point in the parable. The other, concerning the birds which are attracted to its branches, is subsidiary. It is interesting to notice that birds would be attracted to the branches, when we know that mustard was, at that time, mixed with, or used as food for pigeons. And a tree was a familiar Old Testament figure for a mighty kingdom that gave shelter to the nations. Indeed, it is specifically used as an illustration of the Messianic kingdom.

Thus the parable would point to this: that the kingdom of heaven, planted in the field of the world as the smallest seed, in the most humble and unpromising manner, would grow until it far outstripped all other similar plants and gave shelter to all nations under heaven. This is also addressed by the last of the parables addressed at this time to the people, that of the leaven (dough). The point of the parable is that the kingdom of God, when received within, would seem like leaven, hidden, but which would gradually pervade, assimilate and transform the whole of our common life. With this most mysterious characterisation of the kingdom of heaven, the Saviour dismissed the people.

And now he was again alone with the disciples in 'the house' at Capernaum, to which they had returned. Many new and deeper thoughts of the kingdom had come to them. But why had he so spoken to the multitude in such a way? And did they quite understand its solemn meaning themselves? Jesus answered their concerns. The disciples now had knowledge concerning the mysteries of the kingdom.

This mystery of the kingdom was explained to the disciples through those first parables. Closely connected are the two parables of the treasure hid in the field and of the 'pearl of great price' (KJV), now spoken to the disciples. In the first, one who buys a field discovers a treasure hidden there and in his joy parts with all else to become the owner of the field and of the hidden treasure that he had so unexpectedly found. Some difficulty has been expressed regarding the morality of such a transaction. In response, this was in entire accordance with Jewish law. If a man had found a treasure in loose coins among the corn, it would certainly be his, if he could claim ownership of the field.

In the second parable, we have a wise merchant who travels in search of pearls and when he finds one which in value exceeds all else. He returns and sells all that he has to buy this unique gem. The supreme value of the kingdom, the consequent desire to appropriate it and the necessity of parting with all else for this purpose, are the points common to this and the previous parable.

Thus, two different aspects of the kingdom and two different conditions are here set before the disciples. The closing parable of the net was no less important. It was to show that mere discipleship – mere inclusion in the gospel net – was not sufficient. That net let down into the sea of this world would include much which, when the net was at last drawn to shore, would prove worthless or even hurtful. To be a disciple, then, was not enough. Even here there would be separation.

So ended that spring day of first teaching in parables to the people by the lake and in the house at Capernaum to the disciples. We have two questions of decisive character to ask. Undoubtedly, these parables were unfamiliar. This appears, not only from a comparison with the Jewish views of the kingdom but from the fact that their meaning was unintelligible to the hearers of Jesus.

Our first question is: Where did Jesus' teaching concerning the kingdom come from? Our second question goes still further. For, if Jesus was a prophet and also the Son of God and if these parables are a fair description of the kingdom he represented, does this not all point to the inescapable conclusion that Jesus was who he said he was? Decision time was approaching!

Chapter 19: A Day of Storms

MATTHEW 8:18,23-27; MARK 4:35-41; LUKE 8:22-25

(Book 3: Chapter 24)

It was the evening and once more great multitudes were gathering to him. What more will he have to say to those who had heard his teaching in parables that morning? He was desperately tired but his work had to go on. He got in a boat intending to have a good snooze. Weariness, faintness, hunger, exhaustion had taken over. How human is that? In fact, as we will see, every deepest show of his humanity is immediately followed by the highest display of his divinity and each special display of his divine power followed by some marks of his true humanity.

Suddenly the heavens darken, the wild wind swoops down those mountain gorges, howling with hungry rage over the trembling sea; the waves rise and toss and lash and break over the ship and beat into it and the white foam washes at his feet.

What will he do? What could he do? The disciples were fearful. This was a key moment for them. Will he come up short, his kingdom that he had preached that very morning, show up as a fantasy? Or are we going to witness a connection between the teaching of that day and the miracle of that evening?

Now, with which of the words recorded by the Gospel writers had the disciples wakened him? With those for him to save them or with those of impatience, perhaps uttered by Peter himself? Similarly, it has been asked, which came first, the Lord's rebuke of the disciples and after it that of the wind and sea, or the other way round?

Perhaps each recorded that first which had most impressed itself on his mind? For Matthew, who had been in the ship that night, perhaps it was the needful rebuke to the disciples? For Mark and Luke, who had heard it from others, perhaps it was the help first, and then the rebuke?

Yet it is not easy to understand what the disciples had really expected, when they woke Jesus up with 'Lord, save us – we perish!' Certainly fear! But also the dawning of a vague belief in the unlimited possibility of all in connection with Jesus. Edersheim speaks poetically of this belief. He calls it:

> a belief that seems to us quite natural as we look back from our privileged position as we think of the gradually emerging, but still partially cloud-capped height of his Divinity, of which, as yet, only the dim outlines were visible to them.

We have come to a pivotal point in the history of Jesus. On the one hand, there are the attacks on him by the religious authorities, but there is also a growing realisation that his teachings and miraculous acts could only be explained in one way: that he was indeed acting as God himself.

The first great stage in his dealings with humanity was for people to come to a knowledge of what he was, through what he did. The second great stage was to come to an experience of what he did and does, through knowledge of who he is. The former is that of the period when Jesus was on earth; the second is that of the period after his ascension into heaven and the descent of the Holy Spirit.

Allow the following words of Edersheim to conjure up a 'storm' of realisation within your own spirit:

> When 'He was awakened' by the voice of his disciples, 'He rebuked the wind and the sea,' just as he had 'rebuked' the fever and the outbursts of the demonised. For all are his creatures, even when lashed to frenzy by the 'hostile power.' And the sea he commanded as if it were a sentient being. 'Be silent! Be silenced!' And immediately the wind was bound, the panting waves throbbed into stillness and a great calm of rest fell upon the lake. For, when Christ sleeps, there is storm; when he wakes, great peace. But these men

who had wakened him with their cry, now experienced wonder, awe and fear. No longer was it, 'what is this?' but, rather, 'Who, then, is this?'

So here we saw the true humanity of the Saviour along with his divine power; the sleeping Jesus and the almighty word of rebuke and command to the elements. This contrasted with the failure of faith and then the excitement of the disciples; and of the calm of the sleeping and then the majesty of the wakening Christ. With him there can be no difficulty since all is his. One thing only he wonders at – the shortcomings of our faith; and one thing only makes it impossible for him to help – our unbelief.

MATTHEW 8:28-34; MARK 5:1-20; LUKE 8:26-39
(Book 3: Chapter 25)

That day of wonders was not yet ended. We suppose the Saviour and his disciples to have landed on the other side of the lake late in the evening. All the circumstances lead us to regard the healing of the demonised at Gerasa as a night scene, immediately on Christ's arrival from Capernaum and after the calming of the storm at sea.

About a quarter of an hour to the south of Gerasa is a steep bluff, which descends abruptly on a narrow ledge of the shore. A terrified herd running down this cliff could not have recovered its foothold and must inevitably have been hurled into the lake beneath. Again, the whole country around is burrowed with limestone caverns and rock chambers for the dead, such as those which were the dwelling of the demonised. Altogether, the scene forms a fitting background to the narrative. From these tombs, the demonised 'one', who is specially singled out by Mark and Luke, as well as his less prominent companion, came forth to meet Jesus.

According to common Jewish superstition, the evil spirits dwelt especially in lonely desolate places and also among tombs. According to Mark, the man was 'Night and day among the tombs and in the hills', the very order of the words indicating the idea (as in Jewish belief) that it was chiefly at night that evil spirits haunted burial places.

Jesus, who had been labelled by the Pharisees as being the messenger of Satan, is here face-to-face with the extreme manifestation of demonic power and influence. The question which had been raised by his enemies is about to be brought to the issue of a practical demonstration. There are critical epochs in the history of the kingdom of God when the power of evil, standing out in sharpest contrast, challenges that overwhelming manifestation of the divine, as such, to bear down and crush that which opposes it. Periods of that kind are characterised by miraculous demonstrations of power, unique even in Bible history. Such a period was, in the Old Testament, that of Elijah and Elisha, with its altogether exceptional series of miracles; and, under the New Testament, that which followed the first formulated charge of the Pharisees against the Christ.

It was the self-confession of the demons when obliged to come into his presence and do homage, which made the man fall down and, in the well-known Jewish formula recorded by the Gospel writers, say: 'What have I to do with thee…?' (KJV). Jesus had commanded the unclean spirit to come out of the man, asking him to identify himself. 'My name is Legion … for we are many.'

Viewing this miracle, again the thought presented itself, is he not the Son of the Most High God? Contrary to what was commonly the case, when the evil spirits came out of the demonised, there was no outpouring of physical distress. Was it then so, that the more complete and lasting the demoniac possession, the less there were of purely physical symptoms accompanying it?

But now the people come from town and country. We may contrast the scene with that of the shepherds when on Bethlehem's plains; the great revelation had come to them, and they had seen the divine baby laid in the manger and had worshipped. As with these herdsmen, there could be no doubt in their minds that One possessing supreme and unlimited power was in their midst. Also, for the healed demoniac, awe and fear! 'Depart from me; for I am a sinful man' (Luke 5:8) is the natural expression of a mind conscious of sin when brought into contact with the divine. Then, his life's mission lay ahead of him, to go back, now healed, to the whole of the large district of the ten confederate cities, the Decapolis, and speak of the great thing Jesus had done for him. In this, there would be both safety and happiness. 'And all men did marvel' (KJV). Then Jesus himself travelled to that region, having had the way prepared for him.

Chapter 20: Miracles of Faith

MATTHEW 9:18-26; MARK 5:21-43; LUKE 8:40-56

(Book 3: Chapter 26)

There seems remarkable similarity between the two miracles of Jesus on leaving Capernaum and those which he did on his return. The stilling of the storm and the healing of the demonised were manifestations of the absolute power inherent in Christ; the recovery of the woman and the raising of Jairus' daughter, evidence of the absolute value of faith.

On the shore at Capernaum, many were gathered on the morning after the storm. As he again stepped on the well-known shore, he was welcomed, surrounded by the crowd, eager, curious, expectant. It seemed as if he had been away all too long for their impatience. The tidings rapidly spread and reached two homes where his help was needed.

Both Jairus, the ruler of the synagogue, and the woman suffering these many years from disease, had faith. But the weakness of the first came from excess and threatened to turn into superstition, while the weakness of the second was due to defect and threatened to end in despair. In both cases faith had to be called out, tried, purified and so perfected; in both, the thing sought for was, *humanly* speaking, unattainable and the means employed seemingly powerless; yet, in both, the outward and inward results required were obtained through the power of Jesus.

Although Matthew speaks of the daughter as dead at the time of Jairus' request to Jesus, the other two Gospel accounts, giving fuller details, describe her as on the point of death, literally, 'at the last breath'. Unless her disease had been both sudden and very rapid, which is barely possible, it is difficult to understand why her father had not on the previous day approached Jesus, if his faith had been such as is generally supposed. Only in the hour of supreme need, when his only child lay dying, did he turn to Jesus.

115

There was a need to perfect such faith, on the one hand into the perseverance of assurance and on the other into the energy of trustfulness. There was nothing unnatural in the approach of this ruler to Jesus. He must have known of the healing of the son of the court official and of the servant of the centurion, there or in the immediate neighbourhood – as it was said, by the mere word of Jesus. This serves to highlight the important point, *that Christ's miracles were intended to aid, not to supersede, faith*; to direct to the person and teaching of Jesus. Instead of exciting the crowd with acts of power, but rather leading in humble discipleship to the feet of Jesus. That was, as we've seen before, the moral purpose of these miracles.

When Jesus followed the ruler to his house, another approached him from out of that crowd, one whose inner history was far different from that of Jairus. The disease from which this woman had suffered for twelve years would render her Levitically 'unclean'. On one page of the Talmud, no less than eleven different remedies are proposed, of which at most only six can possibly be regarded as proper remedies, while the rest are merely the outcome of superstition. But what is interesting here is that, in all cases where remedies are prescribed, it is ordered that, while the woman takes the remedy, she is to be addressed by the words, 'Arise (*Qum*) from thy flux.' Is it a coincidence that the command 'Arise'[40] (*Qum*) is that used by Jesus in raising Jairus' daughter?

Rather than 'magical cures', Jesus neither used remedies nor spoke the word *Qum* to her who had come to touch 'the fringe of his outer garment' for her healing. This is almost the only occasion on which we can obtain a glimpse of what clothing Jesus wore. There was a rule that rabbis ought to be most careful in their dress and that to wear dirty clothes deserved death, for 'the glory of God was man, and the glory of man was his dress'. It was the general rule to eat and drink below a man's means, but to dress above them. For, in these things, a man's character might be learned.

Perhaps a distinctive garment, most likely head gear, was worn, even by 'rulers' at their ordination. The president of the Sanhedrin also had a

---

40. KJV.

distinctive garment and the head of the Jewish community in Babylon had a distinctive girdle. In referring to the clothing which may on a Sabbath be saved from a burning house – not, indeed, by carrying it, but by successively putting it on – no fewer than eighteen articles are mentioned. If we had an understanding of all the terms, we should know precisely what the Jews at the time of Jesus wore.

Unfortunately, many of these possibilities are disputed. Also, it must not be imagined that a Jew would wear all eighteen of these pieces at one time! Included would be undergarments and overgarments; the latter consisted of types of shoes, headcoverings, the *tallith* or upper cloak, the girdle, the *chaluq* or underdress and the *aphqarsin* or innermost covering. As regarded shoes, it was not the practice to provide more than one pair of shoes, and to this may have been referenced by Jesus to the apostles not to provide shoes for their journey.[41]

Regarding the covering of the head, it was deemed a mark of disrespect to walk with a bare head. The ordinary covering of the head was the so-called *sudar*, a cloth twisted into a turban, which might also be worn around the neck. The *sudar* was peculiarly twisted by rabbis to distinguish them from others. We also read of a sort of cap or hood attached to garments. Three or four articles commonly constituted the dress of the body.

First came the undergarment, commonly the *chaluq*, of linen or of wool. The sages wore it down to the feet. It was covered by the upper garment or *tallith* to within about a handbreadth. The *chaluq* lay close to the body and had no other opening than that round the neck and for the arms. At the bottom, it had a kind of hem. To possess only one such 'coat' or inner garment was a mark of poverty. Hence, when the apostles were sent on their temporary mission, they were directed not to take 'two coats' (Luke 9:3, KJV).

Closely similar to the *chaluq* was the ancient garment mentioned in the Old Testament as Kethoneth, which would have been the garment that

---

41. Matthew 10:10, KJV.

Jesus wore. This might be of almost any material, even leather, though it was generally of wool or flax. It was sleeved, close-fitting, reached to the ankles, and was fastened round the loins, or just under the breast by a girdle.

The upper garment which Jesus wore would be most likely the *tallith*. This garment was provided on the four borders, with the so-called *tsitsith*, or 'fringes'. These were attached to the four corners of the outer dress, in supposed fulfilment of the command, Numbers 15:38-41 and Deuteronomy 22:12. At first, this observance seems to have been comparatively simple. The question as to the number of filaments on these 'fringes' was settled in accordance with the teaching of the School of Shammai. Four filaments (not three, as the Hillelites proposed), each of four finger-lengths and attached to the four corners of what must be a strictly square garment. Such were the earliest rules on the subject.

We can now form an approximate idea of the outward appearance of Jesus on that spring morning amid the throng at Capernaum. He would look like any other Jewish teacher of Galilee. His headgear would probably be the *sudar* (turban), or perhaps the *maaphoreth*, which seems to have served as a covering for the head and to have descended over the back of the neck and shoulders. His feet were probably shod with sandals. The *chaluq*, or more probably the *kittuna*, which formed his inner garment, must have been close-fitting and descended to his feet because it was worn by teachers and was regarded as absolutely necessary for anyone who would publicly read the Scriptures, or exercise any function in the synagogue.

As we know, it 'was without seam, woven from the top throughout' (John 19:23, KJV). Around the middle, it would be fastened with a girdle. Over this he would most probably wear the *tallith*, with the customary fringes of four long white threads with one of hyacinth knotted together on each of the four corners. There is reason to believe that three square garments were made with these 'fringes' although, just to show off, the Pharisees made them particularly wide to attract attention, just as they made their phylacteries broad. Although Jesus only denounced the latter practice, not the phylacteries themselves, it is hard to believe that he ever wore them, either on the forehead or the arm. There was certainly no warrant for them in Holy Scripture and only Pharisee legalism could represent their use as fulfilling Exodus 13:9,16 or Deuteronomy 6:8, 11:18. The admission that neither the officiating priests nor the representatives of the people wore them in the Temple seems to imply that this practice was not quite universal.

Back to our story, can we then wonder that this Jewish woman, 'having heard the things concerning Jesus', with her imperfect knowledge, 'in the weakness of her strong faith', thought that if she might but touch his garment she would be made whole? The Lord cannot be touched by disease and misery without healing coming from him, for he is the God-Man. And he is also the loving, pitying Saviour. We can picture her in our minds as mingling with those who thronged and pressed upon the Lord; she 'touched the border of his garment' (KJV) most probably the long *tsitsith* of one of the corners of the *tallith*. We can understand how, with a disease making her Levitically defiled, she might thus seek to have her heart's desire. What strong faith to expect help where all human help had so failed her! And what strong faith to expect that even contact with him, the bare touch of his garment, would carry such divine power as to make her 'whole'.

Yet, in this very strength lay also its weakness. It was not the garment or even his sacred body, but himself that brings healing. There is the danger of losing sight of what is necessary in faith: personal contact with Jesus. And so it is to us also. As we realise the mystery of the incarnation, we must think only of that which brings us in contact with him. We must avoid all superstition, the attachment of power to anything other than the living God.

No sooner had she so touched the border of his garment than 'she felt in her body that she was healed of that plague'. No sooner, also, had she so touched the border of his garment than he knew what had taken place, the release of power out of him. This was neither unconscious nor unwilled on his part. It was caused by her faith, not by her touch. 'Your faith has healed you.'

As brief as this episode was, it must have caused considerable delay in his progress to the house of Jairus. For the girl had died and the mourning had started. It was designed this way: no outcome of God's Providence is of chance. The first thing to be done by Jesus was to eject the mourners, who had proved themselves unfit to be witnesses of his great miracle. It seems that the father was stupefied, passive rather than active in the matter. The great fear which had come upon him on news of the death still seemed to numb his faith. Jesus took her by the hand and spoke only these two words, '*Talyetha Qum*': Maiden, arise! And immediately she arose.

Soon Jesus left Capernaum, but what of that multitude? The news must have speedily reached them that the daughter of the synagogue ruler was not dead. It is doubtful whether Jewish theology generally attributed to the Messiah the raising of the dead. The consensus was that God only would raise the dead. But even those passages in which this is attributed to the Messiah do not refer to single individuals. To this matter, there is not the faintest allusion in Jewish writings. It was unheard of in Jewish theology. The world was now a very different place.

Chapter 21: The Twelve

MATTHEW 13:54-58; MARK 6:1-6
(Book 3: Chapter 27)

So Jesus left Capernaum and from this time onwards it ceases to be the centre of his activity and is only occasionally visited. Because of opposition from the Pharisees and the nearness of Herod's residence at Tiberias, a permanent stay there is impossible at this stage. He now has no dwelling place, he 'has nowhere to lay his head'.

Jesus travels back to Nazareth, his hometown, where he still finds unbelief. It was disconcerting. If ever men had the means of testing the claims of Jesus, the Nazarenes possessed them, on account of their shared history. Yet in Nazareth, they knew him only as that infant whom his parents, Joseph the carpenter and Mary, had brought with them some time after they had first left Nazareth. And now they only knew of this humble family, that they lived in obscurity and that sons and daughters had joined the family.

Of Jesus, indeed, they must have heard that he was not like others, quite different in all ways, as he 'grew in wisdom and stature, and in favour with God and man' (Luke 2:52). Then came that strange episode on his first visit to Jerusalem, when his parents had to return and found him in the Temple. There are three assumptions that we may make for the subsequent years: that Jesus followed the occupation of his adoptive father; that Joseph had died; that the mother and 'brethren' of Jesus had left Nazareth while his 'sisters' apparently continued there, being probably married to Nazarenes.

When Jesus had first left Nazareth to seek baptism at the hands of John, it could scarcely have attracted much attention. Then came vague reports of his early exploits. His fame had preceded him on that memorable Sabbath when all Nazareth had thronged the synagogue, curious to hear what the child of Nazareth would have to say and still more eager to see what he could do. It didn't go too well, at that time, as they found it difficult to equate this 'child of Nazareth' with this man who claimed to be Messiah.

And now he had come back to them, after nine or ten months, in totally different circumstances. No one could any longer question his claims, whether for good or for evil. As on the Sabbath he stood up once more in that synagogue to teach, they were astonished. But the astonishment with which they heard him on that Sabbath *was that of unbelief.* They knew his supposed parentage and his brothers. His sisters were still with them and for these many years had they known him as the carpenter, the son of the carpenter. Yet they continued in their unbelief. In such circumstances as at Nazareth, miracles were not so forthcoming. He will not return again to Nazareth.

MATTHEW 10:1,5-42; MARK 6:7-13; LUKE 9:1-6

From now on he will begin to send out his disciples to spread the gospel, to share his task and mission. He sent out labourers to the harvest. Those visited by the twelve disciples were like sheep that had no shepherd.[42] And it was to deliver them from the distress caused by 'grievous wolves' (Acts 20:29, KJV) and to gather into his fold those that had been scattered, that Jesus sent out the Twelve with the special commission that we will now discuss. We turn mainly to Matthew 10.

From what he speaks of here, it is clear that he is going far beyond that mission of the Twelve, beyond even that of the early Church, but right up to current times in our dealings with a hostile world. The Twelve were to go forth 'two by two', furnished with 'power and authority' over demons and disease. The special commission, for which they received such power, was to proclaim the near advent of the kingdom and to heal the sick, cleanse the lepers and cast out demons. They were to speak good and to do good in the highest sense. They were not to make any special provision

---

42. Matthew 9:36; Mark 6:34.

for their journey, beyond the absolute immediate present. They were but labourers, their support would come from God, but also others would be expected to help.

Before entering a city, they were to search out who in it was 'worthy' and to ask them for hospitality. If it was given, then the 'Peace with thee!' with which they had entered their temporary home would become a reality. Jesus would make it such. As he had given them 'power and authority', so he would honour any hospitable reception. But even if the house should prove unworthy, the Lord would nonetheless own the words of his messengers and make them real, though, in such cases the peace would return to them who had spoken it.

Yet another case was possible. The house or city into which they had entered might refuse to receive them because they came as Jesus' ambassadors. Great would be their guilt and more terrible would be their future punishment. So Jesus would vindicate the disciples' authority as well as his own, and show the reality of their commission.

In their present mission, they were not to touch either Gentile or Samaritan territory. It would have been fatal to have attempted this and it would have defeated Jesus' desire to make a final appeal to the Jews of Galilee.

Jesus knew the hardships that they – and, indeed, the Church in all ages – would encounter. So he laid it on the line. They would be handed over to the various councils and visited with such punishments as these tribunals had the power to inflict. More than this, they would be brought before governors and kings. The support in those terrible circumstances was the assurance of such help from above. And with this, they had the promise that he who endured to the end would be saved.[43]

It is of the greatest importance to realise the seriousness of this prediction and promise, at whatever period of his ministry, starting with the apostolic preaching in the cities of Israel, right up to the destruction of Jerusalem. But it is not to end there.

---

43. Matthew 24:13.

As regards its manner, the 'second coming' of Christ may be said to correspond to the state of those to whom he comes. To the Jews, his first coming was visible and as claiming to be their King. They had asked for a sign and no sign was given them at the time. They rejected him and placed the Jewish nation in rebellion against 'the King'. To the Jews, who so rejected the first visible appearance of Christ as their King, the second appearance would be invisible but real; the sign which they had asked would be given them, but as a sign of judgement, and his coming would be in judgement.

Neither the mission of the disciples nor their journeying through the cities of Israel was finished until the Son of Man came. There were those standing there who would not taste death until they had seen in the destruction of the city and state the vindication of the Kingship of Jesus, which Israel had disowned. And even in those last teachings when this coming in judgement to Israel merges with the greater judgement on an unbelieving world, this earlier coming to the Jewish nation is clearly marked.

'Truly I tell you, this generation will certainly not pass away until all these things have happened' (Matthew 24:34). And it is most significant that the final utterances of the Lord as to his coming were his answers to questions arising from the predicted destruction of the Temple. The early disciples associated this with the final coming of Christ.

Because of the treatment which their master received, the disciples must expect misrepresentation and verbal abuse. Nor could it seem strange to them, since even the common Rabbinic proverb had it, 'It is enough for a servant to be as his lord.' And very significant is its application by Jesus, 'If they have called the master of the house Beelzebul, how much more ... them of his household' (KJV). This charge, brought of course by the Pharisees had a double significance. The expression 'master of the house' looked back to the claims which Jesus had made on his first purification of the Temple.

We almost seem to hear the coarse Rabbinic witticism in its play on the word 'Beelzebul'. For, Zebhul means in Rabbinic language, not any ordinary dwelling, but specifically, the Temple and Beel-Zebul would be the 'master of the Temple'. On the other hand, Zibbul means 'sacrificing to idols' and so Beelzebul would, in that sense, be equivalent to 'chief of idolatrous sacrificing' – the worst of demons, who presided over, and incited to, idolatry! 'The Lord of the Temple' (which truly was his Church) was to them 'the chief of idolatrous worship'.

Jesus encouraged his followers to set aside all regard for personal safety, even in preference to the duty of preaching the gospel. There was a higher fear than of people, that of God and it should drive out the fear of those who could only kill the body. Two sparrows cost only about a third of a penny, yet even one of them would not perish without the knowledge of God. No illustration was more familiar to the Jewish mind than that of his watchful care even over the sparrows.

Nor could even the additional promise of Jesus, 'even the very hairs of your head are all numbered' surprise his disciples. But it would convey to them the assurance that, in doing his work, they were performing the will of God and were therefore in his keeping.

Even the statement about taking up the cross in following Jesus, although prophetic, would not be a strange idea. Crucifixion was, indeed, not a Jewish punishment, but the Jews must have become sadly familiar with it. The Targum speaks of it as one of the four modes of execution which Naomi described to Ruth as customary, the other three being stoning, burning and beheading. Indeed, the expression 'bearing the cross' is so common, that we read, 'Abraham carried the wood for the sacrifice of Isaac, like who bears his cross on his shoulder.'

Nor could the disciples be in doubt as to the meaning of the last part of Jesus' address. They were old Jewish forms of thought, only filled with the new wine of the gospel. The rabbis taught of the extravagant merit attached to the reception and entertainment of sages. The very expression 'in the name of' a prophet, or a righteous man', is strictly Jewish and means 'for the sake of' or 'with intention'. It appears to us that Christ introduced his own distinctive teaching by the admitted Jewish principle that hospitable reception for a prophet or a righteous man would produce a share in the prophet's or righteous man's reward.

And we are repeatedly assured that to receive a sage or even an elder, was like receiving the Shekhinah itself. But the final promise of Jesus, concerning the reward of even 'a cup of cold water' to 'one of these little ones' in the name of a 'disciple', goes far beyond the furthest conceptions of his contemporaries. These 'little ones' were 'the children' who were still learning the elements of knowledge, and who would by-and-by grow into 'disciples'. For, as the Midrash has it: 'Where there are no little ones, there are no disciples; and where no disciples, no sages: where no sages, there no elders; where no elders, there no prophets; and where no prophets, there does God not cause his Shekhinah to rest.'

We have focused on Jewish parallelisms here because it seemed important to show that the words of the Lord were not beyond the comprehension of the disciples. Starting from forms of thought and expressions with which they were familiar, he carried them far beyond Jewish ideas and hopes. It was of their time, as well as to us and to all times, so we can see how far the teaching of Jesus exceeds any limitations we may put on it.

Chapter 22: John the Baptist

(Book 3: Chapter 28)

Meanwhile, having sent his disciples off on their mission trip, Jesus himself taught and preached for a short time in the towns around Capernaum. He was successful enough to have drawn the attention of Herod Antipas, the Roman tetrarch in the Galilee region and this was the probable reason why the disciples returned earlier than expected and also why the disciples of John the Baptist now arrived on the scene, informing Jesus of his death. Let us now backtrack a little…

JOHN 3:25-30

It was early summertime when John was baptising in Aenon, near Salim, Jesus and his disciples were similarly engaged in the neighbourhood. The Pharisees had arrived on the scene and had a plan to separate Jesus and John by drumming up the jealousy of the latter. John was having none of that. He was happy to defer to the greatness of Christ. In his simple Judean illustration, he was only 'the friend of the bridegroom' (*Shoshebheyna*), not the bride.

Hours of cloud and darkness were to follow.

MATTHEW 14:1-12; MARK 6:14-29; LUKE 3:19-20

The scene has changed and the Baptist has become the prisoner of Herod Antipas. There were three reasons for this. According to Josephus, the tetrarch was afraid that John's absolute influence over the people, who seemed disposed to carry out whatever he advised, might lead to a rebellion. This is suggested by the remark of Matthew 14:5 that Herod was afraid to put the Baptist to death on account of the people's opinion of him. On the other hand, the statement that Herod had imprisoned John on account of his declaring his marriage with Herodias unlawful is consistent also with Josephus. Both motives were relevant, but there is an obvious connection between them.

There is a possibility of a third cause that led to John's imprisonment. The Pharisees may have used Antipas as their tool and worked upon his superstitions to aid their own purposes. The reference to the Pharisees' spying in John 4:1-2, which led to the withdrawal of Jesus into Galilee, seems to imply that the Pharisees had something to do with the imprisonment of John.

MATTHEW 11:2-14; LUKE 7:18-25

John would have been held in a tiny keep in a citadel. Let's let Edersheim paint a picture of the scene:

> This terrible keep had for ten months been the prison of that son of the free 'wilderness,' the bold herald of the coming Kingdom, the humble, earnest, self-denying John the Baptist. And now with this deep dungeon in the citadel on the one side, and, on the other, the luxurious palace of Herod and his adulterous, murderous wife. He could hear the shouts of wild revelry and drunken merriment and must have, in darker moments, thought, was this the Kingdom he had come to announce as near at hand? For which he had longed, prayed, toiled, suffered, utterly denied himself and all that made life pleasant and the rosy morning of which he had hailed with hymns of praise?

Where was the Christ? Was he the Christ? What was he doing? Was Jesus eating and drinking all this time with 'publicans and sinners', while John was suffering for him? Was Jesus in his person and work so quite different from himself? And why was he so?

MATTHEW 9:14-16; MARK 2:18-22; LUKE 5:33-39

In these circumstances, we empathise with John's disciples, as months of this weary captivity pass. In their view, there must have been a terrible contrast between he who lay in the dungeon and he who sat down to eat and drink at a feast of the publicans. Jesus' reception of 'publicans and sinners' they could understand; their own master had not rejected them. But why eat and drink with them? The Pharisees, in their anxiety to create division, must have told them all this again and again and pointed to the contrast, drumming away relentlessly to create division between the two camps. At any rate, it was at the instigation of the Pharisees that the disciples of John asked Jesus this question about fasting.

Rabbinism gave an altogether *external* aspect to fasting. In their view, it was the readiest means of turning aside any threatening calamity, such as drought, pestilence, or national danger. The second and fifth days of the week were those appointed for public fasts because Moses was supposed to have gone up the mountain for the second tablets of the Law on a Thursday, and to have returned on a Monday.

The self-introspection of the Pharisees led many to fast on these two days all year-round. It may well have been on one of those weekly fasts that the feast of Matthew had taken place and that this explains the expression, 'Now John's disciples and the Pharisees were fasting.' This would give credence to their complaint that his disciples did not fast. It is easy to see why Jesus could not promote the practice among his disciples. To understand it we must consider the transformation from the old to the new spirit. Jesus gave two illustrations to highlight this; that of the piece of undressed cloth (or, according to Luke, a piece torn from a new garment) sewed upon an old garment and that of the new wine put into old wine skins.

The old garment will not bear mending with the 'undressed cloth'. Jesus' was not merely a reformation; *all things must become new*. As the old garment cannot be patched from the new, neither can the new wine of the kingdom be restricted by the old wineskins. It would burst those wineskins. Not the old with a little of the new to hold it together where it is rent, but the new... and only the new.

MATTHEW 11:2-6; LUKE 7:18-35

Weeks had passed and the disciples of John had come back and shown their master all these things. He still lay in the dungeon, his circumstances unchanged. Herod was in that spiritually most desperate state. He had heard the Baptist and was most perplexed.

What could have been going on in John's mind? Had there been some terrible mistake on his part? He was now the prisoner of that Herod, to whom he had spoken with authority; in the power of that bold adulteress, Herodias. If he were Elijah, the great Tishbite had never been in the hands of Ahab and Jezebel. And the Messiah, whose Elijah he was, had not come to his aid but, instead, feasted with 'publicans and sinners'! It must have been a terrible hour. At the end of one's life, and that of such self-denial and suffering and with a conscience so alive to God, which had once driven him burning with holy zeal into the wilderness, to have such a question meeting him as: 'Are you he, or do we wait for another? Am I right, or in error and leading others into error?' This must have been truly awful.

This question, 'Are you the one who is to come, or should we expect someone else?' indicated a faith both in the great promise and in him to whom it was addressed. The designation 'The coming one' (*habba*), though a most truthful expression of Jewish expectancy, was not one ordinarily used of the Messiah. But it was invariably used about the Messianic age, as the *Athid labho*, or coming future and the *Olam habba*, the coming world. Jesus responded, through John's messengers, by demonstrating the Messianic kingdom, through healings and preaching. Without interrupting his work, he just told them to report back to John what they have seen. He to whom John had formerly borne testimony, now bore testimony to him.

The scene once more changes. Weeks have passed since the return of

John's messengers. We cannot doubt that the sunlight of faith has again fallen into the dark dungeon. He must have known that his end was at hand and been ready to be offered up. His work had been done and there was nothing further that he could do and the weary servant of the Lord must have longed for his rest. Let Edersheim pick up the story:

> 'I would that you give me in a charger, the head of John the Baptist!' Silence must have fallen on the assembly. Even into their hearts such a demand from the lips of little more than a child must have struck horror. They all knew John to be a righteous and holy man. Wicked as they were, in their superstition few would have willingly lent himself to such work. And they all knew, also, why Salome, or rather Herodias, had made this demand …
>
> The guardsman has left the banqueting hall. Out into the cold spring night, up that slope and into the deep dungeon. As its door opens, the noise of the revelry comes with the light of the torch which the man bears. No time for preparation is given, nor needed. A few minutes more and the gory head of the Baptist is brought to the young woman in a charger and she gives the ghastly dish to her mother. It is all over! As the pale morning light streams into the keep, the faithful disciples, who had been told of it, come reverently to bear the headless body to be buried. They go away forever from that accursed place, which is so soon to become a mass of shapeless ruins. They go to tell it to Jesus and, from that time onwards, remain with him.

Chapter 23: A Day and Night of Miracles

MATTHEW 14:13-21; MARK 6:30-44; LUKE 9:10-17; JOHN 6:1-14

(Book 3: Chapter 29)

Jesus and his disciples needed to get away from Capernaum and rest. They made the short journey to Bethsaida (*Beth-Saida*, 'the house of fishing') on the eastern border of Galilee. What followed was the only event since his last visit to Jerusalem that was recorded in all four Gospels, so it must have been highly significant!

People started to gather and soon swelled to the immense number of 'about five thousand men, besides women and children'. The circumstance was that Passover time was near, so that many must have been starting on their journey to Jerusalem. And this, perhaps together with the effect on the people of John's murder, may also explain their eagerness to gather around Jesus.

As we picture it to ourselves, Jesus with his disciples and perhaps followed by those who had outrun the others, first climb to the top of the hill and there rest. Then, as he saw the gathering of the great multitude, Jesus was 'moved with compassion toward them' (KJV). It was this depth of longing and intensity of pity that now ended his rest and brought him down from the hill to meet the gathering multitude in the 'desert' plain beneath. And what a sight to meet his gaze – these thousands of men, besides women and children. And now the sun had passed its meridian, and the shadows fell longer on the surging crowd.

What would they eat? Were they to buy 200 denarii worth of loaves? No, they were not to buy, but to give what they could, initially! How many loaves had they? Let them go and see. And when Andrew went to see what bounty the young lad carried for them, he brought back the tidings that the boy had 'five small barley loaves and two small fish'. When we read that these five were barley loaves, we realise the poverty of the situation.

These were the crudest and cheapest of all bread. Hence, as the Mishnah puts it, while all other meat-offerings were of wheat, that brought by the woman accused of adultery was to be of barley, because 'as her deed is that of animals, so her offering is also of the food of animals'.

The Gospel of John here uses a rare term for 'fish', *opsarion*, which properly means what was eaten along with the bread and especially refers to the small and generally dried or pickled fish eaten with bread, like sardines. As the head of the household, Jesus took the bread, 'blessed' (KJV) it and 'broke' it. The expression recalls that connected with the Holy Eucharist. Those baskets used, known in Jewish writings as *kephiphah*, were made of wicker or willow and were considered of the poorest kind. There is a touching contrast between this feast for the 5,000 (besides women and children) and the paltry provision of barley bread and the two small fishes; and, again, between the quantity left and the coarse wicker baskets in which it was stored.

The multitude looked on as the disciples gathered up the fragments into their baskets and the murmur ran through the ranks, 'Surely this is the Prophet who is to come into the world.' And so the Baptist's last enquiry, 'Are you the one who is to come?' (Matthew 11:3) was fully and publicly answered, and that by the Jews themselves.

MATTHEW 14:22-36; MARK 6:45-56; JOHN 6:15-21
(Book 3: Chapter 30)

An irresistible impulse seized the people. They would proclaim him King, then and there. Jesus therefore, realising that they were about to come and take him 'by force', withdrew again to the mountain region, to be alone. He withdrew to pray... for a very long time.

And as he prayed, the faithful stars in the heavens shone out. But there on the lake, where the boat which bore his disciples made for the other shore, a great wind started to blow up. And still he was alone on the land but looking out into the evening after them, as the ship was in the midst of the sea and they were distressed. The lake is about six miles wide and they had as yet reached little more than half the distance.

Already it was the 'fourth watch of the night' (KJV) when Jesus seemed to be passing them, *walking upon the sea*. There can be no question of any natural explanation, the truth of the event must be either absolutely admitted, or absolutely rejected. This walking on the water was even to them within the domain of the truly miraculous and it affected their minds equally, perhaps even more than ours. This miracle forms one of a series of similar manifestations. It is closely connected both with what had passed on the previous evening and what was to follow; it is told with a minuteness of detail and without any attempt at gloss, adornment, apology, or self-glorification, as to give the narrative the stamp of truth; while, lastly, it contains much that lifts the story from the merely miraculous into the domain of the sublime and deeply spiritual.

Had the story been mythical or legendary, we should have expected that the disciples would have been described as immediately recognising the Master as he walked on the sea, and worshipping him. Instead of this, they are troubled and afraid. They supposed it was an apparition (this in accordance with popular Jewish superstitions) and 'cried out for fear' (KJV). It seems that the disciples were unprepared for this miracle. He had seen their difficulty, if not danger, in the boat from the contrary wind. This must have determined him to come to their help and so this miracle also was not a mere display of power but came out of a real need.

But, on the other hand, this happened so that they might learn of his mighty power and (symbolically) that he ruled the rising waves. He may not have been King in the way they understood it, only in a far higher, truer sense than the excited multitude would have proclaimed him.

Chapter 24: Tradition of the Elders

MATTHEW 15:1-20; MARK 7:1-23
(Book 3: Chapter 31)

Let's recap. Jesus and his disciples left Capernaum for Bethsaida on a Thursday and the miraculous feeding of the multitude took place that evening, followed by the passage of the disciples to the other side of the lake and him walking on the waters, in the night of Thursday to Friday.

This was followed by a search for him in Capernaum on the Friday. Finally, we have the final teachings of Jesus on the Saturday in Capernaum and in the synagogue. Early that Friday morning the boat carrying Jesus and his disciples arrived at the sandy beach of the plain of Gennesaret. As news spread of his arrival and of the miracles which had so lately been witnessed, the people from the neighbouring villages and towns flocked around him and brought their sick for the healing touch. This took up most of the morning. Then came the Pharisees and scribes 'who had come from Jerusalem' with the purpose to watch and, if possible, to plot his downfall.

As we understand it, they met Jesus and his disciples on their way to Capernaum. This is when they turned on him. This was followed by an open discussion with them. Finally, there would have been his concluding explanation, after they had entered the house at Capernaum. So, what was all the fuss about?

The opening remarks by the scribes may have been provoked by seeing some of the disciples eating without first having washed their hands, but we can also imagine that it reflected on the miraculously provided meal of the previous evening, when thousands had sat down to food without 'following the ritual'. Neither in that case nor in the present had Jesus defended himself. He was, therefore, guilty of participation in their offence. So, this was all that these Pharisees and scribes could see in the miracle of Christ's feeding the multitude – that it had not been done according to Law!

But, in another aspect, the objection of the scribes went a lot deeper. In truth, it represented one of the great charges which the Pharisees brought against Jesus and which determined them to seek his destruction. It has already been shown that they accounted for the miracles of Christ as being through the power of Satan, whose special representative they declared Jesus to be. This would not only turn the evidence provided by these signs into an argument against Jesus but also justify the resistance of the Pharisees to his claims.

The second charge against Jesus was that he was 'not of God;' that he was 'a sinner'. If this could be established, it would, of course, prove that he was not the Messiah, but a deceiver who misled the people and whom it was the duty of the Sanhedrin to unmask and arrest. How they attempted to establish this was by proving that he broke the traditional law and encouraged others to do so too. This, according to their fundamental principles, involved heavier guilt than sins against the actual Torah!

The third and last charge against Jesus will come into play much later on in the story, his 'blasphemous' claim to equality with God, the very Son of the living God.

To each of these three charges, of which we are now watching the opening skirmishes, there was only one answer: *faith in his person.* And in our time, also, this is the final answer to all difficulties and objections.

It was in support of the second of these charges that the scribes now blamed Jesus for allowing his disciples to eat without having previously washed their hands. At the outset, we must realise that this practice is expressly not a Law of Moses but a 'tradition of the elders'. Still, for them, to neglect it was like being guilty of the worst carnal defilement. Its omission would lead to bodily destruction or, at least, to poverty. Bread eaten with unwashed hands was as if it had been filth. Indeed, a rabbi who had held this command in contempt was actually buried in excommunication. Thus, from their point of view, the charge of the scribes against the disciples is very far from being an exaggeration.

It is difficult to account for the origin of this law. It seems to have been first formulated to ensure that sacred offerings should not be eaten in defilement. When once it became an ordinance of the elders, this was, of course, regarded as sufficient ground for obedience. Scriptural support was sought for it. Some based it on the original ordinance of purification in Leviticus 15:11 while others saw in the words 'sanctify yourselves' (Leviticus 11:44, KJV) the command to wash before meat; in the command, 'be holy' (Leviticus 11:44) that of washing after meat. The former alone was, however, regarded as 'a commandment' (*mitsvah*), the other only as 'a duty' (*chobhah*), which some, indeed, explained on sanitary grounds, as there might be dirt or such stuff on the hands which might hurt the eyes.

This washing before meals is regarded by some as referred to in Talmudic writings by the expression 'the first waters' (*mayim rishonim*), while what is called the 'after waters' (*mayim acharonim*) is supposed to represent the washing after meals. As the purifications were so frequent and care had to be taken that the water had not been used for other purposes, or something fallen into it that might discolour or defile it, large vessels or jars were generally kept for the purpose. These might be of any material, although stone is specially mentioned.

The hands were deemed capable of contracting Levitical defilement which, in certain cases, might even render the whole body 'unclean'. This idea of the 'defilement of the hands' received a very curious application. According to one of the eighteen decrees, which date before the time of Christ, the Torah scroll in the Temple defiles all kinds of meat that touched it. The alleged reason for this decree was that the priests often kept the *Terumah* (preserved first-fruits) close to the scrolls, sometimes resulting in them being nibbled by mice! The Rabbinic ordinance was intended to avert this danger. To increase this precaution, it was decreed that all that renders the *Terumah* unfit, also defiles the hands.

Hence, the Holy Scriptures defiled not only the food but the hands that touched them and this not merely in the Temple, but anywhere. What a strange concept, when you think about it! This gave rise to interesting discussions, whether the Song of Solomon, Ecclesiastes, or Esther were to be regarded as 'defiling the hands', that is, as part of the canon. The ultimate decision was in favour of these books; 'all the holy writings defile the hands; the Song of Songs and Ecclesiastes defile the hands.' Even a small portion of the Scriptures was declared to defile the hands if it contained eighty-five letters because the smallest 'section' (*parashah*) in the Law consisted of exactly that number.

The tradition of the elders was not yet so established as to command absolute and universal obedience, while the disputes of Hillel and Shammai, who seemed almost on principle to have taken different views on every question, must have disturbed the minds of many. We have an account of a stormy meeting between the two schools, attended even with bloodshed. It was agreed that there were to be eighteen decrees in total. Such importance was attached to them that, while any other decree of the sages might be altered by a more grave, learned and authoritative assembly, these eighteen decrees might not under any circumstances be modified.

The eighteen decrees were intended to separate the Jew from all contact with Gentiles. Any contact with a heathen, even the touch of their clothes, might involve such defilement, sometimes forcing them to wash thoroughly. Only those who know the complicated arrangements about the defilements of vessels, as these are described in the Mishnah (*Tractate Kelim*), can form an adequate idea of the painful scrutiny with which every little detail is treated.

Earthen vessels that had contracted impurity were to be broken; those of wood, horn, glass, or brass immersed. If vessels were bought from Gentiles they were to be immersed, put into boiling water, purged with fire, or at least polished. Let us now try to realise the attitude of Jesus concerning these ordinances about purification and seek to understand the motives behind his answers.

He neither approved of the conduct of his disciples nor apologised for their breach of the Rabbinic commands. Here we can see his indifference towards traditionalism. This is the more noticeable since the ordinances of the scribes, in general, were declared more precious and of more binding importance than those of Holy Scripture itself. We must realise the infinite distance between Christ and the teaching of the synagogue.

Rabbinism, in the madness of its self-exaltation, represented God as busying himself by day with the study of the Scriptures and by night with that of the Mishnah. And how, in the heavenly Sanhedrin, over which the Almighty presided, the rabbis sat in the order of their greatness and the Halakhah was discussed and decisions taken in accordance with it.

As terrible as this sounds, it is not nearly all. It was carried beyond the verge of profanity, when God is represented as spending the last three hours of every day playing with Leviathan and it is discussed how, since the destruction of Jerusalem, God no longer laughs, but weeps. Also that, in a secret place of his own, the Almighty roars like a lion in each of the three watches of the night. The two tears which he drops into the sea are the cause of earthquakes! Surely this is madness and no wonder Jesus distanced himself from such ramblings!

This explains how Jesus could not simply show indifference towards traditionalism. His attitude to traditionalism was never more pronounced than in what he said in reply to the charge of neglecting 'the washing of hands'. He proceeded to show that in 'many such like things' (KJV) the Halakhah was utterly incompatible with Scripture; that, indeed, they 'nullify the word of God' by their traditions which they had received.

In explaining for the first time the real character of traditionalism and setting himself in open opposition to its fundamental principles, Jesus also made clear, for the first time, the fundamental principle of his own interpretation of the Law. That Law was not a system of externalism, in which outward things affected the inner person. It was moral and addressed itself to humans as moral beings, to their heart and conscience. As the spring of all moral action was within, so the mode of affecting it would be inward. Not from outside to inside, but from inside outwards; such was the principle of the new kingdom, as setting forth the Law in its fulness and fulfilling it. 'What goes into someone's mouth does not defile them, but what comes out of their mouth, that is what defiles them.'

This highlights the fundamental principles of Christian practice in direct contrast to that of Pharisaic Judaism. It is in this essential difference that the unspeakable difference between Christ and all contemporary teachers appears. Nor is this everything! For, the principle laid down by Jesus concerning that which enters from without and that which comes from within covers, in its full application, not only the principle of Christian liberty regarding the Torah but also touches far deeper and permanent questions, affecting not only Jewish people but all people and to all times.

Chapter 25: Parting of the Ways

JOHN 6:22-71
(Book 3: Chapter 32)

Those who had wanted to take Jesus by force and make him their Messiah-King now caught up with him. Yet he was not actually the Messiah they expected. Nevertheless, enthusiasm was such that thousands were determined to give up their pilgrimage to the Passover and then and there proclaim the Galilean teacher Israel's King.

Why then did he strenuously resist it? Their enthusiasm was fickle, it could go either way! From now on there were to be continuous misunderstandings, doubts and defections, growing into opposition and hatred to death. Jesus was even a mystery to many of those closest to him. Many returned to their homes, others went off to Jerusalem for the Passover. Only comparatively few came back to seek him. They could not disbelieve and yet they could not believe and they sought both a 'sign' to guide them and an explanation to give them its understanding.

It was that miraculous feeding that had raised the popular enthusiasm to the highest pitch, but this was tempered by the chilling disappointment of his denial of their 'religious' hopes and dreams for him. They now came seeking Jesus in every sense of the word. They came because they had eaten the bread without seeing in them 'signs'. They were now outwardly prepared for the very highest teaching, but they were not inwardly prepared for it and therefore they could not understand it.

In his own words, they sought him not because they saw signs but because they 'ate the loaves' and, in their coarse love for the miraculous, 'were filled' (KJV) What brought them was not that they had discerned either the higher meaning of that miracle or the identity of the miracle maker, but that they physically ate bread that came from nowhere! Edersheim summarises it succinctly:

> What they waited for was a Kingdom of God, not in righteousness, joy, and peace in the Holy Ghost, but in meat and drink, A kingdom with miraculous wilderness-banquets to Israel and coarse miraculous triumphs over the Gentiles.

Such were the carnal thoughts about the Messiah and his kingdom of those who sought Jesus because they 'ate the loaves and had [their] fill'. What a contrast between them and the Christ, as he pointed them away from the search for such food to work for the food which he would give them, not a merely Jewish Messiah, but as 'the Son of Man'. And yet, in uttering this strange truth, Jesus could appeal to something they knew when he added, 'For on him God the Father has placed his seal of approval.'

The words, which seem almost inexplicable in this connection, become clear when we understand that this was a well-known Jewish expression. According to the rabbis, 'the seal of God was Truth' (*eMeTH*). The three letters of which this word is composed in Hebrew are respectively the first, the middle, and the last letters of the alphabet. Thus the words of Christ would convey to his hearers that for the real meat, which would endure to eternal life, they must come to him because God had impressed upon him his own seal of truth and so authenticated his teaching and mission.

What now follows took place at a somewhat different time, perhaps on the way to the synagogue. The miraculous feeding of the multitude and the thoughts which clustered around it would naturally make them think of manna, the miraculous food. It spoke of Messiah and for all that the first deliverer Moses had done, the second Messiah would also do.

Their fathers had eaten 'manna in the wilderness'. God had given them this bread out of heaven, given through the merits of Moses and ceased with his death. This the Jews had probably in view when they asked Jesus, 'What about you?' This was the meaning of Christ's emphasis that it was not Moses who gave Israel that bread. The Saviour makes a quite different application of the manna.

Moses had not given it. His merits had not earned it for them but his Father gave them the true bread out of heaven. 'For', as he explained, 'the bread of God is the bread that comes down from heaven and gives life to the world.' Again, this very Rabbinic tradition, which described in such glowing language the wonders of that manna, also further explained its other and real meaning to be. If Wisdom said, 'Eat of my bread, and drink of [my] wine' (Proverbs 9:5, KJV) it indicated that the manna and the miraculous water supply were the results of Israel's receiving the Law and the Commandments. *For the real bread from heaven was the Law.*

As Jesus once more directed them to himself, from works of men to the works of God and to faith, for some of them the passing gleam of spiritual hope had already died out. For they had seen him and yet did not believe. With these words of mingled sadness and judgement, Jesus turned away from his questioners.

The solemn sayings which flowed from Jesus once he had identified himself as *the Bread from heaven* could not have been spoken to the multitude. They had the experience of the raising of the young man at Nain and there, at Capernaum, of Jairus' daughter. Besides, believing that Jesus was the Messiah, it might perhaps not be quite strange nor new to them as Jews that he would at the end of the world raise the pious dead. Indeed, one of the names given to the Messiah – that of *Yinnon*, according to Psalm 72:17 – has by some come from this very expectancy. Again, he had said that it was not any law but his person that was the bread which came down from heaven and gave life, not to Jews only, but to the world, and they had seen him and not believed.

When Jesus said, 'And I, when I am lifted up from the earth, will draw all people to myself' (John 12:32), he was well aware of his Jewish audience. The appeal to their own prophets was the more telling, that Jewish tradition also applied these two prophecies (Isaiah 54:13; Jeremiah 31:34) to the teaching by God in the Messianic age. What was new, though, was when he made claims like, 'Everyone who has heard the Father and learned from him comes to me.' There was no application of this through Moses, but Jesus was very different. 'The one who believes has eternal life.'

This Jesus was the Bread of Life. The manna had not been bread of life, for those who ate it had died, their carcasses had fallen in the wilderness. Not so with this, 'the true bread from heaven'. To share in this food was to have everlasting life, a life which the sin and death of unbelief and judgement would not cut short, as it had that of them who had eaten the manna and died in the wilderness.

Edersheim now addresses his concluding thoughts, which we know to have been delivered in the synagogue:

These were not a mere martyrdom for the life of the world, in which all who benefited by it would share, but personal fellowship with him. Eating the flesh and drinking the blood of the Son of Man, such was the necessary condition of securing eternal life. It is impossible to mistake the primary reference of these words to our personal application of his death and passion to the deepest need and hunger of our souls. In this, also, has the hand of history drawn out the telescope and as we gaze through it, every sentence and word sheds light upon the Cross and light from the Cross.

Truly, this was not the Messiah and Messianic kingdom that they expected and wished for. Instead, this was the rock of offence over which they stumbled and fell. And Jesus read their thoughts. How unfit were they to receive all that was yet to happen in connection with the Christ, how unprepared for it! If they stumbled at this, what would happen when they came to contemplate the far more mysterious facts of the Messiah's crucifixion, resurrection and ascension!

It was not just a case of external gestures. Only inward and spiritual understanding was acceptable. It was absolutely impossible to come to him except under the gracious influence from above. And so this was the great crisis in the history of the Christ. We have traced the gradual growth and development of the popular movement until the murder of John the Baptist stirred up deep feelings. With his death, it seemed as if the Messianic hope, awakened by his preaching and testimony to Jesus, were fading from view. It was a terrible disappointment, not easily borne.

Now it must be decided whether Jesus was really the Messiah. His works, despite what the Pharisees said, seemed to prove it. That miraculous feeding – that was just the beginning, or so they thought! All the greater was the disappointment. First, in the repression of the movement, then his voluntary drawing back, his breaking of their treasured traditions. This was not the Messiah many of them expected!

Here, then, we are at the parting of the two ways. Jesus clearly set forth the highest truths concerning himself, in opposition to the views which the multitude entertained about the Messiah. The result was not good. 'From this time many of his disciples turned back and no longer followed him.' This searching trial reached even to the hearts of the Twelve. Would they also go away? It was an anticipation of Gethsemane, its first experience. But one thing kept them true. It was the experience of the past. This was the basis of their present faith and allegiance. They could not go back to their old past, they must cleave to him. So, Peter spoke for them all, 'Lord, to whom shall we go? You have the words of eternal life.' Then, 'We have come to believe and to know that you are the Holy One of God.'

But of these Twelve Christ knew one to be a 'devil'. The apostasy of Judas had already been birthed in his heart. And the greater the popular expectancy and disappointment had been, the greater the reaction and the hatred that followed. The hour of decision was past and the hand on the dial pointed to the hour of his death.

Chapter 26: Among the Heathens

MATTHEW 15:21-28; MARK 7:24-30

(Book 3: Chapter 33)

Jesus needed a break. Too many discussions and opposing voices, disappointments and defections. What was needed now was a strategic withdrawal. He left the region and turned north to the borders of Tyre and Sidon. There he sought shelter in a house and was visited by the Canaanite-Phoenician woman, drawn by his fame and needing help for her demonised daughter.

The disciples were lacking in mercy, 'Send her away, for she keeps crying out after us', they declared. Jesus, naturally, was more merciful. 'Lord, Son of David ...!' she cried. This was the most distinctively Jewish designation for the Messiah and yet it came from the mouth of a heathen! Jesus was happy to bless her for this. Spoken by a heathen, these words were an appeal, not to the Messiah of Israel, for David had never reigned over her or her people. She used these words because the promises to David were fully and spiritually applicable for her, despite being a heathen.

To have granted her the help she needed was both easy and hard. It was easy because he was able to help her in her need; it was hard because it flew in the face of what he was trying to achieve, not for people to see his works of healing merely as works of power.

His miracles were intended as signs to Israel, not the heathens. In her mouth, then, it meant something to which Jesus could not have easily accepted. And yet he could not refuse her petition. And so he first taught her that which she needed to know before she could approach him in such manner, the relationship of the heathen to the Jewish world and of both to the Messiah. And then he gave her what she asked.

If we view this as the teaching of Jesus to this heathen concerning Israel's Messiah, all becomes clear. She had spoken, but Jesus had not answered her. When the disciples asked that she might be sent away because she was troublesome to them, he replied that his mission was only to the 'lost sheep of Israel'. This was absolutely true, as regarded his work while upon earth; and true, in every sense, as we keep in view the worldwide relevance of the Davidic reign and promises and the real relation between Israel and the world. Thus baffled, she cried no longer 'Son of David' but, 'Lord, help me!' She had acknowledged Jesus for who he was!

It was then that the special teaching came in the manner she could understand. No expression was more common in the mouth of the Jews than that which designated the heathens as dogs. Most harsh as it was, as the outcome of national pride and Jewish self-assertion, yet in a sense, it was true, that those within were the children, and those without were 'dogs'. Only, who were they within and who they without? If they are dogs, then they are the master's dogs and under his table and when he breaks the bread to the children, in the breaking of it the crumbs must fall all around. 'The dogs eat the crumbs that fall from their master's table.' Heathenism may be like the dogs when compared with the children's place and privileges; but he is their Master too and although they are under his table, when he breaks the bread there is enough to spare for them.

She now understood what she prayed and she was a daughter of Abraham. And what had taught her all this was faith in his person and work, as not only just enough for the Jews, but enough and to spare for all – children at the table and dogs under it; that in and with Abraham, Isaac, Jacob and David, all nations were blessed in Israel's King and Messiah. And so it was, that the Lord said it: '"Woman, you have great faith! Your request is granted." And her daughter was healed at that moment.' Edersheim summarises:

> He is our Master and, as he breaks the children's bread, it is of necessity that 'the children's crumbs' fall to us, enough, quite enough, and to spare. Never can we be outside his reach, nor of that of his gracious care and of sufficient provision to eternal life.

Yet this lesson also must we learn, that as 'Heathens' we may not call on him as 'David's Son,' until we know why we so call him. We must learn it and painfully first by his silence, that he is only sent to the lost sheep of the house of Israel, what we are and where we are, that we may be prepared for the grace of God and the gift of grace.

MARK 7:31-37

(Book 3: Chapter 34)

This miracle meant that Jesus would get no rest as the fame of the healing spread. Privacy was going to be impossible now wherever he went. He continued his journey into the country of the tetrarch Philip, then on to the Decapolis, the confederacy of 'the Ten Cities'. Heathen territory, where Greek deities were worshipped.

Matthew gives only a general description of what happened there, concluding with those who witnessed his mighty deeds glorifying 'the God of Israel' (Matthew 15:31). Among those brought to Jesus was one deaf and mute. The plea to 'place his hand on him' resulted in Jesus taking him aside from the multitude. In healing him, 'he spat', applying it directly to the diseased organ. We read of the direct application of saliva only here and in the healing of the blind man at Bethsaida (as we shall soon see) and so we perhaps see this as peculiar to the healing of Gentiles. Peculiar, also, is the fact that he sighed, the thrusting of his fingers into the ears and the touch of his tongue.

It is a new era, Israel conquers the heathen world, not by force, but by love; not by outward means, but by the manifestation of power from above. One word was spoken by him, the Jewish word, *'Ephphatha'* (be opened). This teaches us that Jesus must always have spoken the Jews' language, even among the heathens.

MARK 8:22-26

Another miracle is recorded in these parts, also on a heathen. It was in Bethsaida that a blind man was brought to him, with the plea that he would touch him. Here, also, the Saviour took him aside, led him out of the village and 'spat on the man's eyes and put his hands on him'. We mark the similarity of the means employed in both cases. We may here recall that the use of saliva was a well-known Jewish remedy for infections of the eyes.

We can understand how to Gentiles the Messiah of Israel would chiefly stand out as 'the Son of David'. It was the most universal form in which the great Jewish hope could be viewed by them. It provided a contrast to Israel's present fallen state and it recalled the Golden Age of Israel's past and the fulfilment of what to David had only been promises. We remember the leper who knelt before him only said, 'Lord, if you are willing, you can make me clean' (Matthew 8:2) and the two blind men, 'Have mercy on us, Son of David' (Matthew 9:27).

As regards the two blind men (and the healed leper also), it is almost impossible not to connect Jesus' peculiar insistence on their silence with their advanced faith. They had owned Jesus as the 'Son of David', as one able to do all things, even to open by his touch the eyes of the blind. And it had been done to them, as it always is, according to their faith.

But a profession of faith must not be publicly proclaimed. It would and did bring to Jesus crowds which, unable spiritually to understand the meaning of such a confession, would only embarrass and hinder. For confession must only be the result of faith. A worked-up Jewish crowd was not something encouraged by Jesus and no help to the progress of his kingdom. Neither was a world that has no faith in his power, nor experience of his ability and willingness to cleanse the leper and to open the eyes of the blind. Yet the leprosy of Israel and the blindness of the Gentile world are equally removed by the touch of his hand at the cry of faith.

Chapter 27: Sabbath

~~

MATTHEW 12:1-21; MARK 2:23-3:6; LUKE 6:1-11
(Book 3: Chapter 35)

The Jerusalem scribes, who had been relentlessly stalking Jesus, had been away celebrating the Passover during the recent healings. Now, after the two festive days, they were back, returning to their hateful task. Accordingly, we now find them once more confronting him.

The contest steps up and we notice a change in Jesus' methodology. Before he had been chiefly preaching the kingdom and healing body and soul. Now, through the hostility of the leaders of Israel, he enters a new stage. It is marked by the prophetic description, 'They compassed [him] about like bees' but 'are quenched as the fire of thorns' (Psalm 118:12, KJV). The first skirmish concerns the observance of the Sabbath.

On no other subject is Rabbinic teaching more painfully complex and confusing. For them, the Sabbath was meant to be absolute rest from all labour and a delight. The Mishnah includes Sabbath desecration among those most heinous crimes for which a person was to be stoned. This, then, was their prime objective; to make a breach of the Sabbath rest impossible. How far this was carried out, we shall presently see. Their other objective was to make the Sabbath a delight. A special Sabbath dress and the choicest food are preferred, even if one had to work for it all the week, or public charity was to supply it. The strangest stories are told how, by the purchase of the most expensive dishes, the pious poor had gained unspeakable merit and obtained, even on earth, 'heaven's manifest reward'.

And yet there is also that which is touching, beautiful and even spiritual. On the Sabbath there must be no mourning, for this saying applies to the Sabbath, 'The blessing of the LORD, it maketh rich, and he addeth no sorrow with it' (Proverbs 10:22, KJV). Quite alone was the

Sabbath among the measures of time. Every other day had been paired with its fellow; not so the Sabbath. And so any festival, even the Day of Atonement, might be transferred to another day; not so the observance of the Sabbath.

According to legend, the Sabbath complained before God that of all days it alone stood solitary. But God had wedded it to Israel and this holy union was forged when it stood before Mount Sinai and was never to be forgotten. Even the tortures of Gehenna were paused on that holy, happy day. The terribly exaggerated views on the Sabbath entertained by the rabbis and the endless, burdensome rules are going to explain the controversies in which the Pharisees now engaged with Jesus.

Of these, the first was when, going through the cornfields on the Sabbath, his disciples began to pluck and eat the ears of corn. Although this was not the first Sabbath controversy forced upon him, it was the first time that Jesus defied the Pharisees and that he vindicated his position concerning the Sabbath. This also indicates that we have now reached a further stage in the history of his teaching.

This, however, is not the only reason for placing this event so late in his personal history. In Matthew, it is placed out of the historical order, with the view of grouping together what would exhibit Jesus' relation to the Pharisees and their teaching. Accordingly, this first Sabbath controversy is immediately followed by that connected with the healing of the man with the 'withered hand' (KJV).

The different 'setting' in which the three Gospels present the event about to be related illustrates that their aim was to present the events in the history of the Christ in their succession, not of time, but *of relevance*. This is because they do not attempt a biography of Jesus, but a history of the kingdom which he brought.

It was on the Sabbath after the second day of Passover that Jesus and his disciples passed through cornfields. His disciples, being hungry, plucked ears of corn and ate them, having rubbed off the husks in their hands. On any ordinary day, this would have been lawful, but on the Sabbath it involved, according to Rabbinic statutes, at least two sins. For, according to the Talmud, each involved sin, punishment and a sin-offering, as it was an infringement of the Sabbath. Now, in this case there were at least two such acts involved, that of plucking the ears of corn – the sin of reaping – and that of rubbing them, which might be included as any of the following: sifting in a sieve, threshing, sifting out fruit, grinding, or fanning. Nit-picking to the extreme!

The following Talmudic passage came into play – 'in case a woman rolls wheat to remove the husks, it is considered as sifting; if she rubs the heads of wheat, it is regarded as threshing; if she cleans off the side-adherences, it is sifting out fruit; if she bruises the ears, it is grinding; if she throws them up in her hand, it is winnowing.' They had broken Rabbinic Law, not biblical Law. The purpose of Jesus' reply to them was not only to show them their error but to lay down principles that would forever apply to this difficult question.

Unlike the other nine commandments, the Sabbath Law has in it two elements; the moral and the ceremonial; the eternal and that which is subject to time and place; the inward and spiritual and the outward. In its spiritual and eternal element, the Sabbath Law embodied the two thoughts of rest for worship and worship which pointed to rest. The keeping of the seventh day and the Jewish mode of its observance was the outward form in which these eternal principles were presented.

It was a principle that danger to life superseded the Sabbath Law and indeed all other obligations. Among the curious scriptural and other arguments by which this principle was supported, the most relevant scripture is Leviticus 18:5. It was argued that a person was to keep the commandments that they might live, certainly not that by so doing they might die!

Hence, the first argument of our Lord, as recorded by all three Gospels, was taken from biblical history. When, on his flight from Saul, David had eaten consecrated bread, and given it to his followers – although, by the letter of the Levitical Law, it was only to be eaten by the priests,

Jewish tradition vindicated his conduct on the plea that 'danger to life' superseded the Sabbath Law, and hence, all laws connected with it. Then, to show David's zeal for the Sabbath Law, the legend was added that he had reproved the priests of Nob, who had been baking the consecrated bread on the Sabbath.

In truth, the reason why David was blameless in eating the bread was the same as that which made the Sabbath labour of the priests lawful. The Sabbath Law was not one merely of rest, but of rest for worship. The service of the Lord was the object in view. The priests worked on the Sabbath because this service was the object of the Sabbath; and David was allowed to eat of the bread, not because there was a danger to life from starvation, but because he pleaded that he was on the service of the Lord and needed this provision.[44] The disciples, when following the Lord, were similarly in the service of the Lord; ministering to him was more than ministering in the Temple, for he was greater than the Temple.

'The Sabbath was made for man, and not man for the Sabbath.' It is remarkable that a similar argument is used by the rabbis. When insisting that the Sabbath Law should be set aside to avoid danger to life, it is urged: 'The Sabbath is handed over to you; not, you are handed over to the Sabbath.'

Lastly, the three Gospel writers record this as the final outcome of his teaching on this subject, that 'the Son of man is Lord also of the sabbath' (KJV). The service of God and the service of the Temple, by universal consent, superseded the Sabbath Law. But Jesus was greater than the Temple and his service more truly that of God and higher than that of the outward Temple, and the Sabbath was intended for people to serve God. Therefore, Jesus and his service were superior to the Sabbath Law. These Pharisees would understand this, although they would not receive it because they did not acknowledge who Jesus was.

Whether or not the Pharisees had brought the man with the 'withered hand' on purpose, their secret objective certainly was to tempt Jesus into

---

44. 1 Samuel 21:1-6.

breaking the Sabbath Law. But in this, they judged rightly; that he would not witness disease without removing it. Disease could not continue in the presence of him, who was the Life. He read their inward thoughts of evil, and yet he proceeded to do the good which he intended.

Surely on the Sabbath it was lawful to do good? Yes, and to neglect it would have been to do evil. So, according to their own admission, should not a person on the Sabbath save life? Or should he, by omitting it, kill?

We can now imagine the scene in that synagogue. The place is crowded. Jesus probably occupies a prominent position as leading the prayers or teaching. Here, eagerly bending forward are the faces of the Pharisees, full of malice and cunning. They are looking around at a man whose hand is withered, perhaps pushing him forward, drawing attention to him, loudly whispering, 'Is it lawful to heal on the Sabbath?' The Lord takes up the challenge. He tells the man to stand up where they might all see and hear.

He describes the case of a poor man who was in danger of losing his only sheep on the Sabbath. Would he not rescue it and was not a man better than a sheep? They were speechless. He told the man to stretch forth his hand. It was no longer withered when the word had been spoken and fresh life had streamed into it as his hand was restored. The Saviour had broken their Sabbath Law and yet he had *not* broken it, for he healed him without touching him. He had broken the Sabbath rest, as God breaks it, when he sends, or sustains, or restores life, or does good.

You can sense the melancholy in Edersheim's words here:

As he did it. He had been filled with sadness; as they saw it, 'they were filled with madness.' So their hearts were hardened. They went forth and took counsel with the Herodians against him, how they might destroy him.

Chapter 28: Demands and Consequences

MATTHEW 15:32 – 16:12; MARK 8:1-21
(Book 3: Chapter 36)

His ministry in that Gentile district was about to draw to a close. The second mass feeding, of the 4,000, took place in the Gentile Decapolis and those who sat down to the meal were chiefly those who lived there. If we wish to study the symbolism of this event, as compared with the previous feeding of the 5,000 who were Jews, some differences come to mind.

On the former occasion, there were 5,000 fed with five loaves, when twelve baskets of fragments were left. On the second occasion, 4,000 were fed from seven loaves and seven baskets of fragments collected. We notice that the number five in the provision for the Jews is that of the Pentateuch, just as the number twelve corresponds to that of the tribes and of the apostles. On the other hand, in the feeding of the Gentiles, we mark the number four, which is the signature of the world and seven, which is that of the sanctuary. Edersheim makes an interesting observation here:

> We would not by any means press it, as if these were, in the telling of the narrative, designed coincidences; but, just because they are undesigned, we value them, feeling that there is more of undesigned symbolism in all God's manifestations – in nature, in history, and in grace – than meets the eye of those who observe the merely phenomenal. Nay, does it not almost seem, as if all things were cast in the mould of heavenly realities, and all earth's 'shewbread' 'Bread of his Presence'?

On all general points, the two narratives run parallel, but the circumstances are so different. The broad lines of difference as to the number of persons, the provision and the quantity of fragments left, cannot be overlooked.

The first was an evening meal for those who had listened to him all day, but who had come without food of their own. In the second the Gentiles had been three days with him and had run out of food when, in his compassion, the Saviour would not send them to their homes faint with hunger.

Yet another marked difference lies even in the baskets in which the fragments left were gathered. At the first feeding, there were the small wicker baskets which each of the Twelve would carry in his hand. At the second feeding, they were the large baskets, in which provisions, chiefly bread, were stored or carried for longer voyages.

This was because, on the first occasion, when they passed into Israelite territory there was not the same need to make provision for storing necessaries as on the second, when they were on a lengthened journey, and passing through Gentile territory. But the most noteworthy difference seems to us this: that on the first occasion, they who were fed were Jews and on the second, Gentiles.

In this second feeding, the Pharisees and the Sadducees were not present. But they were soon to reappear on the scene, as Jesus came close to the Jewish territory of Herod. We suppose the feeding of the multitude to have taken place in the Decapolis and probably close to the eastern shore of the Lake of Galilee. As Jesus sent away the multitude whom he had fed, he came into the borders of Magadan. It was here that the Pharisees now came 'with the Sadducees' (KJV), tempting him with questions and desiring that his claims should be put to the ultimate test of 'a sign from heaven'.

We can quite understand such a challenge on the part of Sadducees, who would disbelieve the heavenly mission of Christ or, indeed, anything that smacked of the supernatural. But, in the mouth of the Pharisees also, it had a special meaning. Certain supposed miracles had been either witnessed by or testified to them, as done by Jesus. He preached a kingdom quite different from their expectations, that was often at odds with all Jewish customs and was a breaker of the Law, in its most important commandments, as they understood them.

It followed that, according to their view of Deuteronomy 13, he was a false prophet who was not to be listened to. Then, also, must his miracles have been "by the power of Beelzebul", "the lord of idolatrous worship", the very "prince of devils".

But had there been real signs and might it not all have been an illusion? Let him show them a 'sign' and let that sign come directly from heaven! A striking instance from Rabbinic literature will show that this demand of the Pharisees was in accordance with their character and practice. As regards 'a sign from heaven', it is said that Rabbi Eliezer, when his teaching was challenged, successively appealed to certain 'signs'. First, a locust tree moved at his bidding 100 or, according to some, 400 cubits. Next, the channels of water were made to flow backwards, then the walls of the Academy leaned forward and were only stopped at the bidding of another rabbi. Lastly, Eliezer exclaimed, 'If the Law is as I teach, let it be proved from heaven!' when a voice fell from the sky, 'What have you to do with Rabbi Eliezer, for the Halakhah is as he teaches?'

It was, therefore, no strange thing when the Pharisees demanded 'a sign from heaven' from Jesus to support his claims and teaching. The answer which he gave was among the most solemn which the leaders of Israel could have heard and he spoke it in deep sorrow of spirit. They had asked him for some sign of his Messiahship, some striking vindication from heaven of his claims.

It would be given to them only too soon. People could discern by the appearance of the sky whether the day would be fair or stormy. And yet, when all the signs of the gathering storm that would destroy their city and people were clearly visible they, the leaders of the people, would fail to understand them! Israel asked for a 'sign'! No sign should be given the doomed land and city other than that which had been given to Nineveh, 'the sign of Jonah'. The only sign to Nineveh was Jonah's solemn warning of near judgement and his call to repentance and the only sign now, or rather 'unto this generation' (KJV) was the warning cry of judgement and the loving call to repentance.

He left them and departed. The destination was Caesarea Philippi, following his purpose to delay the final conflict. For the great crisis must begin, as it would end, in Jerusalem and at the feast. It would begin at the Feast of Tabernacles and it would end at the following Passover. But even the disciples themselves showed how little they, who had so long and closely followed Jesus, understood his teaching and how spiritually dull they were.

But first, they were together in a boat and when they landed, they carried ashore the empty baskets, apart from a single loaf of bread. Jesus broke the silence, speaking that which was so much on his mind. He warned them of the leaven of the Pharisees and Sadducees that had so corrupted the holy bread of Scripture truth. The disciples, aware that in their hurry and excitement they had forgotten bread, misunderstood these words of Christ.

This misunderstanding was at least rational. They thought that Jesus had purposely forgotten to bring bread in order to conjure up some more miraculous loaves. The mere suspicion showed what was in their minds and pointed to their danger. This explains how, in his reply, Jesus rebuked them, not just for their lack of discernment, but for their 'little faith'. It was their lack of faith – the very leaven of the Pharisees and Sadducees – which had suggested such a thought! Again, if the experience of the past had taught them anything, it should have been to believe that Jesus' provision was not a 'sign', such as the Pharisees had asked, but what faith might ever expect from one who followed him.

Then they understood. It was not of the leaven of bread that he referred to but to the far more real danger of 'the teaching of the Pharisees and Sadducees' which had underpinned the demand for 'a sign from heaven'. Here, as always, Jesus rather suggests than gives the interpretation of his meaning. And this is how he taught. Our modern Pharisees and

Sadducees also too often ask of him 'a sign from heaven' in evidence of his claims. And we also too often misunderstand his warning to us concerning their leaven.

Chapter 29: Proclamations

MATTHEW 16:13-28; MARK 8:27 – 9:1; LUKE 9:18-27

(Book 3: Chapter 37)

They arrived at Caesarea Philippi. It would have taken two days to get there. It was a magnificent location. Nestling amid three valleys on a terrace on a slope of Mount Hermon, it is almost shut out from view by cliffs and woods. Everywhere there is a wild medley of cascades, mulberry trees, fig trees, dashing torrents, festoons of vines, bubbling fountains, reeds and ruins and the mingled music of birds and waters. The vegetation and fertility all around are extraordinary. Here Herod, when receiving the tetrarchy from Augustus, built a temple in his honour. On the rocky wall close by, niches may still be traced, one of them bearing the Greek inscription, 'Priest of Pan'. When Herod's son Philip received the tetrarchy, he enlarged and greatly beautified the ancient town and called it in honour of the Emperor, Caesarea Philippi.

It was into this chiefly Gentile district that the Lord now withdrew with his disciples after that last and decisive question of the Pharisees. It was here that Peter delivered his great confession. It may have been that this rock wall below the castle, under which sprang the Jordan, or the rock on which the castle stood, supplied the suggestion for Jesus' words, 'You are Peter, and on this rock will I build my church'.

Jesus and his disciples spent six days hereafter this confession and here, on one of the heights of snowy Hermon, was later on the scene of the Transfiguration. Isn't it significant that such events should have taken place far away from Galilee and Israel, in the lonely grandeur of the shadows of Hermon and even among a chiefly Gentile population? Not in Judea, nor even in Galilee, but far away from the Temple, the synagogue, the priests, Pharisees and scribes, was the first confession of the Church made, and on this confession its first foundations laid.

The backdrop of all of this had been the public challenge of the Pharisees and Sadducees, that Jesus should validate his claims to the Messiahship through 'a sign from heaven'. Probably, neither his questioners nor his disciples understood his answer or even the meaning of his 'sign'. To the Pharisees, Jesus would seem to have been defeated. He had publicly declined or at least evaded the challenge. He had conspicuously failed! At least, so it would appear to those who could not understand his reply.

But what of the disciples, who (as we have seen) would probably understand the 'sign' of Christ somewhat better than the Pharisees? Jesus' perceived failure in not meeting the challenge of his questioners must have left some impression on them. It must be remembered that his last 'hard' (John 6:60) sayings at Capernaum had led to the defection of many, who until then had been his disciples.

It was after solitary prayer that, with reference to the challenge of the Pharisees ('the leaven' that threatened them), he now gathered up all their experience of the past by asking his disciples the question, what do those who had watched his works and heard his words, regard him as being? The answer came from Peter, the one who most truly represented the Church because he combined with the most advanced experience of the three most intimate disciples the utmost boldness of confession, 'You are the Messiah'.

And so in part was this 'leaven' of the Pharisees purged! Yet not wholly. For it was then that Jesus spoke of his sufferings and death and that the resistance of Peter showed how deeply that leaven had penetrated. And then followed the grand contrast presented by Jesus, between minding the things of humankind and those of God. Six days more of quiet waiting and growth of faith and it was met, rewarded, crowned and perfected by the sight on the Mount of Transfiguration.

Let's return first to the great confession. The popular opinion did not point to Christ as literally the Baptist, Elijah, Jeremiah, or one of the other prophets who had long been dead. For although the literal reappearance of Elijah and probably also of Jeremiah was expected, the

Pharisees did not teach, nor did the Jews believe in, a moving around of souls between bodies. Besides, no one looked for the return of any of the other old prophets, nor could anyone have seriously imagined that Jesus was, literally, John the Baptist, since all knew them to have been contemporaries.

Rather it would mean that some saw in him the continuation of the work of John, as heralding and preparing the way of the Messiah. But, although they regarded Jesus as an extraordinary man or teacher, they did not view him as the Messiah.

The words of the confession are given somewhat differently by the three Gospel writers. From our standpoint, the briefest form (that of Mark): 'You are the Messiah' means quite as much as the fullest (that of Matthew), 'You are the Messiah, the Son of the Living God.' We can thus understand how the latter might be truthfully adopted and would be the most truthful, accurate and suitable in a Gospel primarily written for the Jews. And here we notice that the most exact form of the words seems that in the Gospel of Luke, 'The Christ of God' (KJV)

The full knowledge that he was the Son of the living God came to the disciples only after the resurrection. Previous to the confession of Peter, those who had witnessed his walking on the water had remarked, 'Truly you are the Son of God' (Matthew 14:33) but not in the sense in which a well-informed, believing Jew would hail him as the Messiah, and 'the Son of the living God', designating both his office and his nature.

Again, Peter himself had made a confession of Christ when, after his teaching at Capernaum, so many of his disciples had forsaken him. It had been, 'We have come to believe and to know that you are the Holy One of God' (John 6:69). The mere mention of these words shows both their internal connection with those of his last and crowning confession, 'You are the Messiah, the son of the living God' and the immense progress made.

In the words of this confession, Peter has consciously reached the firm ground of Messianic acknowledgement. It is the first real confession of the Church. The reply of the Saviour is only recorded by Matthew. But its absence in the Gospel of Luke proves that it could never have been intended as the foundation of so important a doctrine as that of the permanent supremacy of St Peter (through the papal system).

Let's examine the meaning of Jesus' reply. The whole form here is Hebraistic. The 'blessed are you' is Jewish in spirit and form. The address, 'Simon Barjonah' (KJV) proves that the Lord spoke in Aramaic, rather than Greek. Lastly, the expression 'flesh and blood' as contrasted with God, occurs in the letters of Paul and in almost innumerable passages in Jewish writings, as denoting humanity in opposition to God. No less Jewish in form are the succeeding words of Christ, 'You are Peter [*Petros*], and on this rock [*Petra*] I will build my church'.

We notice in the original the change from the masculine gender, 'Peter' (*Petros*), to the feminine, '*Petra*' (rock). This seems significant, when we understand that *Petros* is used in Greek for 'stone' and also sometimes for 'rock', while *Petra* always means a 'rock'. The change of gender must therefore be significant.

We recall that when Peter first came to Christ, the Lord had said to him, 'You will be called Cephas [*Kepha* in Aramaic] (which, when translated, is Peter) [*Petros*, a stone, or else a rock].' When the Lord, therefore, prophetically gave the name 'Cephas', it may have been that by that term he gave only a prophetic interpretation to what had been his previous name, Peter. This seems the more likely, since it was the practice in Galilee to have two names, especially when the strictly Jewish name, such as Simon, had no equivalent among the Gentiles.

Believing that Jesus spoke to Peter in Aramaic, we can now understand how the words *Petros* and *Petra* would be purposely used by Jesus to mark the difference, which their choice would suggest. We can understand how, just as his contemporaries may have regarded the world as reared on the rock of faithful Abraham, so Jesus promised that he would build his Church on Peter's faith and confession.

Nor would the term 'Church' sound strange in Jewish ears, being the Greek equivalent of the Hebrew *Qahal*, 'convocation', 'the called'. In Hebrew use, it referred to Israel, not in their national but in their religious unity. As here employed, it would convey the prophecy that his disciples would in the future be joined together in a religious unity; that this religious unity or 'Church' would be a building of which Christ was the Builder; that it would be founded on Peter's faith and confession. And that this religious unity, this Church, was not only intended for a time but would last beyond death and that 'the gates of Hades' would 'not overcome it'. Viewing the Church as a building founded upon Peter's confession, he would be representative of the apostles, the 'stewards of the mysteries of God' (1 Corinthians 4:1, KJV) with 'the keys of the kingdom of heaven'.

No terms were in more constant use in Rabbinic Canon Law than those of 'binding and loosing'. The words are the literal translation of the Hebrew equivalents Asar, which means 'to bind', in the sense of prohibiting and Hittir, which means 'to loose', in the sense of permitting. On the other hand, 'binding and loosing' referred simply to things or acts prohibiting or else permitting them, declaring them lawful or unlawful. This was one of the powers claimed by the rabbis. As regards their laws, it was a principle that while in Scripture there were some that bound and some that loosed, all the laws of the rabbis related to 'binding'. So binding was to do with law-making.

On the other hand, loosing was to do with the administrating of justice, determining guilt or innocence. These two powers – the legislative and judicial – which belonged to the Rabbinic office, Jesus now transferred to his apostles; the first here to Peter as their representative, the second after his resurrection to the Church. In the view of the rabbis, heaven was like earth and questions were discussed and settled by a heavenly Sanhedrin. Now, regarding some of their earthly decrees, they would say that 'the Sanhedrin above' confirmed what 'the Sanhedrin beneath' had done.

All the three Gospel writers record – each with distinctive emphasis – that the open confession of his Messiahship was not to be made public. Among the people, it could only have led to results the opposite of those to be desired. They write it down in plain language, as fully taught them by later experience, that he was to be rejected by the rulers of Israel, slain and to rise again the third day. And there can be as little doubt that Jesus' language must have clearly implied all this because at the time they did not fully understand it.

Chapter 30: The Transfiguration

MATTHEW 17:1-8; MARK 9:2-8; LUKE 9:28-36
(Book 4: Chapter 1)

Peter's confession of Jesus as the Messiah, the Christ,[45] also identified his followers as the Church. It separated them, as it separated him from all around. It gathered them into one and it marked out the foundation on which the building made without hands[46] was to rise. Without a doubt, this confession also *marked the high point of the apostles' faith.* Not until his resurrection did it reach so high. It was necessary that at this stage in the history of the Christ and immediately after his proclamation, the sufferings and the rejection of the Messiah should be prominently brought forward.

Peter's denial of this brought the response, 'Get behind me, Satan! You are a stumbling-block to me' (Matthew 16:23). Peter's remark was surely a re-enactment of the great initial temptation by Satan after the forty days' fast in the wilderness. Six days later we see the Saviour climb the Mount of Transfiguration with the three apostles Peter, James and John. There can scarcely be a reasonable doubt that Jesus and his disciples had not left the neighbourhood of Caesarea and so that 'the mountain' must have been one of the slopes of gigantic, snowy Hermon.

Edersheim paints a picture:

What a background for the Transfiguration; what surroundings for the Vision, what echoes for the Voice from heaven! It was evening when they climbed the path that led up to one of the heights of Hermon. In all the most solemn transactions of earth's history,

---

45. Christ (English) derives from *Christos* (Greek) which derives from Messiah/ *Mashiach* (Hebrew).

46. 2 Corinthians 5:1.

there have been few who have witnessed God's great doings. Alone with his son, as the destined sacrifice, did Abraham climb Moriah; alone did Moses behold the burning bush amid the awful loneliness of the wilderness and alone on Sinai's height did he commune with God; alone was Elijah at Horeb and with no other companion to view it than Elisha did he ascend into heaven. But Jesus, the Saviour of his people, could not be quite alone, save in those innermost transactions of his soul: in the great contest of his first Temptation and in the solitary outpourings of his heart with God. In the most solemn turning points of this history, Jesus could not be alone, and yet was alone with those three chosen ones, those most receptive of him, and most representative of the Church.

As Luke alone informs us, Jesus took them up that mountain 'to pray'. And the Transfiguration was God's answer to that prayer. Jesus needed prayer so that his soul might lie calm and still, perfect in the unruffled quiet of his self-surrender, the absolute rest of his faith and the victory of his sacrificial obedience. And he needed prayer also as the introduction to and preparation for his Transfiguration. By contrast, it was natural for these men of simple habits, after a night-time climb in that strong mountain air, to be heavy with sleep.

It was in a state of semi-stupor when they witnessed what passed between Moses and Elijah and Jesus but they were fully awake to see his Glory and the two men who stood with him. What they saw was their Master, while praying, 'transformed'. The 'form of God' (Philippians 2:6, KJV) shone through the form of a servant. The appearance of his face became other. It shone 'like the sun'. They saw with him two men, who they immediately recognised as Moses and Elijah.

Suddenly, a cloud passed over the clear brow of the mountain, a cloud filled with light. As it laid itself between Jesus and the two Old Testament representatives, it parted and enveloped them. The Presence of God was revealed, yet also concealed by a luminous cloud. And this cloud overshadowed the disciples; the shadow of its light fell upon them. A nameless terror seized them. Such vision had never before been seen by mortals. In the confusion of their terror, they were keen to keep things going, by getting busy in making booths for the heavenly visitors!

A Voice came out of the cloud saying, 'This is my beloved Son: Hear him' (KJV). This was the testimony to seal it all, one Voice to give both meaning and music to what had been the subject of Moses' and Elijah's speaking. That Voice had now come, not in testimony to any fact, but to a Person – that of Jesus as his 'beloved Son'.

So how does the Transfiguration fit in with our story? To begin with, if Jesus was the Christ of God, then this event was a necessary stage in the Lord's history, viewed in the light in which the Gospels present him. Secondly, it was needed for his own strengthening, even as the ministry of the angels after the Temptation. Thirdly, it was good for these three disciples to be there, not only as future witnesses but also for present help. Lastly, the Voice from heaven, in the hearing of his disciples, was of the deepest importance. Coming after the announcement of his death and passion, it sealed that testimony and proclaimed him as the Prophet that Moses had spoken of in Deuteronomy 18:15.

Edersheim provides a solemn epitaph to this episode:

> But, for us all, the interest of this history lies not only in the past; it is in the present also, and in the future. To all ages it is like the vision of the bush burning, in which was the Presence of God. And it points us forward to that transformation, of which that of Christ was the pledge, when 'this corruptible shall put on incorruption'. As of old the beacon-fires, lighted from hill to hill, announced to them far away from Jerusalem the advent of solemn feast, so does the glory kindled on the Mount of Transfiguration shine through the darkness of the world, and tell of the Resurrection-Day. On Hermon the Lord and his disciples had reached the highest point in this history. Henceforth it is a descent into the Valley of Humiliation and Death!

MATTHEW 17:9-21; MARK 9:9-29; LUKE 9:37-43

(Book 4: Chapter 2)

The following morning Jesus and his three disciples moved camp. They had seen his Glory, they had had the most solemn possible witness and they had gained new knowledge of the Old Testament. Perhaps on that morning better than in the previous night, did they realise the vision and feel its calm happiness. It was to their souls like the morning air which they breathed on that mountain. It would be only natural that they may seem distracted to the companions and fellow disciples whom, on the previous evening, they had left in the valley beneath. How much they had to tell them and how glad they would be of the tidings they would hear!

We think here especially of those whom we may think of as the counterpart of the three chosen apostles: Philip, who always sought firm standing ground for faith; Thomas, who wanted evidence for believing; and Judas, whose burning Jewish zeal for a Jewish Messiah had already begun to consume his own soul, as the wind had driven back upon himself the flame that had been kindled. Every question of a Philip, every doubt of a Thomas, every despairing wild outburst of a Judas, would be met by what they had now to tell. But it was not to be so. Evidently, it was not an event to be made generally known, either to the people or even to the great body of the disciples. They could not have understood its real meaning; they would have misunderstood its heavenly lessons. And so it was that the Master laid on the three of them the command to tell no one of this vision until after the Son of Man had risen from the dead.

One thing still troubled them, that they dared not even ask Jesus about, a new and seemingly greater mystery than they had yet heard, the meaning of the Son of Man rising from the dead. Did it refer to the general resurrection? Was the Messiah to be the first to rise from the dead and to waken the other sleepers, or was it only a figurative expression for his triumph and vindication? Evidently, they knew nothing yet of Jesus' personal resurrection as separate from that of others and on the third day after his death. And yet it was so near! So ignorant were they and so unprepared! And they dared not ask the Master of it. This much they had already learned; not to question the mysteries of the future, but *simply to receive them*.

There was another question to ask Jesus, one concerned not by the mysteries of the future, but the lessons of the past. Thinking of that vision, of the appearance of Elijah and of his speaking of the death of the Messiah, why did the scribes say that Elijah should first come and, as was the universal teaching, for the purpose of restoring all things? If, as they had seen, Elijah had come, but only for a brief season, not to abide, along with Moses, as they had fondly wished when they proposed to build booths for them, they had failed to distinguish between the coming of Elijah and its alternative sequence. Truly Elijah had 'already come' in the person of John the Baptist. The divinely intended object of Elijah's coming was to 'restore all things'. If the people had received his message, there would have been the promised restoration of all things. As the Lord had said on a previous occasion 'If you are willing to accept it [or receive, KJV], he is the Elijah who was to come' (Matthew 11:14). Similarly, if Israel had received the Christ, he would have gathered them like a hen gathered her chicks for protection.[47] He would not only have been but have visibly appeared as their King. But Israel did not know their Elijah and did to him whatsoever they wanted; and so would the Son of Man also suffer at their hands.

It was their unbelief that caused their failure to restore the demon-possessed boy. A group of excited people (including scribes) who had tracked the Lord and come upon his disciples in the hour of their greatest weakness, is gathered about a man who had in vain brought his son for healing. This was the hour of triumph for these scribes. The Master had refused the challenge earlier and the disciples, accepting it, had signally failed. There they were discussing the power, authority and reality of the Master.

---

47. Matthew 23:37.

At that very moment, Jesus appeared with the Three. There was immediate calm, preceding victory. Before they could explain themselves, the man came forward and addressed Jesus. At last he had found the One whom he had come to seek and if there was a possibility of help there, oh! Let it be granted. He told them how he had come in search of the Master, but only found the nine disciples and how they had attempted the cure... and failed.

Why had they failed? For the same reason that they had not been taken onto the Mount of Transfiguration, because they were 'faithless' (KJV) – because of their unbelief. They had that outward faith – they believed because of what they had seen; and they were drawn closer to Jesus, at least almost all of them, though in varying measure. But they did not possess that deeper, truer faith.

In such faith, as they had, they tried to imitate their Master. But they totally failed. And it was intended that they should fail, as a lesson to them and to us of the higher meaning of faith as contrasted with power, the inward as contrasted with the merely outward qualification. In that hour of crisis, in the presence of questioning scribes and a wondering populace and in the absence of the Christ, only one power could prevail, that of spiritual faith; and 'this kind' could 'come out only by prayer'.

For one moment we have a glimpse into the Saviour's soul; the poignant sorrow of his disappointment at the unbelief of the 'faithless and perverse generation' (KJV) with which he had so long borne. The next moment Jesus turns to the father. At his command, the boy is brought to him and is healed and, with a strong gentle hand, the Saviour lifted him and with a loving gesture delivered him to his father. All things had been possible for faith; not to that external belief of the disciples, which failed to reach 'this kind' and ever fails to reach such kind, but to true spiritual faith in him.

And so it is to each of us individually and to the Church. 'This kind' – whether it be of sin, of lust, of the world, or of science falsely so-called, of temptation, or of materialism – does not come out by any of our ready-made formulae or dead dogmas. Not so are the flesh and the devil vanquished; not so is the world overcome. It comes out by nothing but by prayer; 'I do believe; help me overcome my unbelief!' Then, although our faith is as the smallest – like a mustard seed – the result to be achieved will be the greatest, most difficult, as in 'removing mountains', *nothing shall be impossible for us.*

Chapter 31: Galilee Revisited

MATTHEW 17:22 –18:22; MARK 9:30-50; LUKE 9:43-50
(Book 4: Chapter 3)

We find Jesus once more with his disciples passing through Galilee, ready for their journey to the Feast of Tabernacles in Jerusalem.

He now speaks clearly of his impending death and resurrection, to prepare them for what is to come. While he would keep his present stay in Galilee as private as possible, he would emphasise this teaching to his disciples so that it should sink in! Yet the announcement only filled their loving hearts with great sorrow; they did not understand it and 'were afraid to ask him about it'.

It is well known that every male in Israel, from twenty years upwards, was expected annually to contribute to the Temple treasury. When it was told in Capernaum that the rabbi of Nazareth had once more come to what seems to have been his Galilean home, it was only natural that they who collected the Temple tribute should have demanded its payment. Possibly, this may have been fuelled by the wish to involve him in a breach of so well-known an obligation. Would he own the duty of paying the Temple tribute? The question which they put to Peter implies, at least, their doubt.

Since the first Passover, which had marked his first public appearance in the Temple at Jerusalem, he had stated that he was the Christ, the Son of God.[48] To have now paid the Temple tribute, without explanation, might have involved a very serious misapprehension. Yet, Jesus would still further vindicate his royal title. He will pay for Peter also and pay, as heaven's King, with a *stater*, or four-drachma piece, miraculously provided.

The event next recorded in the Gospels took place partly on the way from the Mount of Transfiguration to Capernaum and partly in

---

48. Matthew 16:16.

Capernaum itself, immediately after the scene with the tribute money. The disciples were disputing among themselves 'which of them would be the greatest' in the Messianic kingdom of heaven. The honour just bestowed on the Three, in being taken up the mountain, may have roused feelings of jealousy in the others, perhaps through boasting by the three of them.

The spirit which John displayed in his harsh prohibition of the man who did not follow with the disciples and the self-righteous bargaining of Peter about forgiving the supposed or real offences of a brother give evidence of *anything but* the frame of mind which we would have expected after the vision on the mountain. What a disappointment for Jesus! In truth, the apostles were still greatly under the influence of the old spirit.

It was the common Jewish view that there would be distinctions of rank in the kingdom of heaven. Within the charmed circle of Rabbinism, there would be distinctions due to learning, merit and even favouritism. And in the Messianic age, God would assign booths to each according to his rank. How deep-rooted were such thoughts and feelings, appears not only from the dispute of the disciples by the way but also from the request by the 'mother of Zebedee's sons' at a later period (Matthew 20:20-21).

Again, the other disciples only came into Capernaum and entered the house just as Peter had gone for the *stater*, with which to pay the Temple tribute for the Master and himself. And we would suggest that the brother whose offences Peter found it so difficult to forgive, may have been none other than Judas. With his 'Judaistic' ways, such a dispute would have particularly interested him. Perhaps he may have been its chief instigator?

Following on from this is another incident on the journey, which is afterwards related. In this, John seems to have been the principal antagonist. Perhaps in the absence of Peter, he claimed the leading role? They had met one who was casting out demons in the name of Christ, whether successfully or not. So widely had faith in the power of Jesus extended, so real was the belief in the subjection of the demons to him, so reverent was the acknowledgement of him! A man who did this, thus forsaking the methods of Jewish exorcists, could not be far from the kingdom of heaven. John had, in the name of the disciples, forbidden him, because he 'was not one of [them]'.

It was quite in the spirit of their ideas about the Messianic kingdom and of their dispute concerning which of his close followers would be greatest there. There is an eternal principle, 'Whoever is not against us is for us.' He that does not oppose the disciples really is for them. Such a man would not lightly speak evil of Jesus and that was all the disciples should care for really. Jesus was certainly not going to stop him!

'Who, then, is the greatest in the kingdom of heaven?' It was a general question but Jesus could read their hearts. Jesus called a little child – perhaps Peter's little son – and put him in the middle of them. They were not to strive about who was to be greatest, but to be utterly without self-consciousness, like a child. As to the question of greatness in the kingdom, it was really one of the greatness of service and that was the greatest service that implied most self-denial. Suiting the action to the teaching, Jesus took the child in his arms. Not to teach, to preach, to work miracles, nor to do great things, but to do the humblest service for Christ's sake – lovingly, earnestly, wholly, self-forgetfully, simply for Jesus, was to receive Jesus – and therefore to receive the Father.

The love of Christ goes deeper than the act of receiving a child, utterly contrary to what a Pharisee would have done! Someone may enter into the kingdom and do service – yet, if in so doing they disregard the law of love to the little ones, far better their work should be abruptly cut short; better that one of those large millstones, turned by an ass, were hung about their neck and be 'cast into the sea' (KJV).

Chapter 32: The End of the Beginning

~~~

JOHN 7:1-16; LUKE 9:51-56,57-62; MATTHEW 8:19-22
(Book 4: Chapter 4)

We now see Jesus travelling to Jerusalem. Luke takes the wider view where he presents what really were three separate journeys as *one* leading towards the great end. From the moment of his finally quitting Galilee to his final entry into Jerusalem, we see these represented as only one journey. And Luke peculiarly designates this. He now tells us that Jesus sets his face to go to Jerusalem.

The six or seven months between Passover and Tabernacles and all that passed within them, are covered by this brief remark in John 7:1: 'After these things Jesus walked in Galilee: for he would not walk in [Judea] because the Jews sought to kill him' (KJV). A short sentence, but packed with meaning!

But now the Feast of Tabernacles was at hand. The pilgrims would probably arrive in Jerusalem before the opening day of the festival. Remembering that five months had elapsed since the last great feast (that of Weeks), many sacrifices must have been due. Accordingly, the ordinary festive companies of pilgrims, which would travel slowly, must have started from Galilee sometime before the beginning of the feast. These circumstances fully explain the details of the narrative. They also illustrate the loneliness of Jesus in his work.

His disciples had failed to understand his teaching on this. With his impending death, they either displayed gross ignorance or else disputed about their future rank. And 'his own brothers did not believe in him'. The whole course of recent events, especially the ignored challenge of the scribes for 'a sign from heaven' had deeply shaken them.

What was the purpose of his works, if done in the presence of his apostles, in a house, a remote district, or even before an ignorant multitude? If claiming to be the Messiah, he wished to be openly known as such. He must use other means. If he really did these things, let him manifest himself before the world, in Jerusalem, the capital of their world and before those who could test the reality of his works. Let him come forward at one of Israel's great feasts, in the Temple and especially at this feast which pointed to the Messianic ingathering of all nations.

Let him now go to them so that all might have the opportunity of seeing his works. This was not easy then and it is not easy now. One factor is key: do not ignore the world's hatred for the Christ. Discipleship is not the result of any outward manifestation by evidence or demonstration, it requires the conversion of a child-like spirit. For the season of understanding had not yet come, though it would soon arrive. But the world hated him because Jesus was manifested, not to restore an earthly kingdom to Israel, but to bring the heavenly kingdom upon earth, 'to destroy the devil's work' (1 John 3:8).

Here Luke's account begins. Jesus' intention seems to have been to take the more direct road to Jerusalem through Samaria to avoid his enemies. But he was soon frustrated when, in the very first Samaritan village, they found that neither hospitality nor friendly treatment could be extended to him.

This was an act of open hostility to Israel, as well as to Jesus, and James and John, the 'sons of thunder' (Mark 3:17) whose feelings for their Master were, perhaps, the more deeply stirred as opposition to him grew fiercer, proposed to call down divine judgement of fire from heaven to destroy that village. It seems a bit extreme! He who had come not to destroy, but to save, turned and rebuked them and passed from Samaritan into Jewish territory to pursue his journey.

As they were going towards another village, a scribe broke into a spontaneous declaration of readiness to follow him absolutely and everywhere. The intensity of the self-denial involved in following Jesus was immediately further brought out. This scribe had offered to follow Jesus. The expression 'to follow' a teacher would, in those days be universally understood as implying discipleship.

Now, no other duty would be regarded as more sacred than to bury the dead. To this everything must give way, even prayer and the study of the Law. Yet, when Jesus called another disciple to follow him, he was fully aware that at that very moment his father lay dead. Thus, he called him to set aside his obligation and sacred duty. In Jesus' reply, the backdrop was that, according to Jewish Law, the burial and mourning for a dead father and the subsequent purifications would have occupied many days, so that it might have been difficult, perhaps impossible, to make an immediate decision to follow Jesus. We would rather abide by the simple words of Christ. They teach us that there are higher duties than either those of the Jewish Law or even of natural reverence and a higher call than that of people.

LUKE 10:1-16

(Book 4: Chapter 5)

Although we can't be certain as to the order of events, it was on his progress southwards at this time that Jesus designated those Seventy[49] who were to herald his arrival in every town and village. With all their similarity, there are notable differences between the mission of the Twelve sent earlier and this of the Seventy. The mission of the Twelve was on their appointment as apostles; it was evangelistic and missionary and it was in confirmation and manifestation of the 'power and authority' (Luke 9:1) given to them.

On the other hand, no power or authority was formally conferred on the Seventy, their mission being for one definite purpose; to prepare for the coming of the Master in the places to which they were sent. Their selection was from the wider circle of disciples, the number being now seventy instead of twelve. Even these two numbers seem to indicate that the twelve symbolised the princes of the tribes of Israel, while the seventy were the symbolical representatives of these tribes, like the seventy elders appointed to assist Moses.

---

49. Or 'seventy-two', (NIV).

There was something very significant in this appearance of Jesus' messengers, by 'two by two', in every place he was about to visit. As John the Baptist had heralded the coming of Jesus, so now two heralds appeared to solemnly announce his advent at the close of his ministry. As John had prepared his way, so they did the same, as the representatives of the New Testament Church. In both cases, the preparation sought was a moral one. It was the national summons to open the gates to the rightful King and accept his rule.

MATTHEW 9:36-38

Compared with the scope and the urgency of the work, how few were the labourers! Yet, as the field was God's, so also could he alone 'send out workers' willing and able to do his work. It is noticeable that both the introductory and the concluding words addressed to the apostles are missing in what was said to the Seventy. It was not necessary to warn them against going to the Samaritans, since the direction of the Seventy was to those cities of Perea and Judea, on the road to Jerusalem, through which Jesus was about to pass. Nor were they armed with precisely the same supernatural powers as the Twelve.

MATTHEW 11:20-24

A peculiarity in the instructions given to the Seventy seem verbal rather than real; the expression, 'if the son of peace be there' (Luke 10:6, KJV) is a Hebraism, equivalent to 'if the house be worthy' and refers to the character of the head of the house and the tone of the household. Lastly, the direction to eat and drink such things as were set before them is only a further explanation of the command to abide in the house which had received them. Finally, in Luke, the address to the Seventy is followed by a denunciation of Chorazin and Bethsaida. This is evidently in its right place; after the ministry of Jesus in Galilee had been completed and finally rejected. In Matthew 11, it stands immediately after the Lord's rebuke of the popular rejection of the Baptist's message. The 'woe' pronounced on those cities, in which 'most of his mighty works were done' (KJV) is in proportion to the greatness of their privileges.

The denunciation of Chorazin and Bethsaida is the more remarkable in that Chorazin is not otherwise mentioned in the Gospels, nor yet any miracles recorded as having taken place in Bethsaida. This is surely a mark of authenticity of the history being described, rather than just fulfilling a 'legend'. Again, apparently, no record has been preserved in the Gospels of most of Christ's miracles, only those being narrated which were necessary to present Jesus as the Christ, in accordance to the respective plans on which each of the Gospels was constructed. Chorazin and Bethsaida are compared with Tyre and Sidon, which under similar declarations would have repented, while Capernaum which, as for so long the home of Jesus, is compared with Sodom. And such guilt involved greater punishment.

LUKE 10:17-24

Whether or not the Seventy actually returned to Jesus before the Feast of Tabernacles, it is convenient to consider the result of their mission. It had filled them with the joy of assurance. The outcome had exceeded their expectations, just as their faith had gone beyond the mere letter into the spirit of his words. As they reported it to him, even the demons had been subject to them through his name, as Edersheim now declares:

> The great contest had been long decided, it only remained for the faith of the Church to gather the fruits of that victory. The Prince of Light and Life had vanquished the Prince of Darkness and Death. The Prince of this world must be cast out. In spirit, Christ gazed on 'Satan fallen as lightning from heaven.' As the Lord beholds him. He is fallen from heaven from the seat of power and of worship; for his mastery is broken by he who was stronger than he. The authority and power over 'the demons,' attained by faith, was not to pass away with the occasion that had called it forth. The Seventy were the representatives of the Church in her work in preparing for

the Advent of Christ. As already indicated, the sight of Satan fallen from heaven is the continuous history of the Church. What the faith of the seventy had attained was now to be made permanent to the Church, whose representatives they were.

For the words in which Jesus now gave authority and 'power to tread on serpents and scorpions, and over all the power of the enemy' (KJV) and the promise that nothing should hurt them could not have been addressed to the Seventy for a mission which had now come to an end, except in so far as they represented the Church universal. This is for us, too! It is almost needless to add that those 'serpents and scorpions' are not to be literally but symbolically understood.

Yet it is not this power or authority which is to be the main joy either of the Church or the individual, but the fact that our 'names are written in heaven'. And so Jesus brings us back to his great teaching about how the need to become like children is the secret of true greatness in the kingdom. This sentiment almost reached its climax in the thanksgiving, that the Father in heaven had hidden these things from 'the wise and learned' and 'revealed them to little children'. As we view it in the light of those times, we know that 'the wise and learned' – the rabbi and the scribe – could not from their standpoint have perceived them. And so it must ever be, that, not as 'wise and learned' but only as 'little children' can we share in that knowledge which makes us wise unto salvation.

MATTHEW 11:25-30

He had sent forth the Seventy on vital work. He had already prayed for the Father to send forth labourers entrusted to the faith and service of the Church and that prayer still holds now! And the true wisdom, which qualified for the kingdom, was to take up his yoke, which would be found an easy burden, not like that unbearable yoke of Rabbinic conditions and the true understanding to be sought; it was by learning of him.

One of the most common expressions of the time was that of 'the yoke' to indicate submission to an occupation or obligation. And, indeed, this voluntary making of the yoke as heavy as possible, the taking on themselves as many obligations as possible, was the ideal of Rabbinic piety.

LUKE 10:25,38-42; 11:1-4

There was an enquiry on the part of a 'certain lawyer' (KJV) as to what he should do to inherit eternal life. Together with Jesus' parable about the Good Samaritan, this is relevant to the previous teaching about entering into the kingdom of heaven. From this interruption, we turn to a far different scene. It follows in Luke's narrative and we have no reason to consider it out of its proper place. If so, it must mark the close of Jesus' journey to the Feast of Tabernacles, since the home of Martha and Mary was in Bethany, close to Jerusalem, almost one of its suburbs.

One of his disciples asks him to teach them to pray, as the Baptist had similarly taught his followers. This seems to indicate that they were then on the scene of John's former locations, north-east of Bethany and that it occurred on Jesus' return from Jerusalem.

Again, from the narrative of his reception in the house of Martha, we gather that Jesus had arrived in Bethany with his disciples, but that he alone was the guest of the two sisters. It was the beginning of the Feast of Tabernacles and the scene recorded by Luke would take place in the open leafy booth which served as the habitation during the festive week. For, according to law, one lived in such booths during the festive week to eat, sleep, pray and study. We can picture to ourselves Martha moving around on her busy errands and noticing Mary still sitting as a rapt listener and wondering how she could enter so suddenly the master's Presence.

There is no evidence that the household of Bethany had previously belonged to the circle of Jesus' professed disciples. It was, as the narrative shows, a wealthy home. It consisted of two sisters – the elder, Martha, the younger, Mary – and their brother, Lazarus. Although we don't know why, the house was Martha's and she received Jesus into it on his arrival in Bethany. It would have been totally natural for a pious wealthy lady to receive a great rabbi into her house. He was to lodge in one of the booths, the sisters in the house, and the great booth in the middle of the courtyard would be the common meeting place. It could not have been long after his arrival that the sisters felt they had received more than an angel unawares.[50] How best to do him honour was equally the thought of both sisters.

To Martha, it seemed as if she could not do enough in showing him all hospitality. Her younger sister also would do him the highest honour, *but not as Martha*. Mary's homage consisted in *forgetting all else but him, who spoke as none had ever done*. And so, time after time, as Martha passed on her busy way, she still sat listening and living. At last, the sister broke in with what sounds like a complaint, 'Lord, don't you care that my sister has left me to do the work by myself?' Mary had served with her, but she had now left her to do the work alone. Would the Master bid her resume her neglected work? But, with a tone of gentle reproof, affection and reprimand, he taught her in words that are so full that they have entered into everyday conversation: 'Martha, Martha, thou art careful and troubled about many things: But one thing is needful: and Mary hath chosen that good part, which shall not be taken away from her' (KJV). Nevertheless, we see no partiality in this: 'Jesus loved Martha and her sister' (John 11:5).

---

50. See Hebrews 13:2, KJV.

Chapter 33: The Feast of Tabernacles

JOHN 7:11-36
(Book 4: Chapter 6)

Edersheim offers an introduction:

> It was *Chol ha Moed,* as the non-sacred part of the festive week. This was mainly the feast for foreign pilgrims, coming from the farthest distance, whose Temple contributions were then received and counted. As the Jerusalemite would look down on the swarthy strangers, yet fellow-countrymen, or the eager-eyed Galilean curiously stare after them, the pilgrims would, in turn, gaze with mingled awe and wonderment at the novel scene. They could come at this season of the year, not during the winter for the Passover, nor yet quite so readily in summer's heat for Pentecost. But now they came, in the delicious cool of early autumn, when strangers from afar off and countrymen from Judea, Perea, and Galilee, would mingle in the streets of Jerusalem, under the ever-present shadow of that glorious Sanctuary of marble, cedarwood, and gold, up there on high Moriah, symbol of the infinitely more glorious overshadowing Presence of him, who was the Holy One in the midst of Israel.

Quite rightly is the Feast of Tabernacles acclaimed as 'the Feast' (*ha Chag*) and the Jewish historian Josephus describes it as 'the holiest and greatest'.[51] The whole symbolism of the Feast, beginning with the completed harvest, for which it was a thanksgiving, pointed to the future. The rabbis themselves admitted this. The strange number of sacrificial bullocks – seventy in all – they regarded as referring to 'the seventy nations' of the

---

51. Josephus, *Antiquities* VIII, Chapter 4, Part 1.

Gentiles. The ceremony of the outpouring of water, which was considered of such vital importance, is symbolic of the outpouring of the Holy Spirit.

Jesus did not appear in the Temple during the first two festive days. The pilgrims from all parts of the country had expected him there, for everyone would now speak of him on the quiet in Jerusalem, for they were afraid of their rulers. But they sought him and enquired after him. 'Some said, "He is a good man"', while others declared that he only led astray the common, ignorant populace. And now, all at once in *Chol ha Moed*, Jesus himself appeared in the Temple and taught.

We don't know what his teaching was on this occasion. But the effect on the people was one of general astonishment. To the Jews, there was only one kind of learning, that of theology and only one road to it – the schools of the rabbis. Among the Jews, a rabbi's teaching derived authority from the fact of its accordance with tradition, that it accurately represented what had been received from a previous great teacher and so on upwards to Moses and to God himself. On this ground, Jesus claimed the highest authority. His doctrine was not his own invention, it was the teaching of him that sent him. The doctrine was God-received and he was sent directly from God to bring it. He was God's messenger of it to them.

Jesus is defending himself against a charge which naturally came up when he claimed that his teaching was of God and himself God's real and faithful messenger. A general cry 'you have a demon' broke free. But he would not be interrupted and continued, 'I did one miracle, and you are all amazed', referring to his healing on the Sabbath and their utter inability to understand his conduct. *Well, Moses was a messenger of God and I am sent of God.* Moses gave the God-given law of circumcision and, to observe this law, no one hesitated to break the Sabbath since, according to Rabbinic principle, a positive ordinance superseded a negative. And yet, when Jesus, as sent from God, made a man whole on the Sabbath they were angry with him!

The fact that he, whom they sought to kill, was able to speak openly, seemed to them incomprehensible. Could it be that the authorities were shaken in their former idea about him and now regarded him as the Messiah? But it could not be. It was a settled popular belief and, in a sense, not quite unfounded, that the appearance of the Messiah would be sudden and unexpected.

But Jesus could not let it rest there, even for the sake of his poor, weak disciples. He lifted up his voice so that it reached the dispersing, receding multitude. Yes, they thought they knew both him and from where he came. But he had been sent and he that sent him was real! He finished speaking and they had understood his allusions and in their anger would justifiably have 'laid hands on him' (KJV), but 'his hour had not yet come'. Yet others were deeply stirred to faith. As they parted they spoke of it among themselves and the sum of it all was: 'The Christ when he comes, will he do more miracles (signs) than this one did?'

So ended the first teaching of that day in the Temple. And as the people dispersed, the leaders of the Pharisees had watched the effect of his teaching. They conferred with the heads of the priesthood and the chief Temple officials. Orders were given to the Temple guard on the first possible occasion to seize him. Jesus was aware of this and as he was moving in the Temple, watched by the spies of the rulers and followed by a mingled crowd of disciples and enemies, deep sadness could well have filled his heart.

JOHN 7:37 – 8:11

(Book 4: Chapter 7)

It was 'the last and greatest day of the festival' and Jesus was once more in the Temple. We have here the only Jewish festival which has no counterpart in the cycle of the Christian year, just because it points forward to that great, yet unfulfilled hope of the Church, the ingathering of earth's nations to the Christ.

The celebration of the Feast corresponded to its great meaning. Not only did all the priestly families minister during that week, but it has been calculated that no fewer than 446 priests with a corresponding number of

Levites, were required for its sacrificial worship. In general, the services were the same every day, except that the number of bullocks offered decreased daily from thirteen on the first to seven on the seventh day.

The last day was marked by special observances. The pilgrims were all in festive clothing. In their right hand each carried what is called the *Lulabh*, which consisted of a myrtle and willow branch tied together with a palm branch between them. This was supposed to be in fulfilment of the command in Leviticus 23:40. The fruit of the 'goodly trees' (KJV) mentioned in the same verse of Scripture, was supposed to be the *Ethrog*, the so-called paradise-apple (possibly the fruit of the forbidden tree), a species of citron, which each worshipper carried in their left hand.

When the Temple procession had reached the Pool of Siloam, the priest filled his golden pitcher from its waters. Then they went back to the Temple, timing it so that they should arrive just as they were laying the pieces of the sacrifice on the great altar of burnt offering, towards the close of the ordinary morning-sacrifice service. A three-fold blast of the priests' trumpets welcomed the arrival of the priest, as he entered through the 'Water gate' and passed straight into the Court of the Priests. Here he was joined by another priest, who carried the wine for the drink offering. The two priests ascended 'the rise' of the altar and turned to the left. There were two silver funnels here, with narrow openings, leading down to the base of the altar. The wine was poured into the wider east side of the altar and, at the same time, the water poured into the western and narrower opening, the people shouting to the priest to raise his hand, to make sure that he poured the water into the funnel.

For, although they said that the water-pouring was an ordinance instituted by Moses, this was a disputed point between the Pharisees and the Sadducees. The high priest Alexander Jannaeus had on one occasion poured the water on the ground when he was nearly murdered, and in the riot that ensued, 6,000 persons were killed in the Temple.

We can have little difficulty in determining at what part of the services of 'the last and greatest day of the festival' Jesus stood and cried, 'Let anyone who is thirsty come to me and drink.' It must have been with special reference to the ceremony of the outpouring of the water, which was considered the central part of the service. Moreover, all would understand that his words must refer to the Holy Spirit since the rite was universally regarded as symbolic of his outpouring.

These words have remained as the call of Jesus to all that thirst, whatever their need and longing of soul may be. But, as we listen to these words as originally spoken, we feel how they mark that his hour was indeed coming, the preparation past, the manifestation in the present, unmistakable and urgent and the final conflict at hand.

Amid all this, the strongest testimony to his person and mission remains to be told. It came, as so often, from an unexpected place. Those Temple officers, whom the authorities had commissioned to watch for an opportunity to seize Jesus, came back without having done so yet.

But their intentions were clear and there was one standing among the Temple authorities, for whom an uneasy conscience would not allow him to remain quite silent. It was the Sanhedrist Nicodemus, still a secret disciple. He could not hold his peace and yet he dared not speak for Jesus. So he made a compromise of both by speaking as a righteous, rigid Sanhedrist: 'Does our law condemn a man without first hearing him to find out what he has been doing?'

JOHN 8:12-59

(Book 4: Chapter 8)

It was no longer a secret that the leaders of Israel and Jerusalem were plotting the death of Jesus. This underlies all of his words. And he intended to turn this to his advantage, not by appealing to their pity, but by claiming as his right that for which they would condemn him. He was the Messiah, although, to know him and his mission, it needed a true understanding of God and his ways. Did Israel, as such, possess this? They did not; no person possessed it until given to them by God. This was not exactly a new idea by now, but it was now far more clearly stated and developed. Perhaps we have overlooked this teaching of Jesus? It is concerning the corruption of our whole nature by sin and hence the need of understanding 'that which is born of the flesh is flesh; and that which is born of the Spirit is spirit' (John 3:6 KJV); therefore: 'You must be born again' (John 3:7).

That had been Jesus' initial teaching to Nicodemus and it became, with growing emphasis, his final teaching to the teachers of Israel. It forms the very basis of Christianity; it is the ultimate reason for the need for a Redeemer. The Priesthood and the sacrificial work of Christ, as well as the higher aspect of his prophetic office and the true meaning of his Kingship, as not of this world, are based upon it.

It most definitely constitutes the starting point in the fundamental divergence between the leaders of the synagogue and Christ; we might say, for all time between Christians and non-Christians. The teachers of Israel knew not, nor believed in the total corruption of humanity – Jew as well as Gentile – and therefore did not feel the need of a Saviour. They could not understand it – how except someone were 'born again' and 'from above'[52] they could not enter, nor even see, the kingdom of God.

Also, he would teach that Satan was not a merely malicious, impish being, working outward destruction, but that there was a moral power of evil which held us all – not just the Gentile world, but even the most favoured, learned and exalted among the Jews. Satan was the fullest expression of this power, the prince of the power of darkness. This opens up Jesus' reasoning. He presented himself to them as the Messiah and hence as the 'light of the world'. It meant that only by following him would a person not 'walk in darkness' but have the light, not the light of knowledge, but of life.

Edersheim is very clear about this:

On the other hand, it also followed that all who were not within this light, were in darkness and in death. The Pharisees sought to

---

52. See John 3:3 and NIV footnote.

turn it aside by an appeal to the external and visible. They asked for some witness or palpable evidence of what they called his testimony about himself, just as they had formerly asked for a sign from heaven. The Bible is full of what men ordinarily, and often thoughtlessly, call the miraculous. But, in this case, the miraculous would have become the magical, which it never is. If Christ had yielded to their appeal and transferred the question from the moral to the coarsely external sphere. He would have ceased to be the Messiah of the Incarnation, Temptation, and Cross, the Messiah-Saviour. It would have been to un-Messiah the Messiah of the Gospel, for it was only, in another form, a repetition of the temptations in the desert.

The interruption of the Pharisees was thoroughly Jewish and so was their objection. The reply of Jesus was plain. Even if his testimony about himself was unsupported, it would still be true and he was competent to bear it, for he knew where he came from and where he was going, unlike them!

This gave occasion for him to return to the main subject, that the reason for their ignorance of him was that they knew not the Father and that only acknowledgement of him would bring true knowledge of the Father. Such words would only increase their anger towards him. Yet, not until his hour had come!

Soon we find him again teaching 'the Jews'. These would be the Judeans – perhaps Jerusalemites, aware of the murderous intent of their leaders – not his own Galileans. The words are intensely sad, Jesus' farewell to his rebellious people, his tears over lost Israel. 'I am going away, and you will look for me, and you will die in your sin. Where I go, you cannot come.'

How true this was. They thought that he spoke of his death and not of that which came after death. It was this misunderstanding which Jesus briefly, but emphatically, corrected by telling them that the ground of their separation was the difference in their nature; they were from below, he from above; they of this world, he not of this world.

Jesus now turned to his people. They were at a crisis in their spiritual history and he must encourage them. Only if they remained in his Word would they know the truth *and the truth would set them free*. It was not merely believing him, but *abiding in it*. Their own tradition told them that only those who laboured in the study of the Law were free. Yet he spoke not of study but on abiding in his Word. But it was this very thing which they resisted. And so they ignored the spiritual and fell back upon the physical applications of his words.

He would turn to their favourite conceit of being Abraham's seed. Yes, they were, but it was only the moral application that alone was of real value. Abraham's seed? He showed that their father could not have been Abraham, so far as spiritual heritage was concerned. They had now a glimpse of his meaning, but only to misapply it, according to their Jewish prejudice. Their spiritual heritage, they urged, must be of God, since their physical ancestor was Abraham. But Jesus showed them that if theirs was a spiritual heritage from God, then they would not reject his message, nor seek to kill him, but recognise and love him.

He had now said most of what he wanted to say and their objections were degenerating into wrangling. It was time to break it off through a general application. The question, he added, was not of what he said, but of what God said of him. That God, whom they claimed as theirs, and yet knew not.

But, as for Abraham, he had delighted in the thought of the coming day of the Christ and seeing its glory. He was glad. Even Jewish tradition agreed on this! Jesus then spoke the words which could not be mistaken: 'Verily, verily, I say unto you, Before Abraham was, I am' (KJV). It was as if they had only waited for this. Furiously they rushed into the Court of the Gentiles to pick up stones, and to cast them at him. But, once more, 'his hour had not yet come' and their fury proved impotent. Hiding for the moment in one of the many chambers, passages, or gateways of the

Temple, he soon left the scene.

It had been the first open demonstration of his divinity in the presence of his enemies and when most contempt was thrown at him. Soon would that conflict be renewed both in word and by deed, for the end of mercy and judgement had not yet come, but was drawing terribly closer.

Chapter 34: Messianic Miracle

JOHN 9
(Book 4: Chapter 9)

After the scene in the Temple just described, we have, probably on the next day, the healing of the man born blind, at the Temple entrance, the chosen spot for those in need to gather. Because this healing became known very quickly, we presume this is where the healing happened.

It was the Sabbath and Jesus with his disciples was passing by a blind beggar. On the Sabbath, he would, of course, neither ask for nor receive charity, though some would help him privately. The blind were regarded as especially entitled to charity and the Jerusalem Talmud relates some touching instances of the favour displayed towards them.

As the Master and his disciples passed the blind beggar, Jesus saw him, with that look which they who followed him knew to be full of meaning. Yet they were so used to the ways of the Pharisees, that there was no thought of possible mercy, with the following thought pre-eminent, through whose guilt was he so afflicted – his own, or that of his parents?

As this man was 'blind from birth', the possibility of sin before birth would suggest itself, at least as a speculative question, since the 'evil impulse' (*Yetser haRa*) might even then be called into activity. At the same time, both the Talmud and the later charge of the Pharisees, 'in sins were you born altogether' imply that in such cases the alternative explanation would be considered, that the blindness might be caused by the sin of his parents. It was a common Jewish view, that the successes or failures of the parents would appear in the children. In fact, up to thirteen years of age, a child was considered part of his father and as suffering for his guilt. More than that, the thoughts of a mother might affect the moral state of her unborn offspring and the terrible apostasy of one of the greatest rabbis had, in popular belief, been caused by the sinful delight his mother had taken when passing through an idol-grove! Lastly, certain special sins in the parents would result in specific diseases in their offspring, and one is mentioned as causing blindness in the children.

It was their opinion that God does not interfere in the ordinary course of everyday life. But there is another and a higher aspect of it since Jesus has come and is really the *healer of all disease and evil* by being the remover of its ultimate moral cause. This is indicated in his words when, putting aside the clumsy alternative suggested by the disciples, he told them that it was so, in order 'that the works of God might be displayed in him', as we read in verse 3. They wanted to know the 'why'. He told them the 'in order to' of the man's calamity.

He told them the purpose which it and all similar suffering should serve, since Jesus has come, the healer of evil. Thus, he tackled the question in terms of the moral purpose which suffering might serve. And this, because the coming and work of the Christ have made it possible to us all.

He had to work fast during the few hours still left of his brief working day. He may also have anticipated any objection to his healing on the Sabbath. As the 'light of the world' (John 8:12), he could do no else but shine as long as he was in it. And this he demonstrated by the healing of the blind. Saliva was commonly regarded as a remedy for diseases of the eye, although not for the removal of blindness. With this he made clay, which he now used, adding to it the direction to go and wash in the Pool of Siloam, a term which literally meant '*sent*': a symbolism of him who was the 'Sent of the Father'.

The blind man seems to have been ignorant of the character of his healer, and it needed the use of some means to make him receptive. His sight was restored by clay, made out of the ground with his spittle, whose breath had at the first breathed life into clay. And this was then washed away in the Pool of Siloam, from whose waters had been drawn on the Feast of Tabernacles, that which symbolised the pouring forth of the new life by the Spirit.

Lastly, we may ask why such a miracle should have been performed on one without faith, who does not even seem to have known about Jesus? We can only repeat that the man himself was intended to be a symbol, 'that the works of God might be displayed in him'. And so, what the Pharisees had sought in vain was freely offered when there was a need for it. With wonderful simplicity, the man's obedience and healing are recorded.

The formal question now put to him by the Jews was no more than an inquisition rather than the outcome of a wish to learn the circumstances of his healing. And so we notice in his answer the cautious desire not to say anything that could incriminate his benefactor. He tells the facts truthfully and plainly; he emphasises the means by which he had recovered sight.

Then they bring him to the Pharisees, not to take notice of his healing, but to use it as a charge against Jesus. Such must have been their motive, since it was universally known that the leaders of the people had, of course informally, agreed to take the strictest measures, not only against Jesus but also against anyone who professed to be his disciple. The grounds on which the present charge against Jesus would rest was plain: the healing involved a breach of the Sabbath Law. The first of these was that he had made clay. Next, it would be a question of whether any remedy might be applied on the holy day. It was declared lawful to apply, for example, wine to the outside of the eyelid on the grounds that this might be treated as washing; but it was sinful to apply it to the inside of the eye. And as regards saliva, its application to the eye is expressly forbidden, because it was evidently intended as a remedy. There was, therefore, abundant legal grounds for a criminal charge, which the Pharisees initiated.

Firstly, as if not satisfied with the report of those who had brought the man, they made him repeat it. The simplicity of the man's language left no room for evasion or deception. They may have been the accusers but Rabbinism itself was being judged here! The facts could neither be denied nor explained and their only complaint against Jesus was his breaking of their traditional law. Which was approved by God? Their traditional law of Sabbath observance or he who had done such miracles? With this dilemma, they turned to the simple man before them. What was the impression left on the mind of the one who had the best opportunity for judging?

'He is a prophet'! So they turned to the parents. After all, the man might not have been really blind so they decided to cross-examine them. But on this most important point the parents, with all their fear of the anger of the Pharisees, remained unshaken. He had been born blind; but as to the manner of his cure, they declined to offer any opinion. Thus, as so often, the plots of the enemies of Christ resulted in the opposite of those wished for. For to people so wretchedly poor as to allow their son to live by begging, the consequence of being put outside the congregation – which was to be the punishment of any who confessed Jesus as the Messiah – would have been dreadful.

We can understand how everyone would dread such an outcome. The Rabbinists provide twenty-four grounds for excommunication, of which more than one might serve the purpose of the Pharisees. But in general, to resist the authority of the scribes, or any of their decrees, or to lead others either away from 'the commandments', or to what was regarded as a profanation of the divine name, was sufficient to incur the ban.

As nothing was forthcoming from his parents, the man who had been blind was once more summoned before the Pharisees. It was simply to demand a recantation from him, though this was put in the most roundabout manner. You have been healed. Admit that it was only by God's hand miraculously stretched forth and that 'this man' had nothing to do with it. It could not have been Jesus who had done it, for they knew him to be a 'sinner'!

Certainly, this was the condemnation of Jesus but he who had been healed of his blindness was not to be so betrayed into a denunciation of his Great Physician. It was his turn now to bring back the question to the issue which they had originally raised; and we admire it all the more, as we remember the consequences to this poor man of so confronting the

Pharisees. There was the unquestionable fact of his healing of which he had personal knowledge (of course!)

The renewed enquiry now by the Pharisees as to how Jesus had healed him was met by irony from the man. Was it because they felt the wrongness of their own position and that they should become his disciples? It stung them to the quick. They lost all self-possession and with this their moral defeat became complete. This 'ignorant' layman had now the full advantage in the controversy. How come that the leaders of Israel should confess themselves ignorant of the authority of one who had the power to open the eyes of the blind, a marvel which had never before been witnessed?

If he had that power, where did it come from and why? It could only have been from God. They said he was 'a sinner' and yet there was no principle more frequently repeated by the rabbis than that answers to prayer depended on a man being 'devout' and doing the will of God. There could therefore be only one conclusion. *If Jesus had not divine authority, he could not have had divine power.* The Pharisees had nothing to answer and, as not infrequently in similar cases, could only in their fury cast him out with bitter accusations.

Edersheim adds to this:

Would he teach them, he, whose very disease showed him to have been a child conceived and born in sin and who, ever since his birth, had been among ignorant, Law-neglecting 'sinners'? But there was another, who watched and knew him; he whom he had dared to confess and for whom he was content to suffer. Let him now have the reward of his faith, even its completion; and so shall it become manifest to all time, how, as we follow and cherish the better light, it rises upon us in all its brightness and that faithfulness in little brings the greater stewardship.'

Tenderly did Jesus seek him out and asked him, 'Do you now believe on the Son of God, through this experience?' And is it not always so that faith is based on the conviction of personal experience? Thus is faith always the child of experience and yet its father also; faith not without experience and yet beyond experience; faith not superseded by experience, but made reasonable by it.

In language plainer than he had ever before used, Jesus answered and with an immediate confession of faith, the man worshipped him. And so it was, that the first time he saw his deliverer, it was to worship him. What a contrast was this faith and worship of the poor simple man, once blind, now in every sense seeing, to the blindness of judgement which had fallen on those who were the leaders of Israel!

It had been a contest between traditionalism and the work of Christ. They were traditionalists, were they also blind? But they had misunderstood him by leaving out the moral element, thus showing themselves blind indeed. It was not the calamity of blindness, but it was a blindness in which they were guilty and for which they were responsible, which was the result of their deliberate choice. Therefore their sin – not their blindness only – remained!

Chapter 35: Confrontations and Condemnations

JOHN 10:1-21
(Book 4: Chapter 10)

As he left Jerusalem in sorrow, he ploughed on. He now spoke to them an allegory in the form of a parable, to hide the higher truths from those who had not seen but revealing them to those whose eyes had been opened. If the scenes of the last few days had made anything plain, it was the utter unfitness of the teachers of Israel for their professed work of feeding the flock of God.

The Rabbinists also called their spiritual leaders 'feeders' (*Parnasin*), a term which comprised of the two ideas of 'leading' and 'feeding', which are the theme of this allegory. No better illustration could be found for those to whom 'the flock of God' was entrusted. They had entered into God's sheepfold, but not by the door by which the owner, God, had brought his flock into the fold. This entrance had been his free love, his gracious provision, his thoughts of pardoning, his purpose of saving mercy. That was God's Old Testament door into his sheepfold. Not by that door, as had so lately fully appeared, had Israel's rulers come in.

They had climbed up to their place in the fold some other way, as a thief or a robber. What more accurate description could be given to the Pharisees and Sadducees who were responsible for God's flock? How different was Jesus, who comes in and leads us through the door by which God had brought, and ever brings, his flock into his fold! This was the *true shepherd*.

Jesus was the door. And all those who went before him who pretended to be the door – whether Pharisees, Sadducees, or nationalists – were only 'thieves and robbers'. And the sheep, God's flock, did not hear them; for, although they might pretend to lead the flock, the voice was that of strangers. Jesus was the good shepherd, in contrast to others who falsely claimed to be the shepherds. Their objective had been a selfish one and they had pursued it even at the cost of the sheep, of their life and safety. Jesus was the good shepherd who 'lays down his life for the sheep'! What a contrast to a mere hireling, who has no connection with the sheep and who flees at the sight of the wolf.

And all this to be the Shepherd-Saviour, to die and rise for his sheep and thus to gather them all, Jews and Gentiles, into one flock and to be their shepherd. It was a noble closing to the series of those chats in the Temple, designed to show that he was truly sent of God.

In the Talmud (Yoma 66b) we have a series of questions addressed to Rabbi Eliezer ben Hyrcanos, to test his views about Jesus. Rabbi Eliezer, one of the greatest rabbis, was the brother-in-law of Gamaliel II, the son of that Gamaliel at whose feet Paul sat. He may, therefore, have been acquainted with the apostle and we have solid evidence that he met freely with Jewish Christians and took pleasure in their teaching.

One question asked is, 'Is it right for the Shepherd to save a lamb from the lion?' To this the rabbi gives an evasive answer, 'You have only asked me about the lamb.' This was followed by, 'Is it right to save the Shepherd from the lion?', again with an evasive answer, 'You have only asked me about the Shepherd.' Thus, as this is a clear reference to the sheep and the shepherd in Jesus' allegory, the rabbi, by dividing them, cleverly evaded giving an answer to his questioners. This helps us to appreciate the debate that Jesus instigated even in the Jewish writings. It casts a light not only upon the rabbi but also a sidelight on the history of Nicodemus. The question arises of how far many rabbis and laymen may have gone in their belief in Christ.

MATTHEW 12:22-45; LUKE 11:14-36
(Book 4: Chapter 11)

Jesus then travelled to Perea, where he mostly remained until a week before his last Passover in Jerusalem, apart from a short trip to Jerusalem at the Feast of Dedication (*Chanukah*). This is a quiet period. It consists almost exclusively of teachings and parables, with a few narrative portions interspersed. And this is not only because the season of the year must have made travel difficult, but chiefly from the character of his ministry in Perea, which was, substantially, a resumption of his early Galilean ministry, only modified and influenced by the much fuller knowledge of the people concerning Jesus and the greatly developed hatred from their leaders.

This accounts for the recurrence of many things recorded in the earlier part of this history. Thus, to begin with, we can understand how he would, at this initial stage of his Perean ministry, repeat, when asked for instruction concerning prayer, those sacred words ever since known as the Lord's Prayer.

In Luke,[53] the prayer is for the forgiveness of 'sins', while Matthew[54] uses the Hebraic term 'debts', which has passed even into the Jewish Liturgy, denoting our guilt as indebtedness. Again, the 'day by day' (KJV) of Luke, which further explains the petition for 'daily bread' common both to Matthew and Luke, may be illustrated by the beautiful Rabbinic teaching that the manna fell only for each day, so that thought of their daily dependence might call forth constant faith in our 'Father in heaven'.

The first event in this period was when Jesus cast out a demon and restored speech to the demonised. This is one of the cases in which it is difficult to determine whether narratives in different Gospels, with slightly varying details, represent different events or only differing modes of narration. This same event would have taken place on more than one occasion and that, when it occurred, would result in the same charge against Jesus of turning to the 'dark' side.

The leading feature of his reply to the Pharisees is that their crediting satanic activity to what Jesus did was only prompted by hostility to his person. This mode of turning the argument against the arguer was

---

53. Luke 11:2-4.
54. Matthew 6:9-13.

peculiarly Hebraic and he asked them whether their own disciples cast out demons and, if so, by whom are they doing it?

But secondly, he teaches against the flimsy, superstitious and unspiritual views entertained by the religious leaders, concerning both the kingdom of evil and that of God. By their own admission, the casting out of Satan was part of the work of Messiah. Then had the kingdom of God come to them, for in this was the kingdom of God and he was the God-sent Messiah, come not for the glory of Israel, nor for anything outward or intellectual, but to engage in mortal conflict with moral evil and with Satan as its representative.

In that contest, Jesus binds the strong one. It follows that his work is a moral contest waged through the Spirit of God, where all must take a part. But they went further, by representing Jesus' coming as satanic! Such perversion of all that is highest and holiest, such opposition to the Holy Spirit as if he were the manifestation of Satan, represents sin in its absolute completeness and for which there can be no pardon, with no possibility of repentance. The unforgivable sin!

The Pharisees fell back on the old device of asking him for some visible sign. It was an attempt to shift the argument from the moral to the physical. It was the moral that was at fault and no amount of physical evidence or demonstration could have supplied that. He would offer them only one sign, that of Jonah the prophet. He pointed to the allegorical history of Jonah. As he appeared in Nineveh, he was himself 'a sign to the Ninevites', the fact that he had been three days and nights in the whale's belly and that he had been brought back to preach in Nineveh was evidence to them that he had been sent of God. And so would it be again.

Then Jesus returned to his former teaching concerning the kingdom of Satan and the power of evil. Now he applied it not to the individual, but to the Jewish community as a whole. As compared with the other nations of the world, Israel was like a house from which the demon of idolatry had gone out with all his attendants, really the 'Beel-Zibbul' whom they dreaded. And then the house had been swept of all the foulness and

202

uncleanness of idolatry and garnished with all manner of Pharisaic adornments. Yet all this while the house was left really empty, God was not there and so the demon returned to it again, to find that house swept and garnished indeed, but also empty and defenceless!

Coming to the end of his teaching, Jesus spoke of light and lamps. What was the object of lighting a lamp? Surely, that it may give light. But if so, no one would put it into a vault, nor under the bushel, but on the stand. Should we then expect that God would light the spiritual lamp if it be put in a dark vault? It was a blessed lesson with which to close his teaching and one full of light, if only they had not put it into the vault of their darkened hearts. Yet soon would it shine forth again and give light to those whose eyes were opened to receive it.

LUKE 11:37-54
(Book 4: Chapter 12)

Jesus was invited by a Pharisee to the morning meal. This resulted in his second recorded teaching in Perea. It is the last address to the Pharisees in Luke but it was not to set up yet another accusation against him.

What would they have eaten at this meal? The favourite food was young meat, goats, lambs and calves. Bread was regarded as the mainstay of life and in a sense it constituted the meal. For the blessing was spoken over the bread and this was supposed to cover all the rest of the food that followed, such as the meat, fish or vegetables. Similarly, the blessing spoken over the wine included all other kinds of drinks. Otherwise, it would have been necessary to pronounce a separate benediction over each different article eaten or drunk. He who neglected the prescribed benedictions was regarded as if he had eaten of things dedicated to God.

Let us suppose the guests assembled. To such a meal they would not be summoned by slaves, nor be received in such solemn state as at feasts. First, each would observe, as a religious rite, 'the washing of hands'. Next, the head of the house would cut a piece from the whole loaf and speak the blessing. As he generally did, Jesus omitted the 'washing of hands' before the meal.

So what happened at the table of the Pharisee? When the water was presented to him, Jesus would either refuse it or would be expected to first wash his hands. Yet Jesus did nothing and sat down to the meal without this formality. He was true to his teachings that spiritual purification set aside any human ordinances which diverted thoughts of purity into questions of the most childish character.

On the other hand, we can also understand what bitter thoughts must have filled the mind of the Pharisee when his guest neglected to perform this cherished rite. It was an insult to himself, a defiance of Jewish Law, a revolt against the most cherished traditions of the synagogue. Pharisees were taught not to sit down to a meal with such a person. He must have regretted inviting Jesus to his table.

Formerly Jesus had shown how traditionalism came into conflict with the written Law of God. Now, how it superseded the first principles which underlay that Law. Remember, he had laid down the principle that defilement came *not from without inwards, but from within outwards.* And the Phariseeism which pretended to the highest purity was, really, the greatest impurity – the defilement of graves, only covered up, not to be seen of people! It was at this point that one of the scribes at the table spoke up. But, as 'one of the lawyers' rightly remarked, by attacking not merely their practice but their principles, the whole system of traditionalism was condemned.

And so the Lord most definitely meant it. The scribes were the followers of the traditional law; those who bound and loosed in Israel. They did bind on heavy burdens, but they never loosed one; all those grievous burdens of traditionalism they laid on the poor people, but not the slightest effort did they make to remove any of them.

There was a terrible truth and solemnity in what Jesus spoke and in the sorrow with which he denounced them. The next few months would bear witness how truly they had taken upon them this tradition of guilt and all the later history of Israel shows how fully this sorrow has come upon them.

Chapter 36: Hypocrisy!

LUKE 12:1 – 13:17
(Book 4: Chapter 13)

The record of Jesus' last warning to the Pharisees and of their hateful response is followed by a summary of his teaching to the disciples. The tone is still that of warning, but entirely different from that to the Pharisees. It is a warning of sin that threatened, not of judgement that awaited; it was *for prevention, not in condemnation.* He was protective of those who were his people and wanted the very best for them.

'Beware … of the leaven of the Pharisees' (KJV)! There is no need to point out the connection between this warning and the denunciation of Pharisaism and traditionalism at the Pharisee's table. Although the word 'hypocrisy' had not been spoken there, it was the sum and substance of his contention that Pharisaism, while pretending to be what it was not, concealed what it was. And it was this 'leaven' that permeated the whole system of Pharisaism. It wasn't that as individuals they were all hypocrites, but that the very system was hypocrisy.

We think of the differences between this time and when previously Jesus sent out the apostles on their mission. Earlier it had been in the form of a warning; now it was that of comforting reassurance. There it was near the beginning; here near the close of his ministry. Again, as before, it was followed by advice and consolation, followed by a caution to dismiss fear and to speak out publicly what had been told them privately.

On the other hand, when now addressing his disciples, while the same caution is given, it was as spoken to disciples rather than to preachers. Lastly, whereas the Twelve were told not to fear and therefore to speak openly what they had learned privately,[55] the disciples now are forewarned that they were not to be afraid of the possible consequences to themselves.

---

55. Matthew 10:19.

His final teaching to them came in three sections. The first regarded the disciples as servants in the absence of their master. In this parable, he is supposed to be at a wedding and the exact time of his return could not be known. In these circumstances, they should hold themselves in readiness, that whatever hour it might be, they should be able to open the door at the first knocking. Such eagerness and devotion of service would naturally meet its reward, as they watched for his return. Hungry and weary as they were from their zeal for him, he would now, in turn, minister to their personal comfort.

We suppose them to be sleeping when the house might be broken into. Of course, if one had known the hour when the thief would come, sleep would not have been indulged in, but it is just this uncertainty and suddenness – the coming of the Christ into his kingdom would be equally sudden.

Peter interrupted to ask, to whom did this parable apply about 'the good man' and 'the servants' who were to watch? To the apostles, or to all? Jesus was clear that if the apostles or others are rulers, it is as stewards and their reward of faithful and wise stewardship will be advance to higher service. But as stewards, they are servants of the Messiah and ministering servants in regard to the other and general servants. There was a warning and a sober instruction here; the Church had a work to do in his absence, the work for which he had come.

Here he could only repeat what on a former occasion he had said to the Pharisees, let them not think that all this only concerned the disciples. No, the struggle would involve the widest consequences, to all the people. Were they so blinded as not to know how to 'interpret this present time'? Could they not read its signs, they who had no difficulty in interpreting it when a cloud rose from the sea, or the sirocco blew from the south?

It appears that some people told Jesus about some Galileans, whom Pilate had ordered to be cut down while engaged in offering their sacrifices. It seems strange that, although the Jews connected special sins with special punishments, they should have regarded it as the divine punishment of a special sin to have been martyred by Pilate in the Temple, while engaged in offering sacrifices. Very probably these Galileans were ruthlessly murdered because of their real or suspected connection with the nationalist movement, of which Galilee was the focus. Somehow guilt by association was intended here as if Jesus himself was involved in this, so he refuted this with a story of his own.

He drew their attention to the tower at the Pool of Siloam, that had fallen on eighteen persons and killed them, perhaps in connection with that construction of an aqueduct into Jerusalem by Pilate, which provoked violent opposition that the Roman so terribly avenged. As good Jews, they would probably think that the fall of the tower, which now had eighteen unfortunates buried in its ruins, was a just judgement of God! But Jesus argued that it was as wrong to believe that divine judgement had overtaken his Galilean countrymen, as it would be to judge that the tower of Siloam had fallen to punish these Jerusalemites.

The fact was that the whole nation was guilty and the coming storm would destroy all unless there was spiritual repentance on the part of the nation. And yet wider than this is the underlying principle that when a calamity befalls a district or a population, we ought not to judge possible causes, but to think spiritually of its general application. And conversely, this holds true regarding deliverances. Having thus answered the implied objection, the Lord next showed, in the parable of the fig tree, the need and urgency of national repentance.

Next, we are confronted by the clumsy zeal of a chief ruler of a synagogue who is very angry, but not very wise, who admits Jesus' healing power and does not dare to attack him directly but, instead, rebukes, not him, not even the woman who had been healed, but the people who witnessed it, at the same time telling them to come for healing on other days rather than the Sabbath!

He was easily and effectually silenced and all who sympathised with him were put to shame. 'Hypocrites!' spoke the Lord – on your own admissions your practice and your Law condemn your speech. The retort was unanswerable and irresistible; it did what was intended, it covered the adversaries with shame.

Chapter 37: At Chanukah

LUKE 13:22; JOHN 10:22-42
(Book 4: Chapter 14)

It had been about two months since Jesus had left Jerusalem after the Feast of Tabernacles. He returns for a brief stay during the Feast of the Dedication of the Temple (*Chanukah*). This festival was not of biblical origin but had been instituted by Judas Maccabaeus in 164BC, when the Temple, which had been desecrated by Antiochus Epiphanes, was once more purified and rededicated to the service of God. During the feast, the series of Psalms known as the *Hallel* was chanted in the Temple, the people responding as at the Feast of Tabernacles.

The practice of illuminating the Temple and private houses was popular during the eight days of the festival. Tradition had it that when the Temple services were restored by Judas Maccabaeus, the oil was found to have been desecrated. Only one flagon was discovered of that which was pure, sealed with the very signet ring of the high priest. The supply proved just sufficient for the sacred lampstand for one day, but by a miracle, the flagon was continually replenished for eight days until a fresh supply could be brought from Thekoah. In memory of this, it was ordered the following year that the Temple be illuminated for eight days on the anniversary of its 'Dedication'.

It is winter and Jesus is walking in the covered porch in front of the Beautiful Gate, which formed the principal entrance into the Court of the Women. As he walks up and down, the people are literally barring his way. From the circumstances, we cannot doubt that the question which they put, 'How long will you keep us in suspense?', was an accusation rather than a general enquiry!

The more we realise this, the more wonderful is his answer. Briefly, he puts aside their hypocrisy. Does he still need to go over old ground? He had told them before and they disbelieved him then! This was because they were not his sheep. As he had said to them before, it was characteristic of his sheep to hear, recognise and listen to his voice and follow him. He reminds his hearers that his work is really the Father's work, given to him to do, and no one could snatch them out of the Father's Hand.

They understood this but rejected it when they again took up stones intending to stone him – no doubt, because he expressed, in yet more plain terms, what they regarded as his blasphemy. Edersheim explains:

> Once more the Lord appealed from his Words, which were doubted, to His Works, which were indubitable. And so he does to all time. His Divine Mission is evidence of his Divinity. And if his Divine Mission be doubted. He appeals to the 'many excellent works' which he hath 'showed from the Father,' any one of which might, and, in the case of not a few, had, served as evidence of his Mission. And when the Jews ignored, as so many in our days, this line of evidence, and insisted that he had been guilty of blasphemy, since, being a man. He had made himself God, the Lord replied in a manner that calls for our special attention.

He claimed to be one with the Father. Let us see whether the claim was strange. In Psalm 82:6 the titles 'gods' and 'sons of the Most High' had been given to human judges, wielding his delegated authority, since his word of authorisation had come to them. But now authority was not transmitted by 'the Word', but by a *personal and direct mission on the part of God.*

The comparison made was not with prophets, because they only told the word and message from God, but with judges who, as such, did the very acts of God. If these were 'gods', the very representatives of God, could it be blasphemy when he claimed to be the Son of God, who had received authority, not through a word transmitted through long centuries, but a direct personal command to do the Father's work? He had been directly and personally consecrated to it by the Father and directly and personally sent by him, not to say but to do the work of the Father.

The test was whether Jesus really did the works of the Father and if he did the works of his Father, then let them believe, if not the words yet the works, and then would they arrive at the knowledge that 'the Father is in me, and I in the Father'. In other words, recognising the work as that of the Father, they would come to understand that the Father worked in him and that the root of his work was in the Father.

The stones that had been taken up were not thrown, for his words were not deserving of such a punishment, according to Rabbinic Law. But 'they tried to seize him' so as to drag him before their tribunal. His time, however, had not yet come and 'he escaped their grasp'. How he did this, we know not, but it serves to show his total control over the proceedings and narrative. He was totally in charge... if they only knew it!

Chapter 38: More Parables

LUKE 10:25-37; 11:5-13

(Book 4: Chapter 15)

The period now leading up to his last entry into Jerusalem starts with the brief visit to Bethany to raise Lazarus from the dead. The parables of this period look back on the past and forward into the future. Those originally spoken by the Lake of Galilee were purely symbolic. They presented unseen heavenly realities under themes that required to be translated into earthly language. It was quite easy to do so, but only if you possessed the key to the heavenly mysteries; otherwise, they were dark and mysterious. They were easily read from above downwards. Viewed from below upwards, only strangely intertwining outlines could be perceived. In other words, you needed to be in the know first!

It is quite different with this second series of parables. They could, as they were intended, be understood by all. They required no translation. They were not symbolic but practical. Their prevailing character is not descriptive but encouraging and they bring the gospel, in the sense of glad tidings to the lost, most closely and touchingly to the hearts of all who hear them. They are signs in words, as the miracles are signs in works, of what Jesus has come to do and to teach. Most of them bear this character openly and even those which do not, but seem more like a warning, still have an undertone of love, as if divine compassion lingered in tender pity.

The parable of the Good Samaritan is linked to a question, addressed to Jesus by a 'lawyer', an expert in Jewish Canon Law, 'Teacher ... what must I do to inherit eternal life?' At the root of this lay the notion that eternal life was the reward of merit, of works. The only question was, what these works were to be. The idea of guilt had not entered his mind; he had no conception of sin within. It was the old Judaism of self-righteousness speaking without disguise; that which was the ultimate ground of the rejecting and crucifying of the Christ. And so our Lord, using the common Rabbinic expression 'How do you read it?', pointed him to the Scriptures of the Old Testament.

As regards the duty of absolute love to God, indicated by Deuteronomy 6:5, there could be no hesitation in the mind of a Jew. Rabbinism is never weary of quoting its greatest teacher, Hillel, that he had summed up the Law in these words: 'What is hateful to you, that do not to another. This is the whole Law; the rest is only its explanation.' Hillel put it in a negative form, while Jesus put it positively. It is the preaching of the Law that awakens in the mind a sense of sin. Then Jesus was able to show in a parable how far orthodox Judaism was from even a true understanding of the purpose of the Law.

The question that should have been asked is not 'who is my neighbour?' but 'whose neighbour am I?' The gospel answers the question of duty by pointing us to love. Thus is the parable truly Christian and points up to him who, in our great need, became neighbour to us, even at the cost of all he had. And from him, as well as by his Word, are we to learn our lesson of love.

The parable which follows seems closely connected. A man has a friend who, long after nightfall, unexpectedly comes to him. He has nothing in the house, yet he must provide for his need, for hospitality demands it. Accordingly, though it is so late, he goes to his friend and neighbour to ask him for three loaves, stating the case. On the other hand, the friend so asked refuses since, at that late hour, he has retired to bed with his children and to grant his request would imply not only inconvenience to himself but the disturbing of the whole household. The main circumstances, therefore, are a sudden, unthought-of sense of need, obliging to make what seems an unreasonable request. It is a gross misunderstanding to describe it as presenting a mechanical view of prayer, as if it implied, either that God was unwilling to answer or else that prayer, otherwise unheard, would be answered merely for its persistence.

So important is the teaching of this parable that Jesus makes detailed application of it. The emphasis of the parable and its lesson are in the word 'everyone'. Not only this or that but 'everyone' shall so experience it. The reality is of our need ('ask'), the reality of our belief that the supply is there ('seek'), and the intensity and energy of our spiritual longing ('knock'). This applies to 'everyone', whoever they may be, and whatever the circumstances which would seem to make their prayer especially difficult to answer. As we follow Jesus' teaching, we ask for the Holy Spirit and the Holy Spirit, in leading us to him, leads us into 'all the truth' (John 16:13), to all life and to what satisfies all need.

LUKE 12:13-21; 13:6-9; 14:1-24
(Book 4: Chapter 16)

The three parables which follow may generally be designated as those 'of warning'. Each of them is set in a historical frame, having been spoken under significant circumstances.

In the parable of the foolish rich man, it appears that someone among them had the idea that the authority of the Great Rabbi of Nazareth might be used for his own selfish purposes, that he might possibly enlist Jesus as his champion. The Jewish law of inheritance was so clearly defined that if this person had any just or good cause, there could have been no need for appealing to Jesus. Hence, it must have been 'covetousness' in the strictest sense, which prompted it. Such an attempt to derive profit from his spiritual influence accounts for the severity with which Christ rejected the demand.

Jesus teaches him about the wisdom in laying up the good treasure which cannot be taken from us, that 'This is how it will be with whoever stores up things for themselves but is not rich towards God'. It was a barbed arrow out of the Jewish quiver, for we read in the Talmud that a rabbi told his disciples, 'Repent the day before thy death' and when his disciples asked him, 'Does a man know the day of his death?' he replied, that 'on that very ground he should repent today, lest he should die tomorrow. And so would all his days be days of repentance'.

The special warning intended to be conveyed by the parable of the barren fig tree follows on. This parable speaks of Israel in its relation to God; the need for repentance, the nature of repentance and its urgency and the relation of Christ to Israel. The fig tree had been specially planted by the owner in his vineyard, which was the choicest location. Fig trees, as well as palm and olive trees, were regarded as so valuable that to cut them down if they yielded even a small measure of fruit, was popularly deemed to deserve death at the hand of God.

Allegorically, the fig tree in the Old Testament served as the emblem of the Jewish nation, whereas the vineyard in the New Testament is the symbol of the kingdom of God, as distinct from the nation of Israel. So the parable may be thus translated: God called Israel as a nation and planted it in the most favoured spot, as a fig tree in the vineyard of his own kingdom. And it bore no fruit, so the axe beckoned. 'Between the tree and the axe, nothing intervenes but the intercession of the Gardener, who would make a last effort, and even his petition applies only to a short and definite period, and, in case it passes without result, this petition itself merges in the proposal, "But if not, then cut it down."' How speedily and terribly the warning came true. Whether this parable should be applied to all circumstances of nation, community, family, even of individuals, it is not necessary to speak.

The third parable of warning, that of the Great Supper, refers not to the political state of Israel, but to their religious status and their role as the representatives of the kingdom of God. What led up to this parable was his healing of the man with the 'abnormal swelling' in sight of them all on the Sabbath, after he rebuked their perversion of the Sabbath Law and of those characteristics of Pharisaism, which showed how far they were from bringing forth fruit worthy of the kingdom. Jesus had spoken of making a feast, not for one's own, but for the poor and afflicted. This would imply true spirituality, in the giving to strangers, but not condescendingly. The Pharisee's words implied that he fully expected to share in these blessings as a matter of course just because he was a Pharisee. Accordingly, it was to this man personally that the parable was addressed.

One of the principal points in the parable was this: to come to that feast, to enter into the kingdom, implies *the giving up* of something that seems most desirable and the enjoyment of which appears only reasonable.

Be it possession, business and pleasure, the main point is that when the time came, they all refused to enter in, each having some valid and reasonable excuse. But the ultimate ground of their refusal was that they felt no real desire and saw nothing attractive in such a feast; they had no real reverence for the host. Then let the feast be for those who needed it and to whom it would be a feast, the poor and those afflicted, the crippled, blind, lame, on whom those great citizens would look down.

He finishes by saying, 'I tell you, not one of those who were invited will get a taste of my banquet.' And this was the final answer to this Pharisee and to those with him at that table and to all such perversion of Christ's words and misapplication of God's promises of which he and they were guilty.

LUKE 15

(Book 4: Chapter 17)

There is a connection between the three parables here. They are concerned with 'the recovery of the lost', in the first instance through the unwearied labour; in the second, through the anxious care of the owner; and in the third through the never-ceasing love of the Father. To understand these parables, the circumstances must be kept in view. It has formerly been shown that the Jewish teaching concerning repentance was nothing like what was taught by Jesus. Theirs was not a gospel to the lost; they had nothing to say to sinners.

In the parable of the lost sheep the main interest centres *on the lost*; in the second (that of the lost coin), *it centres on the search*. In the first, the danger of being lost arose from the natural tendency of the sheep to wander. In the second parable, it is no longer our natural tendency to which our loss is attributable. The drachma has been lost, but it is still in the house, not like the sheep that had gone astray. It is interesting to note the Jewish parallel to the first parable, where the motivation of the man following the straying animal is Pharisaic fear and distrust in case the Jewish wine that it carried should become mingled with that of the Gentiles.

The third parable, that of the lost son, is more popularly known as the story of the Prodigal Son. Rabbinic tradition supplies a parallel in that while prayer may sometimes find the gate of access closed, it is never shut against repentance and it introduces a parable in which a king sends a tutor after his son who, in his wickedness, had left the palace, with this message, 'Return, my son!' to which the latter replied. 'With what face can I return? I am ashamed!' To which the father sends this message, 'My son, is there a son who is ashamed to return to his father and shall you not return to your father? You shall return.'

In the parable of the lost son, the main interest centres in his restoration. Presumably, the father had only these two sons. The eldest would receive two portions, the younger the third of all movable property. The father could not have disinherited the younger son. On the other hand, a man might, during his lifetime, dispose of all his property to the disadvantage, or even the total loss, of the first born, or of any other children; he might give all to strangers.

The next scene in the history is misunderstood by those who say that the young man's misery is there represented as the result of God's manoeuvrings rather than of his own misdoings. To begin with, his riotous living was fully his responsibility. The main objective is to show that absolute liberty and indulgence of sinful desires and passions ended in anything but happiness. The providence of God had an important part in this.

To a Jew, there was more than degradation in being reduced to feeding swine, since the keeping of swine was prohibited to Israelites under a curse. What perhaps gives additional meaning to the state this son found himself in is the Jewish saying: 'When Israel is reduced to the carob-tree, they become repentant.' It was this pressure of extreme want which first showed to the younger son the contrast between the country and the circumstances to which his sin had brought him and the plentiful provision of the home he had left and the kindness which provided 'bread enough and to spare' (KJV) for even the hired servants. There was only a step between what he said, '[having come] to himself' (KJV) and his resolve to return, though its difficulty seems implied in the expression, 'I will arise' (KJV).

Here it deserves special notice, as marking the absolute contrast between the teaching of Jesus and Rabbinism, that we have in one of the oldest Rabbinic works, a parable exactly the reverse of this, when the son of a friend is redeemed from bondage, not as a son, but to be a slave, so that obedience might be demanded of him. The implication drawn is that the obedience of the redeemed is not that of parental love of the pardoned, but the enforcement of the claim of a master. *How different to the teaching of Christ!*

LUKE 16

(Book 4: Chapter 18)

The last group of parables spoken during this part of Jesus' ministry are connected by a leading thought, *righteousness*. There are three parables of the unrighteous; the unrighteous steward, the unrighteous owner and the unrighteous judge. In Luke 16 we read of the first two.

The parable of the unjust steward was primarily spoken to his disciples, but also those 'publicans and sinners' whom Jesus had received, to the great displeasure of the Pharisees. Them he would teach concerning the 'mammon of unrighteousness' (KJV). And, when the Pharisees sneered at this teaching, he would turn it against them and show that, beneath the self-justification, there lay as deep sin and as great alienation from God as that of the sinners whom they despised.

In this parable, we are told what the sinner when converted should learn from his previous life of sin, though we must not expect to find spiritual equivalents for each of the persons or incidents introduced. The parable itself forms only an illustration of the lessons, spoken or implied, which Jesus would convey to his audience.

Its object is simply to show, in the most striking manner, the prudence of a worldly person, who is only interested in looking after himself. At the same time, the illustration is so chosen as that its matter, 'the mammon of unrighteousness', may serve to teach those new converts who had formerly sacrificed all for the sake of that mammon. The suitability both of the parable and of its application to the audience appears from its similarity to what occurs in Jewish writings.

Thus, the reasoning that the Law could not have been given to the nations of the world, since they have not observed the seven commandments given to Noah (which Rabbinism supposes to have been given to the Gentiles), is illustrated by a Jewish parable in which a king is represented as having employed two administrators; one over the gold and silver and the other over the straw. The latter rendered himself suspected and when he complained that he had not been set over the gold and silver, they said to him: 'you fool, if you have proved yourself unreliable in regard to the straw, shall they commit to you the treasure of gold and silver?' And we almost seem to hear the very words of Jesus: 'He that is faithful in that which is least is faithful also in much' (KJV).

And the ultimate application of all this was that division was impossible in the service of God. It is impossible for the disciple to make a separation between spiritual matters and worldly and to attempt serving God in the one and mammon in the other. There is absolutely no such distinction to the disciple and our common usage of the words 'secular' and 'spiritual' is derived from a terrible misunderstanding and mistake. To the secular, nothing is spiritual; and to the spiritual, nothing is secular. 'No one can serve two masters ... You cannot serve both God and Money [mammon].'

The parable of the rich man and Lazarus was spoken primarily for the disciples. Its first object was to show the great difference between the concepts of 'before men' (KJV) and 'before God'; between the rich man as he appears to people in this world, and as he is before God and will be in the next world. The second main goal of the parable was to illustrate that Pharisaic standing was an abomination before God. The third object of the parable was in the selfish use which they made of their possessions, their mammon.

The parable itself is strictly of the Pharisees and their relation to the 'publicans and sinners' whom they despised. With infinite wisdom and depth, it speaks of their selfish use of the literal riches – their covetousness – and about their selfish use of the figurative riches, their Pharisaic righteousness, which left poor Lazarus at their door to the dogs and to famine, not bestowing on him anything from their supposed rich festive banquets.

On the other hand, it will be necessary in the interpretation of this parable to keep in mind that its details must not be exploited, nor doctrines of any kind derived from them, either as to the character of the other world, the question of the duration of future punishments, or the possible moral improvement of those in Gehinnom. All such things are foreign to the parable, which is only intended as a type, or illustration of what is intended to be taught. If proof were required, it would surely be enough to remind ourselves that this parable is addressed to the Pharisees, to whom Jesus would scarcely have communicated details about the other world, something on which he was so reticent in his teaching to the disciples.

Without going into detail overall, there are some interesting observations to make. The carrying up of the soul of the righteous by angels is certainly in accordance with Jewish teaching. Again, regarding the expression 'Abraham's bosom' (KJV) it occurs, although not frequently, in Jewish writings. Also, the appeal to Abraham as our father is so frequent, his presence and merits are so constantly invoked; notably, he is so expressly designated as he who receives the penitent into Paradise, Gan Eden, the Garden of Eden.

The rich man has died and the next scene is in Hades or Sheol, the place of the disembodied spirits before the final Judgement. It consists of two sections: the one of consolation, with all the faithful gathered to Abraham as their father; the other of fiery torment. Thus far, this is in accordance with the general teaching of the New Testament. As regards the details, they evidently represent the views current at the time among the Jews. According to them, the Garden of Eden and the Tree of Life were the abode of the blessed. We read that the righteous in Gan Eden see the wicked in Gehinnom and rejoice. Similarly, that the wicked in Gehinnom see the righteous sitting beautified in Gan Eden, and their souls are troubled. Marking the vast difference between Jewish ideas and Jesus' teaching, we notice that there is no analogy in Rabbinic writings to the statement in the parable that there is a wide and impassable gulf between Paradise and Gehenna.

LUKE 18:1-14; MATTHEW 18:23-35
(Book 4: Chapter 19)

If one asked how the conduct of the unjust judge could serve as an illustration of what might be expected from God, we answer that the lesson in the parable is not from the similarity but from the contrast between the unrighteous human and the righteous divine judge. In truth, this mode of argument is perhaps the most common in Jewish parables and occurs on almost every page of ancient Rabbinic commentaries. It is called the *Qal vaChomer*, 'light and heavy', and answers from the less to the greater. According to the rabbis, ten instances of such reasoning occur in the Old Testament itself. Thus, it is argued that 'if a King of flesh and blood' did so and so, shall not the King of kings? Or, if the sinner received such and such, shall not the righteous?

In the present parable, the reasoning would be 'if the Judge of Unrighteousness said that he would defend, shall not the Judge of all Righteousness do judgement on behalf of his Elect?'. When describing how at the preaching of Jonah, Nineveh repented and cried to God,[56]

---

56. Luke 11:32.

Jesus' answer to the loud persistent cry of the people is thus explained, 'The bold conquers even a wicked person, how much more the All Good of the world!'

The parable introduces to us a judge in a city and a widow. In the interpretation of this parable the Church, whom she represents, is also widowed in the absence of her Lord. This widow approaches the unjust judge with the urgent demand to be vindicated of her adversary. For reasons of his own, he will not. But, eventually, he complies with her request apparently from fear of bodily harm! Here is the *Qal vaChomer*, if the 'Judge of Unrighteousness' speaks thus, shall not the Judge of all Righteousness – God – do judgment and vindicate his Elect?

Finally, the parable of the unmerciful servant. This concerns a self-righteous, unmerciful spirit, worried about how often we should forgive, forgetting our own need for absolute and unlimited pardon at the hands of God. This is not about the king's command to sell into slavery the first debtor, together with his wife and children. We have three distinct scenes in this story.

In the first, our new feelings towards our brothers and sisters mirror our new relationship with God, as the proper basis of all our thinking, speaking and acting. Notably, as regards forgiveness, we are to remember the kingdom of God so that *we may learn the duty of absolute, not limited, forgiveness* – not that of 'seven' but of 'seventy times seven' (Matthew 18:21-22). We are the debtors of our heavenly King, who has entrusted to us what is his and which we have misused, incurring an unspeakable debt, which we can never discharge and which deserves bondage, misery and utter ruin! But, if in humble repentance we cast ourselves at his feet, he is ready, in infinite compassion, not only to release us from punishment but also to forgive us the debt. It is this new relationship to God that must be the foundation and the rule for our new relationship with our fellow servants.

And this brings us to the second part of this parable. Here the lately pardoned servant takes his fellow-servant by the throat – a not uncommon mode of harshness on the part of Roman creditors – and says, 'Pay up!' It can scarcely be necessary to show the guilt of such conduct. But this is the object of the third part of the parable.

Here the unmerciful servant is summoned and addressed as 'wicked servant' and the words are followed by the manifestations of righteous anger. As he has done, so is it done to him. This is the final application of the parable and he is delivered to the 'tormentors' (KJV). We pause to notice how near Rabbinism has come to this parable, and yet how far it is from its sublime teaching. We recall that unlimited forgiveness was not the doctrine of Rabbinism. It did, indeed, teach how freely God would forgive Israel and it introduces a similar parable of a debtor appealing to his creditor and receiving the fullest and freest release of mercy, and it also draws from it the moral that human beings should similarly show mercy.

But, however beautifully Rabbinism at times may seem to speak on the subject, the gospel conception of forgiveness could only come by the blessed experience of the infinitely higher forgiveness, the incomparably greater mercy which the pardoned sinner has received in Jesus from our Father in heaven.

Chapter 39: Preparations

LUKE 13:23-35; 14:25-35; 17:1-10

(Book 4: Chapter 20)

From the parables, we now turn to some more interactions which Jesus had at this point of his ministry. A question was asked. 'Lord, are they few, the saved ones that are being saved?' The question, whether just a 'few' were to be saved, could not have been put from the Pharisaic point of view if we understood this as personal salvation. On the other hand, if taken as applying to the near-expected Messianic kingdom, it has its distinct parallel in the Rabbinic statement that, as regarded the days of the Messiah (his kingdom), it would be similar to what it had been at the entrance into the land of promise, when only two (Joshua and Caleb), out of all that generation, were allowed to have a part in it.

Regarding entrance into the Messianic kingdom, this Pharisee, and those whom he represented, are told that this kingdom was not theirs, as a matter of course. This entering in through the 'narrow door', was in opposition to the many – the Pharisees and Jews generally – who were seeking to enter in, in their own way, never doubting success, but who would discover their terrible mistake.

The next teaching had been spoken 'at that time'. It was provoked by a pretended warning from 'some Pharisees' to depart the area otherwise Herod would kill him. We expect there to have been secret intrigues between the Pharisaic party and Herod, but we see here a ruse to get rid of him as his works of healing were largely attracting and influencing the people. Pointing to their secret intrigues, he implored them to go back to 'that fox' and tell him that Jesus still had an appointed time to work, and then 'I will reach my goal'. Jesus knew his appointed time... and it wasn't to be now, at the hand of Herod!

Jesus wept over Jerusalem. He knew what things *could* have been like and cried tears of anguish and love over what was yet to come. When Jesus departed from that place, with him 'went great multitudes' (KJV). People still followed him. It was then that he had to remind them of the cost of discipleship. What were they letting themselves in for? Substantially, it was only what Jesus had told the Twelve when he sent them on their first mission. Only it was now cast in a far stronger mould, as befitted the altered circumstances, with the near prospect of his condemnation, with all that this would involve for his followers.

It was now a serious business and discipleship becomes impossible, without actual renunciation of all other competing relationships and, more than that, of life itself. Of course, the term 'hate' does not imply hatred of parents or relatives, or of life in the ordinary sense. But it points to this; outward separation was before them in the near future, so, in the present, inward separation was absolutely necessary. They needed to be in a good place inwardly before they could deal with the trials to come.

Chapter 40: Miracle of Miracles

JOHN 11:1-54

(Book 4: Chapter 21)

The raising of Lazarus marks the highest point in the ministry of our Lord; it is the climax of a history where all is miraculous: the person, the life, the words, the work. As regards Jesus, we have here the fullest evidence alike of his divinity and humanity; as regards those who witnessed it, the highest manifestation of faith and of unbelief. Here we have our first clear outlook on the death and resurrection of Christ, of which the raising of Lazarus was the prelude.

He had indeed raised the dead before, but it had been in far-off Galilee and in circumstances essentially different. But now it would be one so well known as Lazarus, at the very gates of Jerusalem, in the sight of all people. If this miracle is true, we instinctively feel all is true; and seventeenth-century philosopher Spinoza was right in saying that if he could believe the raising of Lazarus, he would tear to shreds his system, and humbly accept the creed of Christians. But is it true? We have reached a stage in this story when such a question might seem almost uncalled for.

Edersheim, though, is emphatic:

> For we have learned to trust the Gospels and, as we have followed him, the conviction has deepened into joyous assurance, that he, who spoke and lived as none other, is in no doubt the Christ of God. And yet we ask ourselves here this question again, on account of its absolute and infinite importance; because this may be regarded as the highest and decisive moment in this story. Because, in truth, it is to the historical faith of the Church what the great Confession of Peter was to that of the disciples.

The fact of miracles runs counter to our everyday experiences and expectations but draws us to the possibility of direct divine interaction. The existence of a God implies at least the *possibility of miracles*. In terms of the raising of Lazarus, we may be asked these three things: firstly, that no other explanation is rationally possible; secondly, that such a view of it is consistent with itself and with all the details of the narrative and thirdly, that it is harmonious with what precedes and what follows the narrative. This is a tall order, so how does it all pan out?

It was while in Perea that a message suddenly reached Jesus from the home at Bethany of Mary and her sister, Martha, concerning their brother, Lazarus. 'Lord, the one you love is ill.' The messenger was apparently dismissed by Jesus with this reply, 'This illness will not end in death. No, it is for God's glory so that God's Son may be glorified through it.' The apostles would naturally now assume that Lazarus would not die and that his restoration would glorify Jesus. Its true meaning was that the death of Lazarus was to be the *starting point* of our story.

Jesus knew that Lazarus had died and yet stayed where he was for another two days. He is never in haste because he is always sure. They eventually prepared for the journey. He next spoke of Lazarus, their 'friend', as 'fallen asleep', in the frequent Jewish (as well as Christian) figurative sense of it and of his going there to wake him out of sleep.

Even his disciples had no clue what he was saying, so much did they need the lesson of faith about to be taught them by the raising of Lazarus! When they arrived, Lazarus had been four days in the grave. According to custom, he would be buried the same day that he had died. Lazarus would not have laid in a cemetery, but in his own private tomb in a cave, probably in a garden, the favourite place of interment.

Jesus arrived at Bethany. As Bethany was only about two miles from Jerusalem many from the city, who were on friendly terms with what was evidently a distinguished family, had come in obedience to one of the most binding Rabbinic directions, that of comforting the mourners. In the funeral procession, the sexes had been separated and the practice probably prevailed even at that time for the women to return alone from the grave. Then began the mourning in the house, which really lasted thirty days, of which the first three were most important; the others, during the seven days, or the special week of sorrow, were of less intense mourning. But on the Sabbath, as God's holy day, all mourning had ceased.

Martha hastened to meet the Master. Even now, when it all seemed too late, it must have been difficult for them. And still, there was the hope that even now God would give Jesus whatsoever he asked.

Jesus is the 'resurrection and the life' and this, the new teaching about the resurrection, was the object and the meaning of the raising of Lazarus. And so this raising of Lazarus prefigures his own resurrection, 'the firstfruits of those who have fallen asleep' (1 Corinthians 15:20).

It seems that the Master called for Mary. She was probably sitting in the chamber of mourning, with its upset chairs and couches and other tokens of mourning, as was the custom, surrounded by many who had come to comfort them. As she heard of his coming and call, she rose quickly and the Jews followed her, under the impression that she was again going to visit and to weep at the tomb of her brother. For it was the practice to visit the grave, especially during the first three days.

When she came to Jesus, she forgot everything and could only fall at his feet. And the Jews who witnessed it were moved and wept with her. And now they were at the cave which was Lazarus' tomb. Jesus told them to roll aside the great stone which covered its entrance. In the awkward silence that followed, one voice only was raised. It was that of Martha. Jesus had not spoken of raising Lazarus. But what was about to be done? She could scarcely have thought that he merely wished to gaze once more upon the face of the dead. Something nameless had seized her. *She dared not believe, she dared not disbelieve.*

Did she, perhaps, not dread a failure? It was the common Jewish idea that corruption commenced on the fourth day, that the drop of gall, which had fallen from the sword of the angel and caused death, was then working its effect and that, as the face changed, the soul took its final leave from the resting place of the body.

Edersheim describes what then happened:

> Only one sentence Jesus spoke, of gentle reproof. And now the
> stone was rolled away. One loud command spoken into that silence,
> one loud call to that sleeper, one flash of God's Own Light into that
> darkness and the wheels of life again moved at the outgoing of The
> Life. And, still bound hand and foot with graveclothes and his face
> with the napkin, Lazarus stood forth, shuddering and silent, in the
> cold light of earth's day.

What happened next? Some of those who had seen it believed in him,
others hurried back to Jerusalem to tell it to the Pharisees, who convened
a meeting of the Sanhedrists, not to judge him, but to plan what to do
next. Here there could be no question that he was really doing these
miracles. But whether really of satanic power or merely a satanic delusion,
one thing, at least, was evident; that if he were left alone, everyone would
believe in him!

And that was unthinkable because, if he then led the Messianic
movement of the Jews as a nation, then the Jewish City and Temple and
Israel as a nation would perish in the fight with Rome. But what was to
be done? They had not the courage for judicial murder until Caiaphas,
the high priest, reminded them of the well-known Jewish adage, that it 'is
better ... that one man die ... than that the whole nation perish'.

This was the last prophecy for Israel's old order. With the sentence of
death on Israel's true high priest, prophecy and the high priesthood died.
It had condemned itself. They had reached the point of no return.

Someone, perhaps Nicodemus, sent word of the secret meeting and
resolution of the Sanhedrists. That Friday and the next Sabbath Jesus
rested in Bethany, then he withdrew and continued with his disciples,
withdrawn from the Jews, until he would make his final entrance
into Jerusalem.

Chapter 41: The Beginning of the End

———

LUKE 17:11-19

(Book 4: Chapter 22)

Jesus prepared for his last journey to Jerusalem. During this journey, great multitudes followed him and he healed and taught them. One of the strangest was the healing of no less than ten lepers! Without either touch or command, Jesus told them to go and show themselves as healed to the priests. For this, it was not necessary to go to Jerusalem. Any priest might declare 'unclean' or 'clean' provided the applicants presented themselves singly, and not in a group for his inspection.

And they went at Christ's bidding, even before they had actually been healed! So great was their faith and as they went, the new life coursed in their veins. Nine of them continued their way – presumably to the priests – while the one Samaritan in the number at once turned back, with a loud voice glorifying God. No longer now was he a stranger, but in great reverence fell on his face at the feet of him to whom he gave thanks.

This Samaritan had received more than new bodily life and health; he had found spiritual life and healing. But why did the nine Jews not return? We may overestimate the faith of these men. As for the other one, that made a man a disciple. For the others, was it simply ingratitude and neglect of the blessed opportunity now within their reach, a state of mind too characteristic of those who know not 'the time of [their] visitation'[57] and which led up to the neglect and final rejection of their Messiah? Certainly, Jesus emphasised the terrible contrast in this between the children of the household and 'this stranger'.

---

57. Luke 19:44, KJV.

MATTHEW 19:1-12; MARK 10:1-12

The teachings concerning the coming of the kingdom came immediately afterwards. The Pharisees encountered Jesus, now on his journey to Judea, and tried to trap him again, this time over the issue of divorce. Most Jewish teachers held that divorce was lawful, the only question being as to its grounds, but the practice was discouraged by many of the better rabbis. To begin with, divorce was regarded as a privilege accorded only to Israel, not to the Gentiles. But on the question, what constituted lawful grounds of divorce, the schools were divided.

No real comparison is possible on this issue between Jesus and even the strictest of the rabbis, since none of them actually prohibited divorce, except in case of adultery. But we can understand how, from the Jewish point of view, testing him, they would put the question, whether it was lawful to divorce a wife for 'every reason'. The Lord appealed straight to the highest authority, God's institution of marriage. He, who at the beginning had made them male and female, had in the marriage-relation joined them together, to the breaking of every other – even the nearest – relationship, to be 'one flesh': that is, to a union which was unity. Such was the fact of God's ordering. It followed that they were one and what God had willed to be one, no one should separate.

MATTHEW 19:13-15; MARK 10:13-16; LUKE 18:15-17

The next incident came straight afterwards. The account of his blessing of 'little children' is a scene of unspeakable sweetness and tenderness, where all is in character, even the conduct of the disciples as we remember their recent inability to fully grasp the teachings of the Master. We can understand how, when one such as Jesus rested in the house, Jewish mothers should have brought their 'little children' to him, that he might put his hands on them and pray. What power and holiness must these mothers have believed to be in his touch and prayer; what life to be in and to come from him; and what gentleness and tenderness must his have been when they dared so to bring these little ones!

This seemed to be incompatible with the supposed dignity of a rabbi, judging by the rebuke of the disciples. Jesus 'was much displeased' (KJV), the only time this strong word is used of him and he said to them, 'Let the little children come to me, and do not hinder them, for the kingdom of heaven belongs to such as these.' Then he gently reminded his own disciples of their grave error, by repeating what they had apparently forgotten that, in order to enter the kingdom of God, it must be received as by a little child; that here there could be no question of intellectual qualification, nor of distinction due to a great rabbi, but only of humility, receptiveness, meekness and simple trust in him.

MATTHEW 19:16-22; MARK 10:17-22; LUKE 18:18-23
(Book 4: Chapter 23)

As we near the goal, the wondrous story seems to grow in tenderness and pathos. It is as if all the love of the Master were to be crowded into these days; all the pressing needs and the human weaknesses of his disciples too. And with equal compassion does he look upon the difficulties of them who truly seek to come to him.

He was stopped by a young man, a ruler, probably of the local synagogue saying, 'Teacher, what good thing must I do to get eternal life?' The actual question of the young ruler occurs repeatedly in Jewish writing, as when it is put to a rabbi by his disciples, and a variety of answers would all point to the observance of the Law. But, in Jesus' reply, this was not the time for lengthened discussion and instruction, but rather for rapid awakening, leading to an earnest drawing towards the Master and real discipleship.

Jesus began with what was admitted as binding, the Ten Commandments, examining that which would be least likely to be broken, then progressing towards that which was most likely to awaken realisation of sin. What this ruler had seen and heard of him had quickened a longing for God and heaven and had brought him to the feet of Jesus. And he saw through to his soul, through to that question, 'What do I still lack?', far deeper down than that young man had ever seen into his own heart.

Edersheim describes the conclusion of this story:

> One thing was needful for this young man, that he should not only become his disciple, but that he should come and follow Christ. He would need to part with all that he had, through willing surrender of all. But without forsaking there can be no following. This is the law of the Kingdom and it is such, because we are sinners, because sin is not only the loss of the good, but the possession of something else in its place. It was a terrible surprise, a sentence of death to his life. And so, with clouded face he gazed down into what he lacked within; but also gazed up in Christ on what he needed.

MATTHEW 19:23-30; MARK 10:23-31; LUKE 18:24-30

Peter seems to remind the Lord that they had forsaken all to follow him. Jesus reminded them of the reward which this would procure, especially for the apostles of Christ. As regarding the apostles personally, some mystery lies on the special promise to them. The rabbis, indeed, speak of a regeneration of the world which was to take place after the Messianic reign. Such a renewal of all things is not only foretold by the prophets and dwelt upon in later Jewish writings, but frequently referred to in Rabbinic literature. But as regards the special rule of the apostles, or ambassadors of the Messiah, we have not any parallel in Jewish writings.

MATTHEW 20:17-19; MARK 10:32-34; LUKE 18:31-34

They were off now to Jerusalem, but we see Jesus apart and alone, busy with thoughts, setting himself ready to do his great work. It says, 'Jesus [was] leading the way, and the disciples were astonished, while those who followed were afraid.' It was then that Jesus took the apostles apart and in language more precise than ever before, told them how all things that were 'written by the prophets about the Son of Man will be fulfilled'. The Lord gave them full details of his betrayal, crucifixion and resurrection. Luke reports, 'they understood none of these things' (KJV). This explains how the events of Passion Week were going to take them by surprise!

MATTHEW 20:20-28; MARK 10:35-45

And now it has fallen on the two chosen disciples, James and John, 'the sons of thunder', to make a request, that they might have their places at his right hand and at his left in his kingdom. With patience Jesus put them right, bearing with the weakness and selfishness which could cherish such thoughts and ambitions even at such a time. To correct them he points to that near prospect when the highest is to be made low. 'You don't know what you are asking'. The King is to be King through suffering; are they aware of the road which leads to that goal? Are they prepared for it, prepared to drink that cup of agony which the Father will hand to him to submit to? In their ignorance, and listening only to the promptings of their hearts, they imagine that they are. Foolish men!

But as for the other ten, when they heard of it, they were far from happy. And so, at a time when unity should have reigned, it was surely ironic (and sad) that the fierce fire of controversy had broken out among them. Would jealousy and ambition have filled those who should have been most humble? Should passions originating from the world, the flesh and the devil have distracted them? It was the rising of that storm on the sea, the noise and tossing of those angry billows, which he hushed into silence when he spoke to them of the grand contrast between the princes of the Gentiles as they 'lord it over them', how, whosoever would be great among them, must seek his greatness in service, not greatness through service, but the greatness of service.

LUKE 19:1-10

(Book 4: Chapter 24)

Finally, Jesus arrives in Judea. Behind him was the ministry of the gospel by word and deed; before him, the final act of his life, towards which all had signposted. Rejected as the Messiah of his people, not only personally but as regarding the kingdom of God which he had come to establish. He was purposefully going up to Jerusalem, there to 'give his life as a ransom for many' (Matthew 20:28).

The first place reached was Jericho, the 'City of Palms', a distance of only about six hours from Jerusalem. News of the approach of Jesus, with the disciples and apostles, would have preceded them. He would have been known to the people of Jericho, just as they must have been aware of the feelings of the leaders of the people, perhaps of the approaching great contest between them and the Prophet of Nazareth.

Close by was Bethany, from where they had all heard of the raising of Lazarus, so well known to all in that neighbourhood. And yet the Sanhedrin, as would have been known, had decided on his death! Jesus was going up to Jerusalem to meet his enemies!

It was the custom when a festive band passed through a place, that the inhabitants gathered in the streets to bid their brethren welcome. Only one in all that crowd seemed unwelcome, alone, and out of place. It was the head of the tax and customs department. As his name shows, he was a Jew, but yet that very name Zacchaeus ('the just' or 'pure') sounded like mockery. We know in what repute publicans were held and what opportunities of wrongdoing and oppression they possessed. And yet Zacchaeus was in the crowd that had come to see Jesus. What had brought him? Certainly not curiosity only. Was it the long working of a conscience or a dim hope of something better? Or was it only the nameless, deep, irresistible inward drawing of the Holy Spirit?

And, since he was too short to see Jesus properly, he climbs up one of those wide-spreading sycamores in a garden, perhaps close to his own house, along the only road by which Jesus can pass, 'to see him'. Jesus looked up at him. Did Jesus know Zacchaeus before? It seemed that God had so appointed it and Jesus came for that very purpose. Let Edersheim explain:

As bidden by Christ, Zacchaeus 'made haste and came down' and, under the gracious influence of the Holy Spirit. He 'received him rejoicing.' Nothing was as yet clear to him and yet all was joyous within his soul. In that dim twilight of the new day and at this new creation the Angels sang and the Sons of God shouted together and all was melody and harmony in his heart. And so the whole current of his life had been turned, in those few moments, through his joyous reception of Christ, the Saviour of sinners. Zacchaeus the public robber, the rich chief of the publicans, had become an almsgiver.

MATTHEW 20:29-34; MARK 10:46-52; LUKE 18:35-43

It was in the morning when he healed the blind man by the wayside, one named 'Bar Timaeus'. What must their faith have been, when there, in Jericho, two blind men not only owned him as the true Messiah but also cried, 'Lord, Son of David, have mercy on us!' And he, who listens to every cry of distress, heard this. He stood still and commanded the blind to be called. In the language of Matthew, 'Jesus had compassion on them and touched their eyes.' In Mark and Luke came the words with which he accompanied the healing, 'your faith has healed you.'

JOHN 11:55-57

Passover approached and so did his arrival in Jerusalem. The chief priests and the Pharisees had given orders that if anyone knew where he was he would report it, 'that they might arrest him'. It would be better for them to seize him where he lodged, before he appeared in public, in the Temple.

MATTHEW 26:6-13; MARK 14:3-9; JOHN 12:1-11

But it was not as they had imagined. Quite openly Jesus came to Bethany, where Lazarus lived. His stay in Bethany became known and, of those who so came, many went away believing. And how, indeed, could it be otherwise? Thus one of their plans was frustrated and the evil seemed only to grow worse. The Sanhedrin could perhaps not be moved to such flagrant outrage of all Jewish Law, but 'the chief priests', who had no such scruples, consulted how they might put Lazarus also to death. Yet, not until his hour had come could anyone do anything against Christ or his disciples.

Jesus had arrived at Bethany six days before the Passover, that is, on a Friday. The day after was the Sabbath, and 'they made him a supper' (KJV). It was the special festive meal of the Sabbath in the house of Simon the Leper – not, of course, an actual leper, but one who had been such. Among the guests were Lazarus, Martha and Mary, who had 'an alabaster jar of very expensive perfume'.

And now the decisive hour had come. Jesus may have told her, as he had told the disciples, what was before him in Jerusalem at the feast and she would be far quicker to understand, 'even as she must have known far better than they how great was the danger from the Sanhedrin'. And it is this understanding of the mystery of his death on her part and this preparation of deepest love for it – this mixture of sorrow, faith and devotion – *which made her deed so precious* that, wherever in the future the gospel would be preached, this also that she had done would be recorded 'in memory of her'.

And the more we think of it, the better can we understand how at that last fellowship meal, when none of the other guests realised – not even his disciples – how near the end was, she would 'come aforehand to anoint [his] body to the burying'. Her faith made it a two-fold anointing; that of the best guest at the last feast and that of preparation for that burial which, of all others, she understood as being so terribly near.

This deed of faith and love now cast the features of Judas in gigantic dark outlines against the scene. He knew the nearness of Jesus' betrayal *and hated the more*; she knew of the nearness of his precious death *and loved the more*. It was not that Judas cared for the poor when he simulated anger that such costly ointment had not been sold and the price given to the poor. For he was essentially dishonest, and covetousness was the underlying passion of his soul. The money, claimed for the poor, would only have been used by himself. Yet such was his pretence of righteousness, such his influence as 'a man of prudence' among the disciples and such their sad weakness, that some of them expressed indignation among themselves and against her who had done the deed of love.

The final words are from Edersheim:

There is something inexpressibly sad, yet so patient, gentle and tender in Christ's 'let her alone.' Surely, never could there be waste in ministry of love to him! There is unspeakable pathos in what he says of his death, as if he would still their souls in view of it. That he, who was ever of the poor and with them, who for our sakes became poor, that through His poverty we might be made rich, should have to plead for a last service of love to himself.

Chapter 42: Palm Sunday

MATTHEW 21:1-11; MARK 11:1-11; LUKE 19:29-44; JOHN 12:12-19

(Book 5: Chapter 1)

The time of the end had come. Jesus was about to make his entry into Jerusalem as King. King of the Jews, as heir of David's royal line, with all the symbolic and prophetic importance attached to it. Yet he was not going to be the Messiah that they expected. The Son of David was to make a triumphal entrance, but on his own terms, as deep and significant expressions of his mission and work. Not in the proud triumph of conquests in war, but in the 'meek' rule of peace.

It is a mistake to regard this entry of Jesus into Jerusalem as implying that he had for the moment expected that the people would receive him as the Messiah. On the contrary, we regard his royal entry to be seen in the light of the crucifixion; his history would not be complete, nor thoroughly consistent, without this connection.

It was right for him to enter Jerusalem because he was a king; and as King to enter it in such manner, because he was such a king and this was in accordance with the prophecy of old. It was a bright day in early spring when the festive procession set out from the home at Bethany. Remembering that it was the last morning of rest before the great contest, we may reverently think of much that may have passed in the soul of Jesus and in the home of Bethany. And now he has left that peaceful resting place.

On his approach, a great multitude 'went forth to meet him' (KJV). This must have mostly consisted, not of citizens of Jerusalem, whose disregard of Jesus was clear, but of those 'that had come for the festival'. With these were also some Pharisees, their hearts filled with bitterest thoughts of jealousy and hatred. Meantime, Jesus and those who followed him from Bethany had slowly entered the well-known caravan road from Jericho to

Jerusalem. It is the most southern of three roads, which converge close to the city, perhaps at the very place where the colt had stood tied.

The announcement that some disciples of Jesus had just fetched the beast of burden on which Jesus was about to enter Jerusalem must have quickly spread among the crowds that thronged the Temple and the city. As the two disciples, accompanied or followed by the multitude, brought 'the colt' to Jesus, two streams of people met – the one coming from the city, the other from Bethany. What followed was so unexpected by those who accompanied Jesus that it took them by surprise.

The disciples, who hadn't yet understood the significance of 'these things', even after they had occurred, seem not even to have realised that Jesus was about to purposefully make his royal entry into Jerusalem. Their enthusiasm seems only to have been kindled when they saw the procession from the town come to meet Jesus with palm branches, cut down by the way, and greeting him with 'Hosanna' shouts of welcome. They spread their garments on the colt and Jesus mounted the beast. Then also in their turn, they cut down branches from the trees and gardens and scattered them as a rude matting in his way, while they joined in the 'Hosanna' of welcoming praise.

We are too apt to judge them from our standpoint, twenty centuries later and after our knowledge of the significance of the event. These people walked in the procession almost as in a dream, or as dazzled by a brilliant light all around, as if compelled by a necessity and carried from event to event.

Gradually the long procession swept up and over the ridge where first begins 'the descent of the mount of Olives' (KJV) towards Jerusalem. At this point, they catch their first view of the south-eastern corner of the city. The Temple and the more northern portions are hidden by the slope of Olivet on the right; what is seen is only Mount Zion which rose, terrace upon terrace, from the Palace of the Maccabees and that of the high priest, a very city of palaces, until the eye rested in the summit on that castle, city and palace, with its frowning towers and magnificent gardens, the royal abode of Herod, supposed to occupy the very site of the palace of David.

They had been greeting him with 'Hosanna's! But enthusiasm, especially in such a cause, is infectious. They were mostly strangers, those who had come from the city, chiefly because they had heard of the raising of Lazarus. And now they must have questioned those who came from Bethany, who in turn related that of which they had been eyewitnesses. We can imagine it all, how the fire would leap from heart to heart. So he was the promised Son of David – and the kingdom was at hand!

'Hosanna to the Son of David! Blessed be he that cometh in the Name of the Lord ... Blessed the Kingdom that cometh, the Kingdom of our father David ... Blessed be he that cometh in the Name of the Lord ... Hosanna ... Hosanna in the highest ... Peace in heaven, and glory in the highest.' They were but broken utterances, partly based upon Psalm 118, the 'Hosanna' or 'Save now' and the 'Blessed be he who comes in the name of the LORD' (Psalm 118:26) forming part of the responses by the people.

It must be remembered that according to Jewish tradition, Psalm 118:25-28 was also chanted as a 'call and response' by the people of Jerusalem, as they went to welcome the festive pilgrims on their arrival, the latter always responding in the second clause of each verse, until the last verse of the psalm, which was sung by both parties in unison, Psalm 103:17 being added by way of conclusion.

Then the Pharisees made a desperate appeal to the Master himself, whom they so bitterly hated, to check and rebuke the honest zeal of his disciples. He had been silent but could be silent no longer. With righteous indignation he pointed to the rocks and stones, telling those leaders of Israel that if the people held their peace, *the very stones would cry out.*

Again the procession advanced. Immediately before was the Kidron Valley, here seen in its greatest depth as it joins the Valley of Hinnom and thus giving full effect to the great peculiarity of Jerusalem, seen only on its eastern side – its situation as of a city rising out of a deep abyss. It is probable that this rise and turn of the road – this rocky ledge – was the exact point where the multitude paused again and 'he wept over it'. This was with loud and deep lamentation. The contrast was, indeed, terrible between the Jerusalem that rose before him in all its beauty, glory and security and the Jerusalem which he saw in vision dimly rising on the skyline, with the camp of the enemy around about it on every side, hugging it closer and closer in a deadly embrace; and yet another scene, the silence and desolation of death by the hand of God – not one stone left upon another!

Edersheim poignantly adds:

> We know only too well how literally this vision has become reality; and yet, though uttered as prophecy by Christ, and its reason so clearly stated, Israel to this day knows not the things which belong to its peace, and the upturned scattered stones of its dispersion are crying out in testimony against it. But to this day, also do the tears of Christ plead with the Church on Israel's behalf and his words bear within them precious seed of promise. We turn once more to the scene just described.

Another point seems to require a comment. The disciples must have been surprised and perplexed as they seem to have been hurried from event to event. But the enthusiasm of the people, their royal welcome of Jesus, how is it to be explained and how reconciled with the speedy and terrible reaction to his betrayal and crucifixion?

Yet it is not so difficult to understand it. It has already been suggested that the multitude who went to meet Jesus must have consisted chiefly of pilgrims. The overwhelming majority of the citizens of Jerusalem were bitterly hostile to Jesus. But we know that even so, the Pharisees dreaded to take the final steps against him during the presence of these pilgrims at the feast, attempting to stifle a movement in his favour. It proved, indeed, otherwise; for these 'country people' were ill-informed; they dared not resist the combined authority of their own Sanhedrin and of the Romans.

Besides, the prejudices of the ordinary people are easily kindled and they readily sway from one extreme to the opposite. Lastly, the very suddenness of the blow which the Jewish authorities delivered would have stunned even those who had deeper knowledge than most of them there.

Again, as regards their welcome of Jesus, we must not attach a deeper meaning to it concerning similarities to the Feast of Tabernacles. It would have been symbolic of much about Israel if they had thus confused the second with the first advent of Christ, the sacrifice of the Passover with the joy of the Feast of Ingathering. But, in reality, their conduct does not support that interpretation. It is true that these responses from Psalm 118, which formed part of what was known as the *Hallel*, were chanted by the people at the Feast of Tabernacles also, but the *Hallel* was equally sung with responses during the offering of the Passover, at the Passover Supper and on the feasts of Pentecost and of the Dedication of the Temple. The waving of the palm branches was the welcome of visitors or kings and not distinctive of the Feast of Tabernacles. At the latter, the worshippers carried, not simple palm-branches, but the *Lulabh*, which consisted of palm, myrtle and willow branches intertwined.

Lastly, the words of welcome from Psalm 118 were (as already stated) those with which on solemn occasions the people also greeted the arrival of festive pilgrims although, as being offered to Christ alone, they may have implied that they hailed him as the promised King and have converted his entry into a triumph in which the people did homage. Let Edersheim complete the scene:

> The Pharisees understood it better and watched for the opportunity of revenge. But, for the present, on that bright spring day, the weak, excitable, fickle populace streamed before him through the City gates, through the narrow streets, up the Temple mount. Everywhere the tramp of their feet and the shout of their acclamations brought men, women and children into the streets and on the housetops. The city was moved and from mouth to mouth the question passed

among the eager crowd of curious onlookers, 'who is he?' And the multitude answered not that this is Israel's Messiah King, but rather 'this is Jesus the Prophet of Nazareth of Galilee.' And now the shadows of evening were creeping up and, weary and sad. He once more returned with the twelve disciples to the shelter and rest of Bethany.

Chapter 43: Passion Week: Day Two

MATTHEW 21:12-22; MARK 11:15-26; LUKE 19:45-48
(Book 5: Chapter 2)

We know how often his nights had been spent in lonely prayer, and surely that would have been the case with the first night in Passion Week. We can then understand that exhaustion and hunger which the next morning made him eager for the fruit on the fig tree on his way to the city. It was very early in the morning of the second day in Passion Week when Jesus and his disciples left Bethany.

In the fresh, crisp, spring air, after the exhaustion of that night, 'he was hungry'. By the roadside, a solitary tree grew in the rocky soil. He saw it far off and it stood out, with its wide-spreading mantle of green against the sky. It was not the season for figs but the tree, covered with leaves, attracted his attention. It is a well-known fact that in that region the fruit appears before the leaves and that this fig tree was advanced, as it was in leaf, which is quite unusual at that season on the Mount of Olives.

The old fruit would, of course, have been edible, but in the present case, there was neither old nor new fruit, but leaves only. It was evidently a barren fig tree ready to be hewn down. We think of the parable of the barren fig tree, which he had so lately spoken.[58] To him, this fig tree, with its luxuriant mantle of leaves, must have recalled, with great vividness, the scene of the previous day. Israel was that barren fig tree and the leaves only covered their nakedness, as they had that of our first parents after their Fall. And the judgement, symbolically spoken in the parable, must be symbolically executed in this leafy fig tree, barren when searched for fruit by the Master. It seems that not only symbolically but in reality that Jesus' word should have laid it low.

---

58. Luke 13:6-9.

Matthew's account has it that, on Jesus' word, the fig tree immediately withered away, though Mark said that it was only the next morning, when they again passed by, that they noticed the fig tree had withered from its very roots. It was the suddenness and completeness of the judgement that had been proclaimed recently which now struck Peter, rather than its symbolic meaning. It was the storm and earthquake rather than the 'still small voice' (1 Kings 19:12, KJV) which impressed the disciples. He noticed that the fig tree had withered in consequence of rather than by the word of Christ.

The same symbolism of judgement was to be directed towards the Temple itself. On the previous afternoon, when Jesus had come to it, the services were probably over and the sanctuary comparatively empty of worshippers. When we examined the first cleansing of the Temple, at the beginning of his ministry, enough has been said to explain the character of that wicked traffic, the profits of which went to the leaders of the priesthood, as also how popular indignation was roused alike against this trade and the traders.

Here he proclaims the transformation of 'the house of prayer' into 'a den of robbers'. If, when beginning to do the 'business' of his Father and for the first time publicly presenting himself as Messiah, it was fitting he should take such authority and first 'cleanse the Temple' of the greedy intruders who, under the guise of being God's chief priests, profaned his house, much more was this appropriate now, at the close of his work, when, as King, he had entered his city and publicly claimed authority.

At the first, it had been for teaching and warning, now it was in symbolic judgement. Now the Temple authorities did not create so much of a fuss to turn the people against him. The contest had reached quite another stage. They heard what he said in their condemnation, and with bitter hatred in their hearts sought for some means to destroy him. But fear of the people restrained their violence. For the people marvelled at his words, astonished at those new and blessed truths. All was so different to the 'usual offerings'!

By his authority, the Temple was cleansed of the unholy, thievish traffic which a corrupt priesthood carried on and so, for the time, was restored to the solemn service of God. That purified house now became the scene of Jesus' teaching, when he spoke those words of blessed truth and of comfort concerning the Father, thus truly achieving the prophetic promise of 'a house of prayer for all nations'.

And as those crooks and thieves were driven from the Temple, then came the poor sufferers, the blind and the lame, to get healing to body and soul. And the boys that gathered about their fathers and looked in turn from their faces of rapt wonderment and enthusiasm to the face of Jesus and then on those healed sufferers, took up the echoes of the welcome at his entrance into Jerusalem as they burst into 'Hosanna to the son of David'.

It rang through the courts and porches of the Temple, this Children's Hosanna. Once more in their impotent anger, the authorities sought to betray him into silencing those children's voices. But the undimmed mirror of his soul only reflected the light. Not from the great, the wise, nor the learned, but 'out of the mouth of babes and sucklings' has he 'perfected praise' (Psalm 8:2, KJV). And this, also, is the music of the gospel.

Chapter 44: Passion Week: Day Three

MATTHEW 21:23-27; MARK 11:27-33; LUKE 20:1-8

(Book 5: Chapter 3)

This third day is so crowded, the actors introduced on the scene are so many, the occurrences so varied and the transitions so rapid, that it is even more than usually difficult to arrange all in chronological order. But we'll do our best! This was, so to speak, Jesus' last working day, the last of his public mission to Israel, the last day in the Temple, the last of teaching and warning to Pharisees and Sadducees, the last of his call to national repentance.

As usual, the day commenced with teaching in the Temple. From the formal manner in which the chief priests, the scribes and the elders are introduced and from the fact that they met Jesus immediately on his entry into the Temple, we assume that a meeting of the authorities had been held to organise measures against the growing danger.

Yet, even so, cowardice, as well as cunning, marked their procedure. They dared not directly oppose him, but endeavoured, through attacking him on the one point, his authority. For them, all teaching must be authoritative, approved by an acceptable authority and handed down from teacher to disciple. The ultimate appeal in cases of discussion was always to some great authority, whether an individual teacher or a decree by the Sanhedrin. In this manner had the great Hillel first vindicated his claim to be the teacher of his time and to decide the disputes then pending. To decide differently from authority was either the mark of ignorant assumption or the outcome of daring rebellion, in either case, to be visited with 'the ban'.

The question, therefore, with which the Jewish authorities met Jesus did not merely challenge him for teaching but also asked for his authority in what he did. They were not there to oppose him but, when a man did as he had done in the Temple, it was their duty to verify his credentials.

He did answer their question, though he also exposed the cunning and cowardice which prompted it. To the challenge for his authority and the dark hint about satanic influences, he replied by an appeal to John the Baptist.

What was their view of the Baptist in preparation for the coming of Christ? They would not, or could not answer! If they said the Baptist was a prophet, this implied not only the authority of the mission of Jesus, but the call to believe in him. On the other hand, they were afraid publicly to disown John! And so their cunning and cowardice stood out self-condemned when they pleaded ignorance – a plea so grossly and manifestly dishonest that Jesus could refuse further discussion with them on this point.

MATTHEW 22:15-22; MARK 12:13-17; LUKE 20:20-26

They next attempted the much more dangerous device of bringing him into collision with the civil authorities. Remembering the ever-watchful jealousy of Rome, the reckless tyranny of Pilate and the low cunning of Herod, who was at that time in Jerusalem, we instinctively feel how even the slightest compromise on the part of Jesus concerning the authority of Caesar would have been absolutely fatal. If it could have been proved, on undeniable testimony, that Jesus had declared himself on the side of the so-called 'nationalist' party, he would quickly have perished!

The plot was most cunningly concocted. The object was to trip him up. They now came to Jesus with flattery, intended to wrong-foot him, appealing to his fearlessness and singleness of moral purpose, to induce him to commit himself without reserve. Here was their question, was it lawful for them 'to give tribute unto Caesar, or not?' (KJV). Were they to pay the tax of one drachma or to refuse it? We know how later Judaism would have answered such a question. It lays down the principle that the right of coinage implies the authority of levying taxes and indeed constitutes such evidence of the government as to make it a duty absolutely to submit to it. To have said 'No' would have been to command rebellion;

to have said simply, 'Yes' would have been to give a painful jolt to his own claim of being Israel's Messiah-King!

When pointing to the image and inscription on the coin, he said, what is Caesar's render to Caesar and what is God's to God. It did far more than rebuke their hypocrisy and presumption; it answered not only that question of theirs to all earnest people of that time, but it settles for all time and for all circumstances the principle underlying it. Jesus' kingdom is 'not of this world' (John 18:36).

It was an answer not only most truthful but of marvellous beauty and depth. It elevated the controversy into quite another sphere, where there was no conflict between what was due to God and to people; in fact, no conflict at all, but divine harmony and peace. Neither did it speak harshly of the nationalist aspirations, nor yet plead the cause of Rome. It did not say whether the rule of Rome was right or should be permanent, but only what all must have felt to be divine. And so they who had come to entangle him, went away, neither convinced nor converted.

MARK 12:41-44; LUKE 21:1-4

From the bitter malice of his enemies and the predicted judgement upon them, we turn to the silent worship of she who gave her all. Truly here was one who, in the simplicity of her humble worship, gave to the Lord what was his! Weary with the arguments, Jesus had climbed the flight of steps that led from the Terrace into the Temple. From these steps he could look into the Court of the Women, into which they opened. He sat down on these steps. Under the colonnades which surrounded the Court of the Women, provision was made for receiving religious and charitable offerings in trumpet-shaped boxes (*shopharoth*).

His gaze was riveted by a solitary figure. It was a poor widow. We can see her coming alone, as if ashamed to mingle with the crowd of rich givers, ashamed to have her offering seen, ashamed, perhaps, to bring it. She looks like a desolate mourner. Her condition, appearance and bearing that of a 'pauper', she held in her hand only the smallest coins, two *perutahs*, and it should be known that it was not lawful to contribute anything less! But it was all her living, perhaps all that she had been able to save out of her scanty housekeeping. And of this, she now made a humble offering to God. Jesus spoke no words of encouragement, for she walked by faith; he did not offer a promise of return, for her reward was in heaven. It must have been a happy day, a day of a rich feast in the heart when she gave up her whole living to God. And so, perhaps, every sacrifice is for God all the more blessed, when we know not of its blessedness.

JOHN 12:20-50

It was then the evening of a long, weary day of teaching. And in those Temple porches, they had been hearing him, those men of other tongues. They were proselytes, Greeks by birth, but stirred up in their inmost being and it was to them that he spoke. Yet they dared not go to Jesus directly but came with their request to Philip of Bethsaida. And he also dared not go directly to Jesus but went to his friend and fellow disciple, Andrew, the brother of Simon Peter.

As we see these 'Greeks' approaching, perhaps we see a flashback to the early days. Not now in the stable of Bethlehem, but in the Temple, are the wise men, the representatives of the Gentile world, offering their homage to the Messiah. But the life which had then begun was now all behind him and yet, in a sense, before him. The hour of decision was about to strike. Edersheim explains further:

But only in one way could he thus be glorified: by dying for the salvation of the world, and so opening the Kingdom of heaven to all believers. On a thousand hills was the glorious harvest to tremble in the golden sunlight; but the corn of wheat falling into the ground, must, as it falls, die, burst its envelope, and so spring into a very manifoldedness of life. Otherwise, would it have remained alone. This is the great paradox of the Kingdom of God – a paradox which has its symbol and analogon in nature, and which has also almost become the law of progress in history: that life which has not sprung of death abideth alone, and is really death, and that death is life. A paradox this, which has its ultimate reason in this, that sin has entered into the world. And as to the Master, the Prince of Life, so to the disciples, as bearing forth the life. If, in this world of sin. He must fall as the seed-corn into the ground and die, that many may spring of him, so must they also hate their life, that they may keep it unto life eternal. Thus serving, they must follow him, that where he is they may also be, for the Father will honour them that honour the Son.

It is now sufficiently clear to us that Jesus spoke primarily to these Greeks and secondarily to his disciples, of the meaning of his impending death. The Jews who heard it, so far understood him, that his words referred to his removal from earth. But they failed to understand his special reference to the manner of it. And yet, because of the peculiarly shameful death on the cross, it was most important that he should refer to it. But, even in what they understood, they had a difficulty. They understood him to imply that he would be taken from the earth; and yet they had always been taught from the Scriptures that the Messiah was, when fully manifested, to abide forever or, as the rabbis put it, that his reign was to be followed by the resurrection.

But Jesus fully replied in what became his last teaching in the Temple. Yes, only for a little while would 'the light' be among them! While they still had the light, the onus was on them to believe in the light, that so they might become the 'children of light'! They were his last words of appeal to them.

Although he had shown so many miracles, Israel still did not believe in him. On the other hand, their wilful unbelief was also the judgement of God in accordance with prophecy. We have seen that rejection of Jesus by the Jews was not an isolated act, but the outcome and the direct result of their whole previous religious development. In the face of the clearest evidence, they did not believe, because they could not believe.

Jesus had come as a light into the world, God had sent him as the 'sun of righteousness' (Malachi 4:2), that by believing in him as the sent one from God, people might attain a moral vision, no longer '[abiding] in darkness' (KJV) but in the bright spiritual light. But as for the others, there were those who heard and did not keep his words and those who rejected him and did not receive his words.

Israel, hardened in the self-chosen course of its religious development, could not and, despite the clearest evidence, *did not* believe. By contrast, we have Jesus absolutely surrendering himself to do the will and work of the Father, witnessed by the Father, revealing the Father, coming as the 'light of the world' (John 8:12) to chase away its moral darkness and speaking to all people, and bringing to them salvation, not judgement.

MATTHEW 22:23-33; MARK 12:18-27; LUKE 20:27-39
(Book 5: Chapter 4)

The Sadducees had only interacted with Jesus once before when, characteristically, they had asked of him 'a sign from heaven'. Their rationalism would lead them to treat the whole movement as beneath serious consideration, the outcome of ignorant fanaticism. Nevertheless, when Jesus assumed such a position in the Temple and was evidently to such extent swaying the people, they could no longer stand by. Their objective was certainly not to argue seriously but to use the much more dangerous weapon of ridicule.

The subject of attack was to be the resurrection. In the view of Christ, their belief was far from 'the belief of the Pharisees'. Yet it was the living cornerstone of that Church which ever pointed all people heavenwards. But they weren't to know this; these thoughts would have been unintelligible at that time even to his own disciples!

He met the arguments of the Sadducees head-on, with words that should have led them onwards and upwards far beyond the standpoint of the Pharisees. The intention of the Sadducees was also covertly to strike at their Pharisaic opponents. The ancient rule of marrying a brother's childless widow had more and more fallen into disrepute, as its original motive ceased to have influence. The Sadducees held the opinion that the command to marry a brother's widow only applied to a betrothed wife, not to one that had actually been wedded. This one was thrown at Jesus.

In his argument against the Sadducees, Jesus first appealed to the power of God, in that he worked in ways quite different than they imagined. The world to come was not to be a reproduction of that which had passed away. What, therefore, in our present relations is of the earth and of our present body of sin and corruption, will cease; what is eternal in them will continue. But the power of God will transform all. Of course, as speaking to the Sadducees, he spoke from the Torah and yet it was not only to the Law but to the whole Bible that he appealed.

The Sadducees were silenced, the multitude was astonished and even from one of the scribes came the admission, 'Teacher, you have beautifully said.' As the scribe spoke later to the Pharisees, he would relate how Jesus had literally gagged and muzzled the Sadducees. There can be little doubt that the report would give rise to mixed feelings, such as that, although Jesus might have wrong-footed the Sadducees, it was now the turn of the Pharisees!

MATTHEW 22:34-40; MARK 12:28-34

'Which is the greatest commandment in the Law?' So challenged, Jesus could have no hesitation in replying. Not to silence him, but to speak the absolute truth. He quoted the familiar words which every Jew was bound to repeat in his devotions and which were ever to be on his lips, living or dying, as the inmost expression of his faith: 'Hear, O Israel: The LORD our God is one LORD' (Deuteronomy 6:4). And then continuing, he repeated the command concerning love to God which is the outcome of that declaration.

But to have stopped here would have been mere Pharisaic worship of the letter of the Law. As God is love, so is love to God – also love to people. 'There is none other commandment greater than these' (KJV). But it was more than an answer, even deepest teaching, when he added, 'On these two commandments hang all the law and the prophets.' They would know what it meant that the Law and the Prophets 'hung' on them, for it was a Jewish expression. He taught them that not any one commandment was greater or smaller, heavier or lighter, than another, but that all sprang from these two as their root and principle and stood in living connection with them.

So noble was the answer that for the moment the generous enthusiasm of the scribe, who had previously been favourably impressed by Jesus' answer to the Sadducees, was kindled. For the moment, at least, traditionalism lost its sway; and, as Jesus pointed to it, he saw the exceeding moral beauty of the Law. He was not far from the kingdom of God.

MATTHEW 22:41-46; MARK 12:35-40; LUKE 20:40-47

Then, without addressing anyone in particular, Jesus set before them all what perhaps was the most familiar subject in their theology, that of the lineage of Messiah; whose Son was he? And when they replied, 'The son of David,' he referred them to the opening words of Psalm 110, in which David called the Messiah 'Lord'.

And this appropriately constitutes Jesus' farewell to the Temple, to its authorities and to Israel.

MATTHEW 23

To begin with, Jesus warned them of the incompetence of Israel's teachers. He neither wished for himself nor his disciples the place of authority which they claimed. On the contrary, as long as they held the place of authority they were to be regarded as sitting in 'Moses' seat' and were to be obeyed, as far as merely outward observances were concerned.

Of the opening accusation about the binding of heavy burdens and 'lay[ing] them on men's shoulders' (KJV), Rabbinism placed the rules of tradition above those of the Law and that, whereas the words of the Law contained what 'lightened' and what 'made heavy', the words of the scribes contained only what 'made heavy'.

It was not a break in the teaching, rather an intensification of it, when Jesus now turned to make his final denunciation of Pharisaism in its sin and hypocrisy. Corresponding to the eight Beatitudes in the Sermon on the Mount with which his public ministry began, he now closed it with eight denunciations of woe. This is the pouring out of his holy wrath, the last and fullest testimony against those whose guilt would involve Jerusalem in common sin and common judgement. Step by step came the accusations and with it the woe of divine wrath announced!

The first woe was on their withholding the kingdom of God from people by their opposition to the Christ. The second woe was on their covetousness and hypocrisy.[59] The third woe was on their proselytism, which issued only in making their converts two-fold more the children of hell than themselves. The fourth woe expresses the moral blindness of these guides rather than their hypocrisy. The fifth woe referred to one of the best-known and strangest Jewish ordinances, which extended the Mosaic Law of tithing, in most burdensome detail.

From tithing to purification, the transition was natural. It constituted the second grand characteristic of Pharisaic piety. Woe to the hypocrisy which only cared for the outside or of outward appearances of righteousness, while heart and mind were full of iniquity. Woe to that hypocrisy that built and decorated tombs of prophets and righteous men to deflect from the guilt of those who had killed them. It was not spiritual repentance but national pride which drove them in this, the same spirit of self-sufficiency, pride and unforgiveness which had led their fathers to commit the murders.

---

59. Matthew 23:14, KJV.

And yet it would not have been Jesus if, while judging them for following the crimes of their fathers, he had not also added to it the passionate lament of a love which, even when spurned, lingered with regretful longing over the lost. And he left the Temple with these words, that they of Israel should not see him again until, the night of their unbelief past, they would welcome his return with a better 'Hosanna' than that which greeted his royal entry three days before. And this was the 'farewell' and the parting of Israel's Messiah from Israel and its Temple. Yet a farewell which promised a coming again and a parting which implied a welcome in the future from a believing people to a gracious, pardoning King!

MATTHEW 19:30 – 20:16
(Book 5: Chapter 5)

It will be convenient here to group together the last series of parables. Most, if not all of them, were spoken on that third day in Passion Week; the first four to a more general audience; the last three[60] to the disciples when, on the evening of that third day, on the Mount of Olives, he told them of the 'last things'.

We begin with the parable of the labourers in the vineyard. It tackles the very character of the kingdom and of work in and for it. The principle which Jesus lays down is that while nothing done for him shall lose its reward, beware of self-righteousness in your expectations. Spiritual pride and self-assertion can only be the outcome either of misunderstanding God's relation to us or else of a wrong state of mind towards others.

We think here of those who were 'last', the Gentiles from the east, west, north and south, the converted 'publicans and sinners' and of others. The labourers who murmured were guilty either of ignorance in failing to perceive the sovereignty of grace – that it is within his power to do with his own as he pleases – or else of malice instead of with grateful joy. 'But many who are first will be last, and many who are last will be first.'

---

60. Matthew 24:45-51; Matthew 25:1-13; Matthew 25:14-20.

MATTHEW 21:28-32

The second parable in this series – or perhaps rather an illustration – introduces a man who has two sons. He goes to the first and, speaking affectionately, bids him go and work in his vineyard. The son rudely refuses, but afterwards he changes his mind and goes. Meantime the father, when refused by the one, has gone to his other son on the same errand. The contrast here is marked. The tone is most polite and the answer of the son contains not only a promise, but we almost see him going – yet he did not go!

The application was easy. The first son represented the tax collectors and prostitutes, whose refusal of the Father's call was implied in their life of reckless sin. But afterwards, they changed their mind and went into the Father's vineyard. The other son, with his politeness of tone and ready promise, but utter neglect of obligations undertaken, represented the Pharisees with their hypocritical and empty professions. And Jesus obliged them to make application of the parable. When challenged by the Lord, which of the two had done the will of his father? They could not avoid the answer.

MATTHEW 21:33-46; MARK 12:1-12; LUKE 20:9-19

Closely connected with the two preceding parables is that concerning the tenants in the vineyard. The object here is to set forth the patience and goodness of the owner, even towards the evil he faced. The meaning of the parable is sufficiently plain. The owner of the vineyard, God, had let out his vineyard to his people of old. The covenant having been instituted, he withdrew, as it were. The former direct communication between him and Israel ceased. Then in due season, he sent 'his servants', the prophets, to gather his fruits. But, instead of returning the fruits, they only ill-treated his messengers, even to death.

In his longsuffering, he next sent on the same errand 'greater' than them, John the Baptist. And when he also received the same treatment, he sent finally his own Son, Jesus Christ. His appearance made them feel that it was now a decisive struggle for the vineyard and so, in order to gain its possession for themselves, they cast the rightful heir out of his own possession and then killed him!

The application was obvious and it was made by Jesus, first, as always, by a reference to the prophetic testimony, showing not only the unity of all God's teaching but also the continuity of the Israel of the present with that of old in their resistance and rejection of God's counsel and messengers.

MATTHEW 22:1-14

The parable of the marriage feast of the king's son and the wedding garment derives from Jewish tradition. In the corresponding Jewish parable, a king is represented as inviting all to a feast, fixing the exact time for it. The wise adorn themselves in time and are seated at the door of the palace, to be in readiness, since no elaborate preparation for a feast can be needed in a palace, while the foolish go away to their work, arguing there must be time enough since there can be no feast without preparation. But suddenly comes the king's summons to the feast, when the wise appear festively adorned, and the king rejoices over them, and they are made to sit down, eat and drink; while he is annoyed with the foolish, who appear squalid and are ordered to stand by and look on in anguish, hunger and thirst.

Then, by contrast, we turn to the parable of Jesus; its meaning is not difficult to understand. The king made a marriage for his son when he sent his servants to call them that were invited to the wedding. Evidently, as in the Jewish parable, and as before in that of the guests invited to the Great Supper, a preliminary general invitation had preceded the announcement that all was ready. But those invited would not come.

These repeated endeavours to call, to admonish and to invite, form a characteristic feature of these parables, showing that it was one of the central objects of our Lord's teaching to exhibit the longsuffering and goodness of God.

The first invitation had been sent to selected guests – to the Jews – who might have been expected to be worthy, but had proved themselves unworthy; the next was to be given, not to the chosen city or nation, but to all that travelled in whatever direction on the world's highway, reaching them where the roads of life meet and part. And, although they had not listened to his call, yet a second class of messengers was sent to them under the New Covenant. And the message of the latter was, that *the early meal* was ready (Christ's first coming), and that all preparations had been made for *the great evening meal* (Christ's reign). Another prominent truth is outlined in the repeated message of the king, which points to the goodness and longsuffering of God.

We can take it further. All are invited to the gospel feast, but they who will partake of it must put on the king's wedding garment of holiness. And whereas it is said in the parable that only one was described without this garment, this is intended to teach that the king will only generally view his guests, but that each will be separately examined and that no one will be able to escape discovery amid the mass of guests if they have not the 'wedding garment' (KJV). In short, in that day of trial, it is not a scrutiny of churches, but of individuals in the Church.

'There shall be the weeping and the gnashing of teeth' (KJV). And here the parable closes with the general statement, applicable alike to the first invited guests, Israel – and to the second, the guests from all the world: 'For [this is the meaning of the whole parable] many are called, but few are chosen' (KJV).

Chapter 45: Passion Week: Day Three: Evening

~~~

MATTHEW 24; MARK 13; LUKE 21:5-38
(Book 5: Chapter 6)

The last denunciation of Jerusalem had been uttered, the last and most terrible prediction of judgement upon the Temple spoken and Jesus and the disciples left the sanctuary and the city, crossed the Kidron Valley and slowly climbed the Mount of Olives. A sudden turn in the road and the sacred building was once more in full view, with its gigantic walls built of massive stones, some of them nearly 24ft long.

Some pointed out to him those massive stones and splendid buildings, others spoke of the rich offerings presented at the Temple. It was but natural that the contrast between this and the predicted desolation should have impressed them; natural, also, that they should refer to it, not as a matter of doubt, but rather as of a question. Then Jesus spoke fully of that terrible contrast between the present and the near future when, as literally fulfilled, not one stone would be left upon another.

In silence, they pursued their way. Upon the Mount of Olives, they sat down, facing the Temple. 'Tell us ... when will this happen ...?' and 'what will be the sign of your coming and of the end of the age?'

When Jesus, on leaving the Temple, said, 'you will not see me again' (Matthew 23:39) he must have referred to Israel in their national capacity. If so, the promise in the text of visible reappearance must also apply to Israel in their national capacity. Accordingly, it is suggested that in the present passage Christ refers to his advent from the Jewish standpoint of Jewish history, in which the destruction of Jerusalem and the appearance of false Christs are the last events of national history, to be followed by the precarious nature of the many centuries of the 'Gentile dispensation'.

Jewish writings speak very frequently of the so-called 'sorrows of the Messiah'. They may generally be characterised as marking a period of internal corruption and of outward distress, especially of famine and war, of which the land of Israel was to be the scene and in which Israel was to be the chief sufferer. When Christ proclaimed the desolation of 'the house' and even placed it in indirect connection with his advent, he taught that which must have been both new and unexpected. This may be the most suitable place for explaining the Jewish expectation connected with the advent of the Messiah.

As regards the answer of the Lord to the two questions of his disciples, it may be said that the first part of his teaching is intended to supply information on the three facts of the future: the destruction of the Temple and his second advent and the 'end of the age', by setting before them the signs indicating the beginning of these events. But even here the exact period of each is not defined.

In the second part, the Lord distinctly tells them what they are not to know and why; and how all that was communicated to them was only to prepare them for that constant watchfulness, which has been to the Church at all times the proper outcome of Jesus' teaching on the subject. This, then, we may take as a guide, that the words of Jesus contain nothing beyond what was necessary for the warning and teaching of the disciples and of the Church.

The first part consists of four sections, of which the first describes 'the beginning of the birth-pains' of the new 'age' about to appear. The expression, 'the end is not yet' (KJV) clearly indicates that it marks only the earliest period of the beginning. The purely practical character of this teaching appears from its opening words. They contain a warning, addressed to the disciples individually, against being 'led astray'. This, more particularly referring to false Christs, with a multitude of impostors who, in the troubled times between the rule of Pilate and the destruction of Jerusalem, will promise Messianic deliverance to Israel.

This also would be a misunderstanding, leading Christians to believe in an immediate reappearance of Christ. There will also be the seductions of false Messiahs or teachers and violent disturbances in the political world. As far as Israel was concerned, these reached their climax in the great rebellion against Rome under the false Messiah Bar Kokhba, in the time of Hadrian.

From the warning to Christians as individuals, Jesus next turns to give warning to the Church as a whole. Here we mark that the events now described must not be regarded as strictly following chronologically those referred to in the previous verses. They form, in fact, the continuation of the 'birth-pains'. As regards the persecutions in prospect, full divine aid is promised to Christians, both to individuals and to the Church. And despite the persecution of Jews and Gentiles, before the end comes 'this gospel of the kingdom will be preached in the whole world as a testimony to all nations'. This is really the only sign of 'the end' of the present 'age'.

Then the Lord proceeds to speak of the destruction of Jerusalem. There can be no question that the warning of the Lord delivered the Church. As directed by him, the members of the Christian Church fled at an early period of the siege of Jerusalem to Pella. As for Jerusalem, the prophetic vision initially fulfilled in the days of Antiochus would once more, and now fully, become reality and the 'abomination of desolation ... stand in the holy place' (KJV). This, together with tribulation to Israel, is unparalleled in the terrible past of its history and unequalled even in its bloody future. So dreadful would be the persecution that, if divine mercy had not intervened for the sake of the followers of Jesus, the whole Jewish race that inhabited the land would have been swept away.

No new Maccabee would arise, no Christ come, as Israel fondly hoped; but over that carcass would the vultures gather and so through all the Age of the Gentiles, until converted Israel should raise the welcoming shout: 'Blessed be he that cometh in the name of the LORD!' (Psalm 118:26).

Now we turn from the future to the present application for the disciples. From the fig tree, under which they may have rested on the Mount of Olives, they were to learn a parable. We can picture Jesus taking one of its twigs, just as its softening tips were bursting into a young leaf. Surely, this meant that summer was nigh – not that it had actually come! The distinction is important. For it seems to prove that 'all these things' which were to indicate to them that it was near, 'even at the doors' (KJV), and which were to be fulfilled before this generation had passed away, could not have referred to the last signs connected with the immediate advent of Christ, but must apply to the previous prediction in Luke 13:34-35 of the destruction of Jerusalem and of the Jewish Commonwealth.

The Church was not meant to know the mystery of that day and hour of the coming of her Lord and Bridegroom. As 'in the days of Noah', the long delay of threatened judgement had led to just getting on with life, ignoring Noah's warnings, so would it be in the future. But that day would come certainly and unexpectedly, to the sudden separation of those who were engaged in the same daily business of life, of whom one might be taken up, the other left to the destruction of the coming judgement.

LUKE 12:35-48; MATTHEW 24:45-51

Now for the first of the three parables speaking of the 'last things'. Jesus had taught that each one had work to do for him and this was not to be neglected. The faithful steward, to whom the Master had entrusted the care of his household to supply his faithful ones, is to be rewarded by advancement to a far more responsible work. On the other hand, belief in the delay of the Lord's return would lead to neglect of the Master's work, to unfaithfulness, tyranny, self-indulgence and sin. And when the Lord suddenly came, as certainly he would come, there would be not only loss, but damage, hurt and the punishment awarded to the hypocrites. Hence, let the Church be ever on her watch, let her ever be in readiness! And how terribly the moral consequences of unreadiness and the punishment threatened have ensued, as the history of the Church during these twenty centuries has only too often and too sadly shown.

MATTHEW 25:1-13

(Book 5: Chapter 7)

The parable of the ten virgins is only an illustration of the last part of Christ's teachings. Its great practical lessons had been: the *unexpectedness* of the Lord's coming, the *consequences* to be understood from its delay and the need for personal and constant *preparedness*. Let Edersheim explain:

> It is late and the coming of the Bridegroom must be near. The day and the hour we know not, for the Bridegroom has been far away. Only this we know, that it is the evening of the marriage which the Bridegroom had fixed and that his word of promise may be relied upon. The personal application of this parable to the disciples, which the Lord makes, follows almost of necessity. 'Watch therefore for ye know not the day, nor the hour.' Not enough to be in waiting with the Church; his coming will be far on in the night; it will be sudden; it will be rapid. Be prepared therefore, be ever and personally prepared! Christ will come when least expected – at midnight – and when the Church, having become accustomed to his long delay, has gone to sleep. So sudden will be his Coming, that after the cry of announcement there will not be time for anything but to go forth to meet him; and so rapid will be the end!

MATTHEW 25:14-30; LUKE 19:11-28

The parable of the talents refers to the personal work of the disciples. It refers generally to all that someone has to serve Jesus; for, all that the Christian has – their time, money, opportunities, talents, or learning, belongs to Jesus *and is entrusted to us* to further the progress of his kingdom. And to each of us he gives according to our capacity for working – mental, moral and even physical – to one five, to another two and to another one 'talent'. This capacity for work lies not within our own power, but it is in our power to use for Jesus whatever we may have.

A deeper, and in some sense more mysterious, truth comes to us in connection with the words, 'You have been faithful with a few things; I will put you in charge of many things.' Surely, then, if not after death, yet in that other 'dispensation' there must be work for Jesus to do, for which the preparation is in this life, be it much or little. This gives quite a new and blessed meaning to the life that now is.

Chapter 46: Passion Week: Day Four

MATTHEW 26:1-5; MARK 14:1-2

(Book 5: Chapter 8)

The three busy days of Passion Week were past. We now have a day of rest, a Sabbath to his soul before its great agony. Then he would refresh himself and prepare for the terrible conflict before him. And he did so as the Lamb of God, meekly submitting himself to the will and hand of his Father and so fulfilling all types, from that of Isaac's sacrifice on Mount Moriah to the Passover lamb in the Temple. He would be bringing the reality of all prophecy from that of the woman's seed that would crush the serpent's head[61] to that of the kingdom of God in its fullness when its golden gates would be flung open to all people and heaven's own light flow out to them as they sought its way of peace.

Only two days more! Jesus knew it well and he passed that day of rest and preparation in quiet retirement with his disciples, perhaps in some hollow of the Mount of Olives, near the home in Bethany, speaking to them of his crucifixion on the Passover. They sorely needed his words; they, rather than he, needed to be prepared for what was coming. And all the time he thought only of them. Such thinking and speaking are not that of humankind, it is that of the incarnate Son of God, the Christ of the Gospels.

He had, indeed, before that, gradually prepared them for what was to happen on the following night. He had pointed to it at the very opening of his ministry, on the first occasion that he had taught in the Temple, as well as to Nicodemus. He had hinted at it when he spoke of the deep sorrow when the Bridegroom would be taken from them, of the need to take up his cross, of the fulfilment in him of the Jonah-type, of his flesh which he would give for the life of the world, as well as in what might

---

61. Genesis 3:15.

have seemed the teaching on the Good Shepherd, who 'lays down his life for the sheep' and the heir whom the evil servants cast out and killed.[62]

But he had also spoken of it *quite directly* and this always when some high point had been reached and the disciples might otherwise have been carried away into Messianic expectations of exaltation without humiliation, a triumph not a sacrifice. We remember that the first occasion on which he spoke so clearly was immediately after that confession of Peter, which laid the foundation of the Church, against which the 'gates of hell' should not 'prevail' (Matthew 16:18, KJV); the next, after descending from the Mount of Transfiguration; the last, on preparing to make his triumphal Messianic entry into Jerusalem.

And now the Master was telling it to them in plain words; he was calmly contemplating it and that not as in the dim future, but in the immediate present – at that very Passover, barely two days away.

MATTHEW 26:14-16; MARK 14:10-11; LUKE 22:1-6

Much as we wonder at their brief scattering on his arrest and condemnation, those humble disciples must have loved him much to sit around him in mournful silence as he spoke and to follow him to the end. But to one of them, in whose heart the darkness had long been gathering, this was the decisive moment. Jesus' prediction, which Judas as well as the others must have felt to be true, extinguished the last glimmering of such light of Christ as his soul had been capable of receiving. In its place flared up the lurid flame of hell. By the open door out of which he had thrust the dying Jesus, 'Satan entered Judas'.

Judas, the man of Kerioth was, so far as we know, the only disciple of Jesus from the province of Judea. The fact that he was treasurer and administrator of the small group of disciples and that he was both a hypocrite and a thief are well known to us. It must be admitted, mostly all our temptations come to us from our greatest weaknesses, and when

---

62. John 2:19; John 3:14; Matthew 9:15; Matthew 10:38; Matthew 12:40; John 6:51; John 10:11,15; Matthew 21:38.

Judas was alienated and unfaithful in heart, this very thing became also his greatest temptation and indeed, hurried him to his ruin. But only after he had first failed inwardly. And so, as ever in like circumstances, the very things which might have been most of blessing become most of curse.

If we were pressed to name a definite moment when the process of disintegration began, we would point to that Sabbath morning at Capernaum, when Jesus had preached about his flesh as the food of the world and so many of his followers ceased to follow after him; when the leaven so worked even in his disciples, that he turned to them with the searching question, whether they also would leave him?[63]

And so, on that sunny afternoon, Judas left them out there, to seek them who were gathered, not in their ordinary meeting place, but in the high priest's palace. Even this indicates that it was an informal meeting, consultative rather than judicial. For, it was one of the principles of Jewish Law that, in criminal cases, the sentence must be spoken only in the regular meeting place of the Sanhedrin. The same assumption is strengthened by the circumstance that the captain of the Temple guard and his immediate subordinates seem to have been taken into the council, no doubt to coordinate the plans for the actual arrest of Jesus.

They were deliberating how Jesus might be taken and killed. Probably they had not yet fixed on any definite plan. Probably in consequence of the popular acclamations at his entry into Jerusalem and of what had since happened, they decided that nothing must be done during the feast, for fear of some popular uprising. They knew only too well the character of Pilate and how in any such tumult all parties might experience terrible vengeance. It must have been intense relief when, in their perplexity, the traitor now presented himself before them with his proposals.

They treated Judas not as an honoured associate, but as a common informer and a contemptible betrayer. This was not only natural but the wisest policy, to save their own dignity and to keep the most secure hold on the betrayer. And, after all, to minimise his services, Judas could really

---

63. John 6:67.

not do much for them, only show them how they might seize him to avoid the possible disruption of an open arrest.

We mark the deep symbolic significance of the 'thirty pieces of silver', in that the Lord was paid for out of the Temple money which was destined for the purchase of sacrifices and that he, who took on him the form of a servant,[64] was sold and bought at the legal price of a slave.

---

64. Philippians 2:7.

Chapter 47: Passion Week: Day Five

MATTHEW 26:17-19; MARK 14:12-16; LUKE 22:7-13; JOHN 13:1
(Book 5: Chapter 9)

When Judas returned from Jerusalem the Passover was close at hand. It began on the 14th Nisan; that is from the appearance of the first three stars on Wednesday evening (the 13th) and ended with the first three stars on Thursday evening (the 14th). The absence of the traitor so close to the feast possibly wouldn't have been noticed by the others. Necessary preparations might have to be made, even though they were to be guests in an unknown house. These matters would, of course, be financially organised by Judas. Everyone in Israel was thinking about the feast. For the previous month, it had been the subject of discussion in the academies and, for the last two Sabbaths at least, that of teachings in the synagogues.

Everyone was going to Jerusalem, or had those near and dear to them there, or at least watched the festive processions to the metropolis of Judaism. It was a universal gathering in remembrance of the birth of the nation when friends from afar would meet and new friends made; when offerings long due would be brought and long-needed purification obtained and all worship in that grand and glorious Temple, with its grand and awesome ritual.

Let us now follow closely the footsteps of Jesus and his disciples and watch closely. The first preparations for the feast would commence shortly after the return of the traitor. The evening of the fifth day marked the beginning of the 14th of Nisan when a solemn search was made with a lit candle throughout each house for any leaven that might be hidden or has fallen aside by accident. Such was put by in a safe place and afterwards destroyed with the rest.

It was probably after the early meal and when the eating of leaven had ceased, that Jesus began preparations for the Passover Supper. 'Then came the day of Unleavened Bread on which the Passover lamb had to be sacrificed.' The suggestion that in that year the Sanhedrin had postponed the Passover Supper from Thursday evening (the 14th-15th Nisan) to Friday evening (15th-16th Nisan), to avoid the Sabbath following on the first day of the feast and that the Passover lamb was therefore in that year eaten on Friday, the evening of the day on which Jesus was crucified, is an assumption void of all support in history or Jewish tradition. Equally untenable is it that Jesus had held the supper a day in advance of that observed by the rest of the Jewish world since the Passover lamb could not have been offered in the Temple and, therefore, no Passover Supper held, outside of the regular time.

Perhaps the strangest attempt to reconcile the Gospel accounts (in that Matthew, Mark and Luke seem to be at odds with John regarding timings) is that while the rest of Jerusalem, including Jesus and his apostles, partook of the Passover Supper, the chief priests had been interrupted in, or rather prevented from it by their proceedings against Jesus; that, in fact, they had not touched it when they feared to enter Pilate's Judgement Hall. Such would have been contrary to one of the plainest commands, 'the Pascha is not eaten but during the night, nor yet later than the middle of the night'.

Evidently, neither the house where the Passover was to be kept nor its owner was to be named beforehand within Judas' hearing, to stop him from informing the authorities. That last meal with its institution of the Holy Supper was not to be interrupted, nor their last retreat betrayed, until all had been said and done, even to the last prayer of agony in Gethsemane. We can see the divine hand in this.

On their entrance into Jerusalem, they would meet a man carrying a pitcher of water. They were to follow him and, when they reached the house, to deliver to its owner the message that this is to be the place for the Last Supper. The disciples were told to ask for the place in the house where the beasts of burden were unloaded, and shoes and staff, or dusty garments and burdens put down. He who was born in a 'hostelry' (*katalyma*) was content to ask for his last meal in a *katalyma*.

It was a common practice that more than one group partook of the Passover Supper in the same apartment. This was unavoidable, for all partook of it, including women and children, apart from those who were unclean according to the Law. And, though each group might be small, it was not to be so big that each couldn't share at least a small portion of the Passover lamb. But, while he only asked for his last meal in the *katalyma*, Jesus would have a private gathering, to eat the Passover alone with his apostles.

Not even the wider company of disciples, such as the owner of the house nor yet even Mary, might be present. And 'the upper room' (KJV) was large, furnished and ready. From Jewish authorities, we know that the average dining apartment was around 15ft square. All that the disciples would have to 'make ready' (KJV) would be the Passover lamb and perhaps that first *chagigah*, or festive sacrifice which, if the lamb itself would not suffice for supper, was added to it.

To us at least it seems most likely that it was the house of Mark's father (then still alive) – a large one, as we gather from Acts 12:13. For, the most obvious explanation of the introduction by Mark alone of such an incident concerning the young man who was accompanying Christ as he was led away captive, and who, on fleeing from those who would have laid hold on him, left in their hands his inner garment as he had rushed into Gethsemane. This was none other than Mark himself. If so, we can understand it all; how the traitor may have first brought the Temple guards who had come to seize Jesus to the house of Mark's father where the supper had been held, and that, finding him gone, they had followed to Gethsemane, for 'Judas ... knew the place, because Jesus had often met there with his disciples' (John 18:2). And how Mark, startled from his sleep by the appearance of the armed men, would hastily cast about him his loose tunic and run after them; then, after the flight of the disciples, accompany Jesus, but escape intended arrest by leaving his tunic in the hands of his would-be captors.[65]

---

65. Mark 14:51.

If the owner of the house had provided all that was needed for the supper, Peter and John would find there the wine for the four cups, the cakes of unleavened bread and probably also the bitter herbs, which were to be dipped once in saltwater, or vinegar, and another time in a mixture called *charoseth* (a compound made of nuts, raisins, apples and almonds). The wine was the ordinary red wine of the country; it was mixed with water, generally in the proportion of one part to two of water. The quantity for each of the four cups is stated by one authority as five-sixteenths of a log, which may be roughly computed at half a tumbler, mixed of course with water.

All things being ready in the furnished upper room, it would only remain for Peter and John to see to the Passover lamb and anything else required for the supper, possibly also to what was to be offered as *chagigah*, or festive sacrifice, and afterwards eaten at the supper. If the latter were to be brought, the disciples would, of course, have to attend earlier in the Temple. The cost of the lamb, which had to be provided, was very small.

And now it would be time for the ordinary evening service and sacrifice. Ordinarily, this began at about 2.30 p.m., the daily evening sacrifice being actually offered up about an hour later. But on this occasion, the service was an hour earlier on account of the feast. As at about 1.30 p.m. of our time, Peter and John climbed the Temple Mount to obtain their lamb. In all that crowd, how few were sympathetic to them, how many enemies there were! The Temple courts were thronged to the utmost by worshippers from all countries and from all parts of the land. The Priests' Court was filled with white-robed priests and Levites – for on that day all the twenty-four courses were on duty and all their services would be called for, although only the course for that week would that afternoon engage in the ordinary service, which preceded that of the feast. Almost mechanically they would witness the various parts of the ceremony.

There must have been a particular meaning to them, a mournful significance, in the language of Psalm 81, as the Levites chanted it that afternoon in three sections, broken three times by the three-fold blast from the silver trumpets of the priests. Before the incense was burnt for the evening sacrifice, or yet the lamps in the golden candlestick were trimmed for the night, the Passover lambs were slain. The worshippers were admitted in three divisions within the Court of the Priests. When the first company had entered, the massive Nicanor Gates – which led from the Court of the Women to that of Israel – and the other side gates into the Court of the Priests were closed. A three-fold blast from the priests' trumpets indicated that the lambs were being slain. This each Israelite did for himself.

We can be fairly sure that Peter and John would be in the first of the three groups into which the offerors were divided; for they must have been anxious to be gone, and to meet the Master and their brethren in that upper room.

Peter and John had slain the lamb. In two rows the officiating priest stood, up to the great altar of burnt offering. As one caught up the blood from the dying lamb in a golden bowl, he handed it to his colleague, receiving in return an empty bowl; and so, the blood was passed on to the great altar, where it was poured out at the base of it. While this was going on, the *Hallel* was being chanted by the Levites. We remember that only the first line of every psalm was repeated by the worshippers; while they responded to every other line with a *Halleluyah* until Psalm 118 was reached, when, besides the first, these three lines were also repeated: 'Save now, I beseech thee, O LORD: O LORD, I beseech thee, send now prosperity; Blessed be he that cometh in the name of the LORD' (KJV).

As Peter and John repeated them on that afternoon, the words must have sounded deeply significant. But their minds must also have reverted to that triumphal entry into the city a few days before when Israel had greeted with these words the advent of their King. The sacrifice now rested on the shoulders of Peter and John, flayed, cleansed and the parts which were to be burnt on the altar removed and prepared for burning.

The second group of offerors could not have proceeded far in the service, when the apostles, bearing their lamb, were wending their way back to the home of Mark, there to make final preparations for the supper. The lamb would be roasted on a pomegranate spit that passed right through it, special care being taken that, in roasting, the lamb did not touch the oven. Everything else, also, would be made ready; the *chagigah* for supper (if such was used); the unleavened cakes, the bitter herbs, the dish with vinegar and that with *charoseth* would be placed on a table which could be carried in and moved at will; finally, the festive lamps would be prepared. It was probably as the sun was beginning to decline on the horizon that Jesus and the other ten disciples descended once more over the Mount of Olives into the Holy City.

It was the last day which the Lord could enjoy free and unhindered, in the Holy City until his resurrection. Once more, in the approaching night of his betrayal, would he look upon it in the pale light of the full moon. He was going forward to accomplish his death in Jerusalem; to fulfil type and prophecy and to offer himself up as the true Passover Lamb, 'the Lamb of God, which taketh away the sin of the world' (John 1:29, KJV).

Edersheim paints the scene:

> They who followed him were busy with many thoughts. They knew that terrible events awaited them and they had only shortly before been told that these glorious Temple buildings, to which they had directed the attention of their Master, were to become desolate, not one stone being left upon the other. Among them, revolving his dark plans, and goaded on by the great Enemy, moved the betrayer. And now they were within the city. Its Temple, its royal bridge, its splendid palaces, its busy marts, its streets filled with festive pilgrims, were well known to them, as they made their way to the house where the guest chamber had been prepared. Meanwhile, the crowd came down from the Temple Mount, each bearing on his shoulders the sacrificial lamb, to make ready for the Passover Supper.

Chapter 48: The Last Supper

MATTHEW 26:17-20; MARK 14:12-17; LUKE 22:7-13; JOHN 13:1
(Book 5: Chapter 10)

The first three stars had become visible and the three-fold blast of the silver trumpets from the Temple Mount rang it out to Jerusalem and far away that the Passover had once more commenced. In the upper chamber of Mark's house, the Master and the Twelve were now gathered.

LUKE 22:14-16

'For I tell you, I will not eat it again until it finds fulfilment in the kingdom of God.' His last Passover provides the foundation of that other feast in which he is ever-present with his Church, not only as its food but as its Host. With a sacrament did Jesus begin his ministry; it was that of separation and consecration in baptism. With a second sacrament did he close his ministry; it was that of gathering together and fellowship in the Lord's Supper. And as in the Passover Supper, all Israel were gathered around the Passover lamb in commemoration of the past, in celebration of the present, in anticipation of the future, and in fellowship in the Lamb, so has the Church been ever since gathered together around its better fulfilment in the kingdom of God.

LUKE 22:24-30

As the Jewish Law directed, they reclined on pillows around a low table, each resting on his left hand, to leave the right free. Sadly, humiliating as it reads and almost incredible as it seems, the supper began with 'a strife among them, which of them should be accounted the greatest' (KJV). We can have no doubt that its occasion was the order in which they should occupy places at the table. We know that this was a subject of general contention among the Pharisees and that the disciples followed suit, desiring to be seated according to their rank.

From the Gospels, we assume that John must have reclined next to Jesus, on his right-hand side, since otherwise he could not have leaned back on him. This would be at one end, the head of the table. We can form a picture of the arrangement. Around a low table, oval or rather, elongated, two parts covered with a cloth and standing or else suspended, the single divans or pillows are ranged in the form of an elongated horseshoe, leaving free one end of the table.

The chief place next to Jesus would be that to his left and we believe it to have been actually occupied by Judas. So, when Jesus whispered to John by what sign to recognise the traitor, none of the other disciples heard it. It also explains how Jesus would hand the sop to Judas first, beginning with him as the chief guest at the table, without attracting special notice. As regards Peter, we can quite understand how, when the Lord with such loving words rebuked their self-seeking and taught them of the greatness of Christian humility, he should, feeling shameful, have rushed to take the lowest place at the other end of the table. Finally, we can now understand how Peter could beckon to John, who sat at the opposite end and ask him across the table, who is the traitor?

The rest of the disciples would occupy such places as were most convenient or suited their fellowship with one another. Having reminded them of the qualities needed by those in the kingdom, he pointed them to himself as their example. The reference here is not to the act of symbolic foot-washing, but to the nature of his whole life and the object of his mission, as of one who served, not as one who *was* served.

LUKE 22:17-18

The supper began, as always, by the head of the company taking the first cup and speaking the thanksgiving over it. The form presently in use consists really of two blessings, the first over the wine, the second for the return of this feast day and for being preserved once more to witness it.

What the Lord added, as he passed the cup around the circle of the disciples, was that no more would he speak the blessing over the fruit of the vine – not again utter the thanks that they had been 'preserved alive, sustained, and brought to this season'.

JOHN 13:2-17

The next part of the ceremony was for the head of the company to rise and wash hands. It is this part of the ritual of which John records the adaptation and transformation on the part of Jesus. The washing of the disciples' feet is evidently connected with the ritual of 'handwashing'. Now this was done twice during the supper; the first time by Jesus alone, immediately after the first cup; the second time by all present, at a much later part of the service, immediately before the actual meal.

The foot-washing, which was intended both as a lesson and as an example of humility and service, was evidently connected with the dispute about which of them should be accounted to be greatest. If so, the symbolic act of our Lord must have followed close on the strife of the disciples and on his teaching what in the Church constituted rule and greatness, which was evidently very different to what they imagined it to be.

MATTHEW 26:21-24; MARK 14:18-21; LUKE 22:21-23; JOHN 13:18-26

Then follows the account of what happened during supper, beginning with Judas. Thankfully, we feel that the human heart was not capable of originating the betrayal of Christ; humanity had fallen, but not so low. It was the devil who had cast it into Judas' heart, with force and overwhelming power. We come here upon these words of deepest mystery, 'I know whom I have chosen: but that the scripture may be fulfilled, He that eateth bread with me hath lifted up his heel against me' (KJV). We must understand it as meaning that Jesus had, from the first, known the inmost thoughts of those he had chosen to be his apostles; but that by this treachery of one of their number, the terrible prediction of the worst enmity, that of ingratitude, true in all ages of the Church, would receive its complete fulfilment.

In the meantime, the supper was proceeding. After the 'washing', the dishes were to be brought to the table immediately. Then the head of the company would dip some of the bitter herbs into the saltwater or vinegar, speak a blessing, and partake of them, then hand them to each in the company. Next, he would break one of the unleavened cakes, of which half was put aside for after supper. This is called the *aphiqomon*, or after-dish, and as we believe that 'the bread' of the Holy Eucharist was the *aphiqomon*, some particulars may here be of interest. The dish in which the broken cake lies (not the *aphiqomon*) is elevated and these words are spoken: 'This is the bread of misery which our fathers ate in the land of Egypt. All that are hungry, come and eat; all that are needy, come, keep the Passover.'

'On this, the second cup is filled and the youngest child present asks for the meaning of all the observances of that night and the liturgy provides full answers about the festival, its occasion and ritual. We do not suppose that the ritual has remained exactly the same over the centuries; even so, there wouldn't have been a major deviation from that followed at the Last Supper. So much stress is laid in Jewish writings on the duty of fully rehearsing at the supper the circumstances of the first Passover and the deliverance connected with it, that we can assume that the Last Supper followed this pattern.

After this, the cup is elevated and then the service proceeds somewhat lengthily, the cup being raised a second time and certain prayers are spoken. This part of the service concludes with the first two psalms in the series called the *Hallel*, when the cup is raised a third time, a prayer spoken, and the cup drunk. This ends the first part of the service. And now the meal begins by all washing their hands.

It was, we believe, during this time that Jesus became 'troubled in spirit'. His soul could not but have been troubled as he fully knew what was ahead of him. But he saw more than even this. He saw Judas about to take the last fatal step and his soul yearned in pity over him. Jesus also saw how the terrible tempest of fierce temptation would that night sweep over them; how it would lay low and almost uproot one of them and scatter all. It was the beginning of the time of Christ's utmost loneliness, of which the climax was reached in Gethsemane.

MATTHEW 26:25; JOHN 13:26-38

And so did he solemnly testify to them of the near betrayal. 'Master, is it I?' (KJV). This question on the part of the eleven disciples, who were conscious of innocence of any purpose of betrayal and conscious also of deep love to the Master gives us one of the clearest glimpses into that night of terror. We can now better understand their heavy sleep in Gethsemane, their forsaking him and fleeing, even Peter's denial.

MATTHEW 26:26-29; MARK 14:22-25; LUKE 22:19-20

We now approach the most solemn part of that night, the institution of the Lord's Supper. It almost seems as if the Gospel writers had intended, by their studied silence concerning the Jewish feast, to indicate that with this celebration and the new institution, the Jewish Passover had forever ceased. The absence of a record by John is compensated by the narrative of Paul in 1 Corinthians 11:23-26, to which must be added as supplementary the reference in 1 Corinthians 10:16 to 'the cup of blessing which we bless' (KJV) as 'fellowship of the blood of Christ', and 'the bread which we break' (KJV) as 'fellowship of the body of Christ'.

We have thus four accounts. If we now ask ourselves at what part of the supper the new institution was made, we cannot doubt that it was before the supper was completely ended. We have seen that Judas had left the table at the beginning of the supper.

According to the Jewish ritual, the third cup was filled at the close of the supper. This was called 'the cup of blessing', partly because a special 'blessing' was pronounced over it. It is described as one of the ten essential rites in the Passover Supper. Next, grace after meat was spoken.

If we are asked what part of the service corresponds to the 'breaking of bread' we note that while the Passover lamb was still offered, it was the law that declared that after partaking of its flesh, nothing else should be eaten. But since the Passover lamb had ceased, it is the custom after the meal to break and feast on the *aphikomon*, or after-dish, of that half of the unleavened bread which had been broken and put aside at the beginning of the supper.

Jesus now connected the institution of the breaking of bread in the Holy Eucharist with the breaking of the unleavened bread at the close of the meal. What did this institution really mean, and what does it mean to us? We cannot believe that it was intended as merely a sign for remembrance of his death. Such remembrance is often equally vivid in ordinary acts of faith or prayer. It seems difficult to account for the institution of a special sacrament and that with such solemnity and as the second great rite of the Church, that for feeding its members. Again, if it were a mere token of remembrance, why the cup as well as the bread?

The Holy Eucharist *feeds the soul* as well as the body. Receiving of the bread and the cup in the Holy Communion is spiritually to the soul what the outward elements are to the body; *that they are both the symbol and the vehicle of true, inward, spiritual feeding on the body and blood of Christ.* Edersheim continues:

Most mysterious words these, our feeding on Christ spiritually and in faith. And ever since has this blessed Institution lain as the golden morning-light far out even in the Church's darkest night – not only the seal of his Presence and its pledge, but also the promise of the bright Day at his Coming. 'For as often as we eat this Bread and drink this Cup, we do show forth the Death of the Lord' for the life of the world, to be assuredly yet manifested, 'until he come.' 'Even so, Lord Jesus, come quickly!'

Chapter 49: His Final Teachings

(Book 5: Chapter 11)

The establishment of the Lord's Supper was not the final act at that Passover table. According to the Jewish ritual, the cup is filled a fourth time and the remaining part of the *Hallel* is repeated. Then follows Psalm 86 and several prayers and hymns. The institution of the Holy Supper was probably followed by the teaching recorded in John 14. Then the concluding psalms of the *Hallel* were sung, after which the Master left the upper chamber. The teachings in John 16 and his prayer were certainly uttered after they had risen from the supper and before they crossed the Kidron brook. In all probability, they were, however, spoken before they left the house.

JOHN 14

We can scarcely imagine such a teaching and still less such a prayer to have been uttered while traversing the narrow streets of Jerusalem on the way to Kidron. In any case, there cannot be a doubt that this was spoken while still at the supper table. It connects itself closely with that statement which had caused them so much sorrow and perplexity, that where he was going, they could not come.[66]

Firstly, we remember the very common Jewish idea that those in glory occupied different abodes, corresponding to their ranks. If the words of Jesus about the place where they could not follow him had awakened any such thoughts, the explanation which he now gave must effectually have dispelled them. Let not their hearts be troubled at the prospect. As they believed in God, so let them also have trust in him. It was his Father's house of which they were thinking and although there were 'many mansions' (KJV) in it – and the choice of this word may teach us

---

66. John 8:21.

something – yet they were all in that one house. The object of his going was the opposite of what they feared; it was to prepare by his death and resurrection a place for them. His present going away meant the ultimate gathering to himself, not final separation.

Jesus was the way to the Father; the full manifestation of all spiritual truth and the spring of the true inner life were equally in him. Other than through him, no one could consciously come to the Father. Thomas had asked what was the goal and what was the way to it? In his answer, Jesus significantly reversed this order and told them first what was the way – himself; and then what was the goal. If they had spiritually known him as the Way, they would also have known the goal, the Father.

Working by faith and praying in faith is in obedience to his commandments. And for such faith, there will be a need of divine presence ever with them. Now that his outward presence was to be withdrawn from earth and he was to be their paraclete or advocate in heaven with the Father, God would send them another paraclete, who would continue with them forever. To the guidance and pleadings of that advocate, they could implicitly trust themselves, for he was 'the Spirit of truth'.

The world would not listen to his pleadings, nor accept him as their guide, for the only evidence by which they judged was that of outward sight and material results. But they would know the reality of his existence and the truth of his pleadings by the continual presence with them as a body of this paraclete and by his dwelling in them individually.

Here begins the essential difference between believers and the world. The Son was sent into the world; not so the Holy Spirit. Again, the world receives not the Holy Spirit, because it knows him not; the disciples know him because they possess him. Because of this promised advent of the other advocate, Christ could tell the disciples that he would not leave them 'orphans' in this world.

One outstanding fact here attracted the attention of the disciples. It was contrary to all their Jewish ideas about the future manifestation of the Messiah, and it led to the question, 'Lord, what has happened, that to us you will manifest yourself and not to the world?' Again, they thought of an outward manifestation, while he spoke of a spiritual and inward manifestation.

As he had explained it, his departure to the Father was the necessary condition of his coming to them in the permanent presence of the other paraclete, the Holy Spirit. That paraclete, however, would, in the economy of grace, be sent by the Father alone.

JOHN 15

If in the teaching recorded in John 14 the God-centred aspect of Christ's impending departure was explained, in that of John 15 the new relationship between Jesus and his Church is set forth. And this may be summarised in these three words: union, communion and disunion.

The *union* between Christ and his Church is corporate, vital and effective. This union manifests in *communion*; of Christ with his disciples, of his disciples with him and of his disciples among themselves. The principle of all these is love; the love of Christ for the disciples, the love of the disciples for Christ and the love in Christ of the disciples for one another.

Lastly, this union and communion has for its necessary counterpart disunion, separation from the world. The world repudiates them for their union with Christ and their communion. But, for all that, there is something that must keep them from going out of the world. They have a mission in it, initiated by and carried on in the power of the Holy Spirit – that of uplifting the testimony of Christ.

When Christ said, 'I am the vine, the true one, and my Father is the gardener' or again, 'you are the branches' what he meant was that he, the Father and the disciples stood in exactly the same relationship as the vine, the gardener and the branches. That relationship was of a corporate union of the branches with the vine to produce fruit for the gardener, who for that purpose pruned the branches.

Nor can we forget in this connection that, in the Old Testament and partially in Jewish thought, the vine was the symbol of Israel, not in their national but in their 'Church-capacity'. Jesus, with his disciples as the branches, is 'the vine, the true one' – the reality of all types, the fulfilment of all promises. They are many branches, yet a grand unity in that vine; there is one Church of which he is the head, the root, the sustenance, the life. And in that vine will the object of its planting of old be realised, to bring forth fruit unto God.

Yet, though it is one vine, the Church must bear fruit not only in her corporate capacity but also individually in each of the branches. The proper, normal condition of every branch in that vine was to bear much fruit, of course. This was done by abiding in him, since 'apart' from him they could do nothing. If the corporate and vital union was effective, if they were abiding in him and his words were abiding in them, then 'whatever you ask in my name the Father will give you'. It is very noteworthy that prayer is limited or, rather, conditioned, by our abiding in Jesus and his words in us just as in John 14:12-14 it is conditioned by fellowship with him and in John 15:16 by permanent fruitfulness.

For it was the most dangerous fanaticism and entirely opposed to the teaching of Christ, to imagine that the promise of Jesus implies such absolute power, as if prayer were magic, that a person might ask for anything, no matter what it was, in the assurance of obtaining his request. Our relationship with Jesus and his word in us, union and communion with him, and the obedience of love are the indispensable conditions of our privileges. The believer may, indeed, ask for anything, because they may always and absolutely go to God; but the certainty of special answers to prayer is proportionate to the degree of union and communion with Jesus.

To keep his commandments was to be his friend. And they were his friends. No longer did he call them servants, for the servant knew not what his Lord did. He had now given them a new name, and with good reason: 'I have called you friends, for everything that I learned from my Father I have made known to you.'

The hatred by the world was going to be a factor. For evil or for good, they must expect the same treatment as their Master. Was it not their privilege to realise that all this came upon them for his sake? And should they not also remember that the ultimate ground of the world's hatred was ignorance of him who had sent Jesus?

JOHN 16

The last of the parting teaching of Jesus, in John 16, was interrupted by questions from the disciples. In general, the subjects treated in it are: the new relationship arising from the departure of Jesus and the coming of the other advocate. The chapter appropriately opens by reflecting on the predicted enmity of the world. Jesus had so clearly foretold this in case it should prove a stumbling block to them. They needed to know that they would not only be put out of the synagogue but that everyone who killed them would deem it 'to offer a religious service to God'.

Although they had in a general way been prepared for it before, he had not told it all so definitely from the beginning, because he was still there. But now that he was going away, it was absolutely necessary to do so. But the advent of the 'advocate' would mark a new era, as regarded the Church and the world. It was their mission to go forth into the world and to preach Christ. That other advocate would go into the world and convict on the three cardinal points on which their preaching turned: sin, righteousness and judgement. And on these would the new advocate convict the world.

Taking, then, the three great facts in the history of Christ: his first coming to salvation, his resurrection and ascension and his sitting at the right hand of God, of which his second coming to judgement is the final issue. The advocate of Christ will in each case convict the world of guilt. A whole new order of things was before the apostles; the abolition of the old ways, the establishment of the Christian dispensation and the relation of the New to the Old, together with many similar questions. As Christ's representative and speaking not from himself, the Holy Spirit would be with them, to guide them so they didn't stray into error and to be their leader into all truth.

Up until then, they had not yet asked in his name. Now let them ask! They would receive and so their joy be completed. Beforehand he had only been able to speak to them in parables and allegory, but then would he declare to them in all plainness about the Father. And, as he would be able to speak to them directly and plainly about the Father, so would they then be able to speak directly to the Father. They would ask directly in the name of Christ; and no longer would it be needful, as at present, first to come to him that he may enquire of the Father about them. For God loved them as lovers of Christ and as recognising that he had come forth from God.

Edersheim adds:

> Yet, even so, his latest as his first thought was of them; and through the night of scattering and of sorrow did he bid them look to the morning of joy. For, the battle was not theirs, nor yet the victory doubtful. We now enter most reverently what may be called the innermost sanctuary. For the first time we are allowed to listen to what was really 'the Lord's Prayer' and, as we hear, we humbly worship. That Prayer was the great preparation for his Agony, Cross, and Passion; and, also, the outlook on the Crown beyond.

JOHN 17

We see the Great High Priest first solemnly offering up himself and then consecrating and interceding for his Church and for her work. The final hour had come. In praying that the Father would glorify the Son, he was really not asking anything for himself, but that the Son might 'glorify' the Father. For, the glorifying of the Son – his support, and then his resurrection – was really the completion of the work which the Father had given him to do.

And then he claimed what was at the end of his mission: his return to that fellowship of essential glory, which he possessed together with the Father before the world was. The gift of his consecration could not have been laid on a more glorious altar. Such a cross must have been followed by such a crown. And now again his first thought was of them for whose sake he had consecrated himself. These he now solemnly presented to the Father.

He introduced them as those whom the Father had specially given to him out of the world. As such, they were really the Father's and given over to Christ. And now he brought them in prayer before the Father. He was interceding, not for the 'world' that was his by right of his Messiahship, but for them whom the Father had specially given him. They were the Father's in the special sense of covenant and mercy, and all that in that sense was the Father's was the Son's and all that was the Son's was the Father's. He sought not now his blessing on them, but on those whom, while he was in the world, he had shielded and guided.

They were to be left behind in a world of sin, evil, temptation and sorrow and he was going to the Father. And this was his prayer: 'Holy Father, protect them by the power of your name, the name you gave me, so that they may be one as we are one.' Those whom the Father had given him, by the effective drawing of his grace within them, he guarded, and none from among them was lost, except 'the son of perdition' (KJV) – and this, according to prophecy. But now he went to the Father. He prayed that in this unity of holiness the joy that was his might be 'fulfilled' (KJV) in them.

In its last part, this intercessory prayer of the Great High Priest covered the work of the disciples and its fruits. As the Father had sent the Son, so did the Son send the disciples into the world, in the same manner, and on the same mission. And for their sakes he now solemnly offered himself, consecrated or sanctified himself, that they might in truth be consecrated.

We remember the unity of the Church – a unity in him and as that between the Father and the Son – as we listen to this: 'those whom you have given me, I will that, where I am, they also may be with me, so that they may gaze on the glory that is mine, which you have given me; because you loved me before the foundation of the world.' And we all would place ourselves in the shadow of this final consecration of himself and of his Church by the Great High Priest.

Chapter 50: Gethsemane

MATTHEW 26:30-56; MARK 14:26-52; LUKE 22:31-53;
JOHN 18:1-11
(Book 5: Chapter 12)

Edersheim sets the scene:

> The last teachings had been spoken, the last prayer had been
> offered and Jesus prepared to leave the city for the Mount of Olives.
> The streets still bustled, lamps were still lit from homes on the way
> and everywhere were the preparations for going up to the Temple,
> the gates of which were thrown open at midnight. Passing out by
> the gate north of the Temple, we descend into a lonely part of the
> Kidron valley, at that season swelled into a winter torrent. Crossing
> it, we turn somewhat to the left, where the road leads towards
> Olivet. Not many steps farther we turn aside from the road to the
> right and reach what tradition has since earliest times pointed out
> as 'Gethsemane' the 'Oil-press.' It was a small enclosed property, 'a
> garden' in the Eastern sense, where probably, amidst a variety of
> fruit trees and flowering shrubs, was a lowly and quiet summer-
> retreat connected with the olive press.

It was here that the Lord addressed himself first to the disciples generally.
It had been foretold of old that the shepherd would be smitten and the
sheep scattered.[67] Did this prophecy of his suffering fill the mind of the
Saviour? Such Old Testament thoughts must have concerned him when,
as the Lamb of God, he went to the slaughter.

They had now reached the entrance of Gethsemane. It may have been
that it led through the building with the oil press and that the eight

---

67. Zechariah 13:7.

apostles were left there as he went onwards and prayed. The other three – Peter, James and John, companions before of his glory, both when he raised the daughter of Jairus and on the Mount of Transfiguration – he took with him further. As if in that last contest his human soul craved for the presence of those who stood nearest him and loved him best.

And now all of a sudden, the cold flood broke over him. Within these few moments, he had passed from the calmness of assured victory into the anguish of the contest. Increasingly, with every step forward, he became full of sorrow and desolate. He told them of the deep sorrow of his soul 'even unto death' (KJV) and asked them to stay there to watch with him. Jesus went forward to enter the contest with prayer. They only saw the beginning of the battle, they only heard the first words in that hour of agony. For, as was the case on the Mount of Transfiguration, irresistible sleep crept over them. Jesus was now well and truly alone.

Edersheim stirs us up:

But what was the cause of this sorrow unto death of the Lord Jesus Christ? Not fear, either of bodily or mental suffering, but death. Man's nature, created of God immortal, shrinks from the dissolution of the bond that binds body to soul. Yet to fallen man death is not by any means fully death, for he is born with the taste of it in his soul. Not so Christ. It was the Unfallen Man dying; it was he, who had no experience of it, tasting death and that not for himself but for every man, emptying the cup to its bitter dregs. It was the Christ undergoing death by man and for man; the Incarnate God, the God-Man, submitting himself vicariously to the deepest humiliation and paying the utmost penalty, death. His going into Death was his final conflict with Satan for man and on his behalf. By submitting to it he took away the power of death.

Alone must the Saviour enter in this final contest, as in his first conflict with the Evil One in the temptation in the wilderness. With great agony of soul he now began to take upon himself the sins of the world and in taking, dealt with them. We may learn from this account of what passed, when 'with strong crying and tears unto him that was able to save him from death' he 'offered up prayers and supplications' (Hebrews 5:7, KJV).

And now, on his knees prostrate on the ground, prostrate on his face, began his agony. His very words bear witness to it. It is the only time, so far as recorded in the Gospels, when he addressed God with the personal pronoun, 'My Father'.

The object of the prayer was, that, if it were possible, the hour might pass away from him. The subject of the prayer was that the cup itself might pass away, yet always with the limitation, that not his will but the Father's might be done. The petition of Christ, therefore, was subject not only to the will of the Father but also to his own will that the Father's will might be done. We are here in full view of the deepest mystery of our faith, the two natures in one Person.

It was in this extreme agony of his soul almost unto death, that the angel appeared (as in the temptation in the wilderness) to 'strengthen' and support his body and soul. And so, the conflict went on, with increasing earnestness of prayer, in that terrible hour. For the appearance of the angel must have indicated to him, that the cup could not pass away. And at the close of that hour, the disciples would have seen the terrible toll, as his sweat, mingled with blood, fell in 'great drops' (KJV) on the ground.

And when the Saviour returned to the three, he found them in deep sleep. While he lay in prayer, they lay in sleep. The conflict had been decided virtually but not finally when the Saviour went back to the three sleeping disciples. He now returned to complete it, though both the attitude in which he prayed (no longer prostrate) and the wording of his prayer indicate how near it was to perfect victory. And once more, on his return to them, he found them in a state of doziness and they didn't know how to answer him. Yet a third time he left them to pray as before. And now he returned victoriously. After three assaults had the tempter left him in the wilderness; after the three-fold conflict in the garden, he was vanquished.

Jesus emerged triumphantly. The hour had come when the Son of Man was to be 'betrayed into the hands of sinners' (KJV). A very brief period of rest was soon broken by the call of Jesus to rise and go to where the other eight had been left, at the entrance of the garden – to go forward and meet the band which was coming under the guidance of the betrayer. And while he was speaking, the heavy tramp of many men and the light of lanterns and torches indicated the approach of Judas and his band. During the hours that had passed, all had been prepared. The scene was now set for the next stage in the drama.

Later on, when, according to arrangement, he appeared at the high priestly palace, or more probably at that of Annas, who seems to have had the direction of affairs, the Jewish leaders first communicated with the Roman garrison. By their own admission, they no longer possessed the power of pronouncing a capital sentence. Because of this fact (so fully confirmed in the Gospels), it was clear that the Sanhedrin had sought formally to pronounce on Jesus what, admittedly, they had not the power to execute.

Nor, indeed, did they, when appealing to Pilate, plead that they had pronounced sentence of death, but only that they had a law by which Jesus should die. The Sanhedrin, not possessing the power of the sword, had, of course, no way of carrying this out. The Temple guard under their officers served merely for policing purposes and were neither regularly armed nor trained. Neither would the Romans have tolerated a regular armed Jewish force in Jerusalem. We can now understand the progress of events.

In the fortress of Antonia, close to the Temple and connected with it by two stairs, lay the Roman garrison. During the feast, the Temple itself was guarded by an armed cohort, consisting of from 400 to 600 men, to prevent or quell any tumult among the numerous pilgrims. It would be to the captain of this cohort that the chief priests and leaders of the Pharisees would, in the first place, apply for an armed guard to arrest Jesus, on the grounds that it might lead to a popular uprising. This band was led not by a centurion, but by a *chiliarch* which, as there were no intermediate grades in the Roman army, must represent one of the six tribunes attached to each legion.

This Roman detachment, armed with 'swords and clubs' was accompanied by servants from the high priest's palace and other Jewish officers, to direct the arrest of Jesus. They bore torches and lamps placed on the top of poles, to prevent any possible concealment. Having joined them, Judas proceeded on his errand. A signal by which to recognise Jesus seemed necessary with so large a band and where escape or resistance might be apprehended. It was – terrible to say – *none other than a kiss*. As soon as the act was done, the guard was to seize and lead him safely away.

We thus picture to ourselves the succession of events. As the band reached the garden, Judas went somewhat in advance of them and reached Jesus just as he had roused the three and was preparing to go and meet his captors. He saluted him, 'Greetings, Rabbi' so as to be heard by the rest and not only kissed 'but covered him with kisses, kissed him repeatedly, loudly, effusively'. The Saviour submitted to the indignity, not stopping, but only saying as he passed on, 'Do what you came for, friend.'

Leaving the traitor and ignoring the signal which he had given them, Jesus advanced to the band and asked them, 'Whom is it you want?' To the brief spoken, perhaps somewhat contemptuous, 'Jesus of Nazareth,' he replied with infinite calmness and majesty, 'I am he'. But his appearance and calmness were too overpowering in its effects on those ignorant soldiers, who perhaps were most reluctant in the work they had in hand. The closest of them fell backwards to the ground.

But Christ's hour had come. They laid hands on Jesus and took him. Then Peter, seeing what was coming, drew the sword which he carried and struck at Malchus, the servant of the high priest – perhaps the Jewish leader of the band – cutting off his ear. But Jesus immediately restrained all such violence. He pointed to the fact how easily he might have commanded angelic legions. He touched the ear of Malchus and healed him.

Their leaders now bound Jesus. It was to this last, most undeserved and uncalled for indignity that Jesus replied by asking them, why they had come against him as against a robber – one of those wild, murderous Sicarii?[68] Had he not all that week been daily in the Temple teaching? Why not then seize him? But this 'hour' of theirs that had come, and 'the power of darkness' (KJV) – this also had been foretold in Scripture! And as the ranks of the armed men now closed around the bound Messiah, none dared to stay with him, in case they also should be bound as resisting authority. So, they all 'deserted him and fled'. But there was one there who didn't flee but remained, a deeply interested onlooker. When the soldiers had come to seek Jesus in the upper chamber of his home, Mark, roused from sleep, had hastily cast about him the loose linen garment that lay by his bedside and followed the armed band to see what would come of it. He now lingered in the rear and followed as they led Jesus away, never imagining that they would attempt to lay hold of him since he had not been with the disciples nor yet in the garden. But they had noticed him. They attempted to grab him when, disengaging himself from their grasp, he left his garment in their hands and fled. So ended the first scene in the terrible drama of that night.

---

68. Jewish zealots.

Chapter 51: The Jewish Trial

~~

JOHN 18:12-14

(Book 5: Chapter 13)

They led the bound Jesus probably through the same gate that he passed with his disciples after the supper, up to the well-known Palace of Annas, on the slope between the Upper City and the Tyropoeon. The streets of Jerusalem would have been quiet at that late hour and the rhythmic bustle of the Roman guard must have been too often heard to startle sleepers or to lead to questions: why that glare of lamps and torches? Who was this prisoner, who had to be guarded on that holy night by both Roman soldiers and servants of the high priest?

Here's a question that could have been asked. Why have they brought Jesus to the house of Annas, since he was not at that time the actual high priest? That office now belonged to Caiaphas, his son-in-law, who had been the first to declare the political necessity for the judicial murder of Christ.[69] There had been no pretence on his part of religious motives or zeal for God; he had cynically put it in a way to override the scruples of those old Sanhedrists by raising their fears.

What was the use of discussing forms of Law? It must, in any case, be done; even the friends of Jesus in the council, as well as the fastidious observers of Law, must regard his death as the lesser of two evils. Caiaphas spoke as the bold, unscrupulous, determined man that he was; Sadducee through and through, a worthy son-in-law of Annas.

No figure is better known in contemporary Jewish history than that of Annas; no person deemed more fortunate or successful, but none also more generally loathed than the ex-high priest. He had held the office for only six or seven years, but it was filled later by not fewer than five of his sons, by his son-in-law Caiaphas and by a grandson.

---

69. John 11:49-50.

He was as resolutely bent on Jesus' death as his son-in-law, though with his characteristic cunning and coolness, not in the hasty, bluff manner of Caiaphas. It was probably from a desire to get involved in the matter or perhaps it was for even more practical reasons – the Palace of Annas was nearer to the place of Jesus' capture – and that it was desirable to dismiss the Roman soldiers as quickly as possible, that Jesus was first brought to Annas and not to the actual high priest.

MATTHEW 26:57-58; MARK 14:53-54; LUKE 22:54-55

No account is given of what passed before Annas. It is only mentioned in the fourth Gospel. As the disciples had all forsaken him and fled, we can understand that they had no idea of what was actually spoken there until afterwards, after Peter and John 'followed him … unto the high priest's palace'.

For the Palace of Caiaphas, the high priest, was the scene of Peter's denial. Of what occurred in the Palace of Caiaphas we have two accounts. John seems to refer to a more private interview between the high priest and Jesus but the second account of the other three writers refers to the examination of Jesus at dawn by the leading Sanhedrists, who had been hastily summoned for the purpose.

JOHN 18:19-23

The questions of Caiaphas focused on two points: concerning the disciples of Jesus and his teaching. The former was to incriminate Christ's followers, the latter to incriminate the Master. To the first enquiry, it was only natural that he should not have condescended to answer. The reply to the second was characterised by that openness which he claimed for all that he had said. His was no secret doctrine.

As Jesus answered these questions, a blow came. Let us hope that it was a Roman, not a Jew, who so lifted his hand. Humanity itself seems to reel and stagger under this blow. Jesus could have retaliated with a phalanx of angels but submitted without murmur or complaint, and answered patiently in such manner to convict the man of his wrongdoing, or at least to have left him speechless.

MATTHEW 26:69-72; MARK 14:66-70; LUKE 22:56-58; JOHN 18:17-18,25

John was no stranger to the Palace of Caiaphas. We have already seen that, after the first panic of Jesus' sudden capture and their own flight, Peter and John seem to have rallied speedily. We get the impression that Peter, so far true to his word, had been the first to stop in his flight and to follow 'afar off' (Matthew 26:58, KJV). He had now been joined by John and the two followed the melancholy procession that escorted Jesus to the high priest. John seems to have entered the court along with the guard, while Peter remained outside until John, who apparently was well known in the high priest's house, had spoken to the maid who kept the door – the male servants being probably all gathered in the court – and so was able to enter.

Peter advanced into the middle of the court where, in the chill spring night, a coal fire had been lit. The glow of the charcoal threw a peculiar sheen on the bearded faces of the men as they crowded around it and talked of the events of that night. It was a chilly night when Peter approached the group around the fire. He would hear what they had to say. It was not safe to stand apart as he might be recognised as one of those who had only escaped capture in the garden by hasty flight.

Was he right in having come there at all? But now it was very chilly, to both body and soul and Peter remembered it all; not, indeed, the warning, but that of which he had been warned. What good could his confession do? Perhaps much possible harm. And why was he there? Peter was very restless and yet he must seem very quiet. He sat down among the servants, then he stood up among them. It was this awkward restlessness that attracted the attention of the maid who had first admitted him. As in the uncertain light she scanned the features of the mysterious stranger, she boldly charged him with being one of the disciples of the Man who stood incriminated up there before the high priest.

And in the chattering of his soul's fever, into which the chill had struck, Peter made a strong denial. Perhaps he spoke too much, inviting suspicion. What had he to do there? And why should he incriminate himself, or perhaps Jesus, by a needless confession to those who had no relevance to him? That was all he now remembered and thought; nothing about any denial of Jesus. And so, as they were still chatting together, Peter withdrew.

We cannot judge how long time had passed, but this we gather, that the words of the woman had either not made any impression on those around the fire, or that the bold denial of Peter had satisfied them. Presently, we find Peter walking away. He was not thinking of anything else now than how chilly it felt and how right he had been in not being entrapped by that woman. And just at this moment 'a cock crowed' (Matthew 26:74).

Edersheim describes what followed:

But there was no sleep that night in the High Priest's Palace. As he walked down the porch towards the outer court, first one maid met him; and then, as he returned from the outer court. He once more encountered his old accuser, the door-portress; and as he crossed the inner court to mingle again with the group around the fire, where he had formerly found safety. He was first accosted by one man, and then they all around the fire turned upon him, and each and all had the same thing to say, the same charge, that he was also one of the disciples of Jesus of Nazareth. But Peter's resolve was taken; he gave the same denial, briefer now, for he was collected and determined, but more emphatic – even with an oath.

MATTHEW 26:59-68; MARK 14:55-65; LUKE 22:67-71

Caiaphas' private examination would be placed between the first and second denial of Peter. The Sanhedrists would have arrived immediately after his second denial. The private enquiry of Caiaphas had been unsuccessful and, indeed, it was only preliminary. The leading Sanhedrists must have been warned that the capture of Jesus would be attempted that night and to hold themselves in readiness when summoned to the high priest.

This was no formal, regular meeting of the Sanhedrin and all Jewish order and law would have been grossly infringed in almost every way if this had been a formal meeting of the Sanhedrin. In those days there were three tribunals and the highest tribunal was that of seventy-one, or the Great Sanhedrin, which met first in one of the Temple chambers, the so-called *Lishkath haGazith* – or Chamber of Hewn Stones – and at the time of which we write, in 'the booths of the sons of Annas'. The judges of all these courts were equally set apart by ordination (*semikhah*), originally that of the laying on of hands.

With the highest tribunal, the Great Sanhedrin, 'the disciples' or students sat facing the judges. The latter sat in a semicircle, under the presidency of the *nasi* ('prince') and the vice-presidency of the *Ab-beth-din* ('father of the Court of Law'). At least twenty-three members were required to form a quorum. Facing the semicircle of judges, we are told, there were two shorthand writers to note down, respectively, the speeches in favour and against the accused.

It is of great importance to enquire how far legal instructions and ordinances were carried out under the iron rule of Herod and that of the Roman procurators. We can well believe that neither Herod nor the procurators would wish to abolish the Sanhedrin, but would leave to them the administration of justice, especially in all that might in any way be connected with purely religious questions. Equally, they would be deprived of the power of the sword and of decision-making on all matters of political or supreme importance. In all cases if he saw fit to interfere, Herod would reserve to himself the final decisions, and so would the procurators, who especially would not have tolerated any attempt at jurisdiction over a Roman citizen.

In short, the Sanhedrin would be accorded full jurisdiction in inferior and in religious matters, with the greatest show, but with the least amount of real rule or of supreme authority. Lastly, as both Herod and the procurators treated the high priest, who 'was their own man', as the real head and representative of the Jews and as it would be their policy to curtail the power of the independent and fanatical rabbis, we can understand how, in great criminal causes or in important investigations, the high priest would always preside, the presidency of the *nasi* being reserved for legal and ritual questions and discussions.

Even this brief summary about the Sanhedrin would be needless if it were a question of applying its rules of procedure to the indictment of Jesus. For the fact remains that Jesus was not formally tried and condemned by the Sanhedrin. It is admitted on all hands, that forty years before the destruction of the Temple, the Sanhedrin ceased to pronounce capital sentences. This alone would be sufficient. But, besides, the trial and sentence of Jesus in the Palace of Caiaphas would have outraged every principle of Jewish criminal law and procedure. Such causes could only be tried, and capital sentence pronounced, in the regular meeting place of the Sanhedrin – not, as here, in the high priest's palace.

Also, no such process might be begun in the night, not even in the afternoon, although if the discussion had gone on all day, the sentence might be pronounced at night. Again, no process could take place on sabbaths or feast days, or even on the eves of them, although this would not have nullified proceedings and it might be argued on the other side, that a process against one who had seduced the people should preferably by carried on and sentence executed at the great public feasts, for the warning of all.

Lastly, in capital cases, there was a very elaborate system of warning and cautioning witnesses, while it may safely be affirmed that at a regular trial Jewish judges, however prejudiced, would not have acted as the Sanhedrists and Caiaphas did on this occasion. But as we examine it more closely, we see that the Gospels do not speak of a formal trial and sentence by the Sanhedrin. Such references as to 'the Sanhedrin' ('council'), or to 'all the Sanhedrin' must be taken in the wider sense, which will presently be explained. On the other hand, the four Gospels equally indicate that the whole proceedings of that night were carried on in the Palace of Caiaphas and that during that night no formal sentence of death was pronounced.

When in the morning they led Jesus to the Praetorium, it was not as a prisoner condemned to death of whom they asked the execution, but as one against whom they laid certain accusations worthy of death. When Pilate asked them to judge Jesus according to Jewish Law,[70] they did not admit that they had done so already, but that they had no competence to try capital cases. But although Jesus was not tried and sentenced in a formal meeting of the Sanhedrin, there can be no question that his condemnation and death were the work of the whole body of the Sanhedrin, with only very few exceptions.

We bear in mind that the resolution to sacrifice Jesus had already been taken. They first sought a false witness against him. Since this was throughout a private investigation, this witness could only have been sought from their own people. Hatred, fanaticism and unscrupulous exaggeration would readily misrepresent and distort certain of his sayings, or falsely impute others to him. But the witnesses contradicted themselves so grossly, or their testimony so notoriously broke down, that for very shame such trumped-up charges had to be abandoned. The majestic calm of his silence must have greatly contributed to this result. On directly false and contradictory testimony, it must be best not to cross-examine at all, but to leave the false witness to destroy itself. Abandoning this line of testimony, the priests next brought forward probably some of their own order, who on the first 'purgation of the Temple'[71] had been present when Jesus, in answer to the challenge for 'a sign' in evidence of his authority, had given them that mysterious 'sign' of the destruction and upraising of

---

70. John 18:31.
71. See John 2:13-20.

the Temple of his body.[72] They had quite misunderstood it at the time and its inclusion now as the ground of a criminal charge against Jesus must have been directly due to Caiaphas and Annas.

We remember that this had been the first time that Jesus had come into collision, not only with the Temple authorities but also with the avarice of the family of Annas. We can imagine how the incensed high priest would have challenged the conduct of the Temple officials, and how, in reply, he would have been told what they had attempted, and how Jesus had met them. Perhaps it was the only real enquiry that a man like Caiaphas would care to put forward about what Jesus said.

And here it was, in its grossly distorted form and it was actually brought forward as a criminal charge! Cleverly manipulated, the testimony of these witnesses might lead up to two charges: to show that Christ was a dangerous seducer of the people, whose claims might have led those who believed them to lay violent hands on the Temple. Also, the supposed assertion that he was able to build the Temple again within three days, might be made to imply divine or magical pretensions. No charge could be so effective as that of being a fanatical seducer of the ignorant populace, who might lead them on to wild, tumultuous acts. But this charge also broke down,[73] through the disagreement of the two witnesses whom the Mosaic Law required and who, according to Rabbinic ordinance, had to be separately questioned.

Only one thing now remained. Jesus knew it well, and so did Caiaphas. It was to put the question, which Jesus could not refuse to answer and which, once answered, must lead either to his acknowledgement or to his condemnation. As we suppose, the simple question was first addressed to Jesus, whether he was the Messiah? He replied by referring to the needlessness of such an enquiry since they had predetermined not to credit his claims. He had, only a few days before in the Temple, refused to discuss them.[74]

---

72. See Matthew 26:59-61.

73. Matthew 26:59-60.

74. Matthew 22:41-46.

Edersheim draws us into the unfolding drama:

> It was upon this that the High Priest, in the most solemn manner, adjured the True One by the Living God, whose Son he was, to say it, whether he were the Messiah and Divine – the two being so joined together, not in Jewish belief, but to express the claims of Jesus. No doubt or hesitation could here exist. Solemn, emphatic, calm, majestic, as before had been his silence, was now his speech. And his assertion of what he was, was conjoined with that of what God would show him to be, in his Resurrection and Sitting at the Right Hand of the Father, and of what they also would see, when he would come in those clouds of heaven that would break over their city and polity in the final storm of judgment.

They all heard it and, as the Law directed when blasphemy was spoken, the high priest rent both his outer and inner garment.[75] Jesus would neither explain, modify, nor retract his claims. They had all heard it; what use was there of witnesses? He had spoken *giddupha* (blaspheming). Then, turning to those assembled, he put to them the usual question which preceded the formal sentence of death. As given in the Rabbinical original, it is: "what think you gentlemen? And they answered, if for life, "For life!" and if for death, "For death.""

But the formal sentence of death which, if it had been a regular meeting of the Sanhedrin, must now have been spoken by the president, was not pronounced. On that night of terror, when all the hatred of humanity and the power of hell were unchained, even the falsehood of such malevolence could not lay any crime to Jesus' charge, nor yet any accusation be brought against him other than the misrepresentation of his symbolic words. What testimony to him this solitary false witness! Again, 'they all condemned him to be guilty of death' (Mark 14:64).

---

75. Matthew 26:65.

LUKE 22:63-65[76]

Edersheim would have been in tears as he recounts the shameful episode:

> It was after this meeting of the Sanhedrists had broken up, that the revolting insults and injuries were perpetrated on him by the guards and servants of Caiaphas. All now rose in combined rebellion against the Perfect Man. These insults, taunts, and blows which fell upon that lonely Sufferer, not defenceless, but undefending, not vanquished, but uncontending, not helpless, but majestic in voluntary self-submission for the highest purpose of love. So far as recorded, not a word escaped his Lips; not a complaint, nor murmur; nor utterance of indignant rebuke, nor sharp cry of deeply sensitive, pained nature. We have seen that, when Caiaphas and the Sanhedrists left the chamber, Jesus was left to the unrestrained licence of the attendants. Even the Jewish Law had it, that no 'prolonged death' (*Mithah Arikhta*) might be inflicted and that he who was condemned to death was not to be previously scourged. At last, they were weary of insult and smiting and the Sufferer was left alone, perhaps in the covered gallery, or at one of the windows that overlooked the court below.

MATTHEW 26:73-75; MARK 14:70-72; LUKE 22:59-62; JOHN 18:26-27

About one hour had passed since Peter's second denial had been interrupted by the arrival of the Sanhedrists. The chattering of Peter betrayed him. This one also was with Jesus the Nazarene; truly. He was of them – for he was also a Galilean! So spoke the bystanders; while, according to John, a fellow servant and kinsman of that Malchus, whose ear Peter, in his zeal, had cut off in Gethsemane, asserted that he actually recognised him. To one and all these declarations, Peter returned only a stronger denial, accompanying it this time with oaths to God. The echo

---

76. This seems out of sequence, but is according to Edersheim's original narrative.

of his words had scarcely died out when loud and shrill the second cock-crowing was heard.

Edersheim bares Peter's heart to the world:

He now remembered the words of warning prediction which the Lord had spoken. He looked up; and as he looked. He saw, how up there, just at that moment; the Lord turned round and looked upon him – yes, in all that assembly, upon Peter! His eyes spoke his Words, they searched down to the innermost depths of Peter's heart and broke them open. Forth they burst, the waters of conviction, of true shame, of heart-sorrow, of the agonies of self-condemnation and, bitterly weeping. He rushed from under those suns that had melted the ice of death and burnt into his heart – out from that cursed place of betrayal by Israel, by its High Priest – and even by the representative Disciple. Out he rushed into the night.

Chapter 52: The Roman Verdict

MATTHEW 27:1-2,11-14; MARK 15:1-5; LUKE 23:1-5

(Book 5: Chapter 14)

The pale grey light had passed into that of early morning, when the Sanhedrists once more assembled in the Palace of Caiaphas, to consider how the informal sentence might best be carried into effect. It was this, and not the question of Jesus' guilt, which was the focus of discussions on that early morning. The result of it was to 'bind' Jesus and hand him over as a criminal to Pilate, with the intention, if possible, not to frame any definite charge but, if this became necessary, to lay all the emphasis on the purely political, not the religious aspect of the claims of Jesus. That was the plan, anyway!

The Jewish leaders brought the bound Jesus to the Praetorium, the quarters occupied by the Roman governor. It is recorded that they who brought him would not themselves enter that forsaken place, 'lest they should be defiled; but that they might eat the passover' (John 18:28, KJV). It may have been about seven in the morning, probably even earlier, when Pilate went out to those who summoned him to dispense justice. His question to them seems to have startled and fazed them. Their deliberations had been private but Roman law demanded that they were in public. Accordingly, Pilate's first question was, what accusation had they brought against Jesus?

Their answer displays humiliation, ill-humour and an attempt at evasion. Pilate proposed that the Sanhedrists should try Jesus according to the Jewish Law. On the previous evening, the governor had given a Roman guard for the arrest of the prisoner and thinking also of the dream and warning of Pilate's wife (Matthew 27:19), a peculiar impression is conveyed to us. Tradition has given her the name Procula, while an apocryphal Gospel describes her as a convert to Judaism. What if the truth lay between these statements and Procula had not only been a proselyte but known about Jesus and spoken of him to Pilate on that evening? This would best explain his reluctance to condemn Jesus.

The onus was now on the Sanhedrists to formally charge him. It was, that Jesus had claimed to be the Christ, a king. By so saying they falsely attributed to Jesus their own political expectations concerning the Messiah. But even this is not all. They also claimed that he perverted the nation and forbade to give tribute to Caesar. The latter charge was so grossly unfounded that we can only regard it as in their mind a necessary conclusion of the premise that he claimed to be King.

Pilate now called Jesus and asked him: 'Are you the king of the Jews?' There is that mixture of contempt for all that was Jewish and of that general cynicism that could not believe in the existence of anything higher. Out of all that the Sanhedrists had said, Pilate took only this, that Jesus claimed to be a king. Jesus, who had not heard the charge of his accusers, now ignored it, in his desire to be merciful to Pilate. He asked Pilate whether the question was his own, or merely the repetition of what his Jewish accusers had told him.[77]

The governor quickly disowned any personal interest. How could he raise any such question? He was not a Jew, and the subject had no general interest. Jesus' own nation and its leader had handed him over as a criminal; what had he done? Pilate's answer left nothing else for him who, even in that supreme hour, thought only of others, rather than himself.

It was not, as Pilate had implied, a Jewish question. It was one of absolute truth; it concerned all people. The kingdom of Christ was not of this world at all, either Jewish or Gentile. Had it been otherwise, he would have led his followers in an uprising and not have become a prisoner of the Jews.

One thought only struck Pilate. 'You are a king, then!' (John 18:37). He was incapable of understanding the higher thought and truth. We mark in his words the same mixture of scoffing and misgiving. Pilate should now be in no doubt as to the nature of the kingdom. Jesus gave an explanation

---

77. John 18:34.

of his claims that a heathen such as Pilate could understand. His kingdom was 'not of this world' (John 18:36). Here was the truth!

But these words struck only a hollow void as they fell on Pilate. It was not merely cynicism, but utter despair of all that is higher which appears in his question, 'What is truth?' (John 18:38). He had understood Jesus, but it was not in him to respond to his appeal. He, who in reality was a stranger to 'the truth', could not sympathise with the grand aim of Jesus' life and work. But even the question of Pilate seems an admission, an implied homage to Christ.

JOHN 18:18-28

Edersheim continues:

> Then came a perfect hailstorm of accusations from the assembled Sanhedrists. As we picture it to ourselves, all this while the Christ stood near, perhaps behind Pilate, just within the portals of the Praetorium. And to all this clamour of charges he made no reply. It was as if the surging of the wild waves broke far beneath against the base of the rock, which, untouched, reared its head far aloft to the heavens. But as he stood in the calm silence of majesty, Pilate greatly wondered. Did this Man not even fear death; was he so conscious of innocence, so infinitely superior to those around and against him, or had he so far conquered Death, that he would not condescend to their words?

LUKE 23:6-12

And so, when he caught the name 'Galilee' as the scene of Jesus' labours, Pilate gladly seized on the prospect of switching the responsibility to another. Jesus was a Galilean and therefore belonged to the jurisdiction of King Herod. So, Jesus was now sent to Herod who had come for the feast to Jerusalem, living in the old Maccabean palace close to that of the high priest.

The opportunity now offered was welcome to Herod. It was a mark of reconciliation between himself and the Roman, and in a manner flattering to himself since the first step had been taken by the governor. In fact, Herod had long wished to see Jesus, of whom he had heard so many things. In that hour, curiosity and the hope of seeing some magic performances were the only feelings that moved the tetrarch. But in vain did he batter Jesus with questions. He was as silent with him as formerly against the virulent charges of the Sanhedrists.

MATTHEW 27:15-18

And so, Jesus was once more sent back to the Praetorium, to which Pilate had summoned the Sanhedrists and the people. The crowd was growing. It was not only to see what was about to happen but also to witness another spectacle, that of the release of a prisoner. For it seems to have been the custom that at the Passover the Roman governor released some notorious prisoner who had been condemned to death. A very significant custom of release, this, for which they now began to clamour.

This was also known by the Sanhedrists who mingled among them. For if the stream of popular sympathy might be diverted to Bar-Abbas, the doom of Jesus would be the more securely fixed. On the present occasion, it might be easier to influence the people, since Bar-Abbas was that kind of villain who, under the colourful pretence of political aspirations, committed robbery and other crimes. But these movements were strongly rooted in popular sympathy.

A strange name and figure, Bar-Abbas. That could scarcely have been his real name. It means 'son of the Father'. Was he a political antichrist? And why, if there had not been some connection between them, should Pilate have proposed the alternative of Jesus or Bar-Abbas, and not rather that of one of the two thieves who were actually crucified with Jesus? But when the governor, hoping for some popular sympathy, put this alternative to them on the ground that neither he nor yet Herod had found any crime in Jesus and would even have appeased them by offering to submit him to the cruel punishment of scourging, it was in vain.

MATTHEW 27:20-31; MARK 15:11-20; LUKE 23:18-25

It was now that Pilate sat down on the judgement seat. But before he could proceed, came that message from his wife about her dream, and the warning to have nothing to do 'with that innocent man'. An omen such as a dream and an appeal connected with it, especially in the circumstances of that trial, would powerfully impress a Roman. And for a few moments, it seemed as if the appeal to popular feeling on behalf of Jesus might have been successful. But once more the Sanhedrists prevailed.

Apparently, all who had been followers of Jesus had been scattered. None of them seems to have been there and if one or another feeble voice might have been raised for him, it was hushed in fear of the Sanhedrists. It was Bar-Abbas they wanted to set free. To the question – half-bitter, half-mocking – what they wished him to do with him whom their own leaders had in their accusation called 'King of the Jews', surged back, louder and louder, the terrible cry, 'Crucify him!'

That cry has since created a terrible echo through the centuries, right up to modern times. In vain, Pilate reasoned and appealed. Popular frenzy only grew as it was opposed. All reasoning having failed, Pilate had recourse to one last resort which, under ordinary circumstances, would have been effective.

When a judge rises from his seat and knowingly condemns an innocent man, surely no jury would persist in demanding a sentence of death. But in the present instance, there was even more. Although we find allusions to some such custom among the Romans, that which here took place was an essentially Jewish practice, which must have appealed the more forcibly to the Jews that it was done by Pilate. And, not only the practice, but the very words were Jewish.

They recalled not merely the rite prescribed in, for example, Deuteronomy 21:6 to mark the freedom from guilt of the elders of a city where untracked murder had been committed, but the very words of such Old Testament expressions as in 2 Samuel 3:28 and Psalm 26:6 and

Psalm 73:13. As the administrator of justice in Israel, Pilate must have been aware of this rite.

Could a judge, especially in the circumstances recorded, free himself from guilt? Certainly, he could not, but such conduct on the part of Pilate appears so utterly unusual that we can only account for it by the deep impression which Jesus had made upon him. All the more terrible would be the guilt of Jewish resistance. Something is overawing in Pilate's 'see ye to it' (KJV). The Mishnah tells us that, after the solemn washing of hands of the elders and their disclaimer of guilt, a priest responded with this prayer: 'Forgive it to Thy people Israel, whom Thou hast redeemed, O Lord, and lay not innocent blood upon Thy people Israel!'

Edersheim remarks:

> But here, in answer to Pilate's words, came back that deep, hoarse cry, 'His Blood be upon us,' and – God help us! – 'on our children!' Some thirty years later and on that very spot, was judgment pronounced against some of the best in Jerusalem; and among the 3,600 victims of the Governor's fury, of whom not a few were scourged and crucified right over against the Praetorium, were many of the noblest of the citizens of Jerusalem. A few years more and hundreds of crosses bore Jewish mangled bodies within sight of Jerusalem. And still have these wanderers seemed to bear, from century to century, and from land to land, that burden of blood; and still does it seem to weigh 'on us and our children.'

JOHN 19:1-16

Bar-Abbas was at once released. Jesus was handed over to the soldiers to be scourged and crucified, although final and formal judgement had not yet been pronounced. Indeed, Pilate seems to have hoped that the horrors of the scourging might still move the people to desist from the ferocious cry for the cross. For the same reason, we may also hope that the scourging was not inflicted with the same ferocity as in the case of Christian martyrs when, with the object of encouraging them to incriminate others, or else recantation, the scourge of leather thongs was loaded with lead, or armed with spikes and bones, which lacerated the back and the chest and face, until the victim sometimes fell down before the judge a bleeding mass of torn flesh.

But, however modified, and without repeating the harrowing realism of a Cicero, scourging was the terrible introduction to crucifixion – 'the intermediate death'. Stripped of his clothes, his hands tied and back bent, the victim would be bound to a column or stake, in front of the Praetorium.

The scourging ended, the soldiers would hastily cast upon him his upper garments and lead him back into the Praetorium. Here they called the whole cohort together and the silent, faint Sufferer became the object of their coarse jesting. They tore the clothes from his bleeding body and in mockery clothed him in scarlet or purple. For a crown, they wound together thorns and for a sceptre, they placed in his hand a reed.[78] Then alternately, in mock proclamation, they hailed him King, or worshipped him as God, and smote him or heaped on him other indignities.

Such a spectacle might well have brought some sympathy. And so Pilate had hoped, when, at his bidding, Jesus came forth from the Praetorium, garbed as a mock-King and the governor presented him to the populace in words which the Church has ever since treasured, 'Behold the man!' (KJV).

But, so far from appeasing, the sight only incited to fury the chief priests and their subordinates. This man before them provided the occasion that on this Passover day a Roman dared in Jerusalem itself to insult their deepest feeling and mock their most cherished Messianic hopes! 'Crucify! Crucify!' resounded from all sides. Once more Pilate appealed to them when, unwittingly and unwillingly, it brought this from the people, that Jesus had claimed to be the Son of God. If nothing else, what light it casts on the mode in which Jesus had borne himself amid those tortures and

---

78. Matthew 27:29, KJV.

insults, that this statement of the Jews filled Pilate with fear and led him to talk with Jesus within the Praetorium.

The impression which had been made at the first and been deepened all along had now passed into the terror of superstition. His first question to Jesus was, where did he come from? And when, as was most fitting, Jesus returned no answer, the feelings of the Roman became only the more intense. Would he not speak; did he not know that he had absolute power 'to free ... or to crucify' him?

Pilate was no imposter. No ordinary man. He had the power of life and death over him. He knew what was the right thing to do, but his cynicism and disbelief thwarted him. Yet he was still moved to release Jesus.

But proportionately, the louder and fiercer cry of the Jews was for his blood, until they threatened to implicate Pilate himself in the charge of rebellion against Caesar if he persisted in showing mercy. Such danger, a Pilate would never face. He sat down once more in the judgment seat, outside the Praetorium, in the place called 'Pavement' (*Gabbatha*). And at the close Pilate once more in mockery presented to them Jesus: 'Behold your King!' (KJV).

Have ever more solemn words been expressed, as Edersheim pronounces judgement:

Once more they called for his Crucifixion – and, when again challenged, the chief priests burst into the cry, which preceded Pilate's final sentence, to be presently executed, 'We have no king but Caesar!' With this cry Judaism was, in the person of its representatives, guilty of denial of God, of blasphemy, of apostasy. It committed suicide; and, ever since, has its dead body been carried in show from land to land, and from century to century: to be dead, and to remain dead, until he come a second time, who is the Resurrection and the Life.

Chapter 53: Crucifixion

MATTHEW 27:31-43; MARK 15:20-32; LUKE 23:26-38; JOHN 19:16-24

(Book 5: Chapter 15)

The terrible crime of slaying their Messiah-King rests, sadly, on Israel. Once more was he unrobed and robed. The purple robe was torn from his wounded body, the crown of thorns from his bleeding brow. He was led forth to execution. Only about two hours and a half had passed since the time that he had first stood before Pilate when the melancholy procession reached Golgotha.

The terrible preparations were soon made; the hammer, the nails, the cross, the very food for the soldiers who were to watch under each cross. Four soldiers would be detailed for each cross, the whole being under the command of a centurion. As always, the cross was borne to the execution by him who was to suffer on it, perhaps his arms bound to it with cords. But there is happily no evidence – rather, every indication to the contrary – that, according to ancient custom, the neck of the sufferer was fastened within the *patibulum*, two horizontal pieces of wood, fastened at the end, to which the hands were bound.

Ordinarily, the procession was headed by the centurion, who proclaimed the nature of the crime and carried a white, wooden board, on which it was written. Jesus came forth bearing his cross. He was followed by the two 'thieves'. These two, also, would bear his own cross and probably be attended each by four soldiers. Crucifixion was not a Jewish punishment and even Herod, with all cruelty, did not resort to this mode of execution. Nor was it employed by the Romans until after the time of Caesar when, with the fast-increasing cruelty of punishments, it became fearfully common in the provinces.

This cruel punishment characterises the domination of Rome in Judea under every governor. During the last siege of Jerusalem, hundreds of crosses appeared daily, until there seemed not sufficient room nor wood for them, and the soldiers diversified their horrible amusement by new modes of crucifixion. The crucifixion of Israel's King put an end to the punishment of the cross, and instead, made the cross the symbol of humanity, civilisation, progress, peace and love.

In common with most abominations of the ancient world, whether in religion or life, crucifixion was of Phoenician origin, although Rome adopted and improved on it. The usual modes of execution among the Jews were strangulation, beheading, burning and stoning. In all ordinary circumstances, the rabbis were most reluctant to pronounce a sentence of death. The place where criminals were stoned (*Beth haSeqilah*) was on an elevation about 11ft high, from where the criminal was thrown down by the first witness. If he had not died by the fall, the second witness would throw a large stone on his heart as he lay. If not yet lifeless, the rest of the people would stone him.

At a distance of 6ft from the place of execution the criminal was undressed, only the covering absolutely necessary for decency being left. In the case of Jesus, we have reason to think that, while the mode of punishment to which he was subjected was un-Jewish, every concession would be made to Jewish custom, and therefore we thankfully believe that on the cross he was spared the indignity of naked exposure.

And so, the procession moved on towards Golgotha. Not only the location, but even the name of that which appeals so strongly to every Christian heart, is a matter of controversy. The name cannot have been derived from the skulls which lay about, since such exposure would have been unlawful, and must have been due to the skull-like shape and appearance of the place. Accordingly, the name is commonly explained as the Greek form of the Aramaic *Gulgalta* or the Hebrew *Gulgoleth*, which means a skull. Certain it is that Golgotha was outside the gate and near the city. In all likelihood, it was the usual place of execution. Lastly, we know that it was situated near gardens, where there were tombs and close to the highway. This all points to the north of Jerusalem.

From the ancient Palace of Herod, the procession descended and probably passed through the gate in the first wall and so into the busy quarter of Acra. As it proceeded, the numbers who followed from the Temple, from the dense business quarter through which it moved, increased. Shops, bazaars and markets were, indeed, closed on the holy feast day. But quite a crowd of people would come out to line the streets and to follow; and, especially, women, leaving their festive preparations, raised loud laments, not in spiritual recognition of Christ's claims, but in pity and sympathy.

Jesus bore his cross up to the last gate which led from the suburb towards the place of execution. Then his strength gave way under it and a man was ordered to help him. This was Simon, who was coming from the opposite direction, one from that large colony of Jews which, as we know, had settled in Cyrene. He seems to have been well known, at least afterwards, in the Church – and his sons Alexander and Rufus even more so than he.

While the cross was laid on the unwilling Simon, the women who had followed closed around, raising their cries. At his entrance into Jerusalem, Jesus had wept over the daughters of Jerusalem; as he left it for the last time, they wept over him. But far different were the reasons for his tears from theirs of mere pity.

It was nine o'clock when the sad procession reached Golgotha and the even sadder preparations for the crucifixion commenced. The punishment was invented to make death as painful and as lingering as the power of human endurance could bear. First, the upright wood was planted in the ground. It was not high and probably the feet of the sufferer were not above 1 or 2ft from the ground. Thus, could the conversation described in the Gospels take place between him and others. Next, the transverse wood was placed on the ground and the sufferer laid on it with his arms extended, drawn up and bound to it.

Then a strong, sharp nail was driven, first into the right, then into the left hand. Next, the sufferer was drawn up using ropes, perhaps ladders;

the transverse either bound or nailed to the upright, with a rest or support for the body (*sedile*) fastened on it. Lastly, the feet were extended and either one nail hammered into each or a larger piece of iron through the two.

And so might the crucified hang for hours, even days, in the unutterable anguish of suffering, until consciousness at last failed. It was a merciful Jewish practice to give to those who were led to execution a draught of strong wine mixed with myrrh to deaden consciousness. This charitable office was performed at the cost of, if not by, an association of women in Jerusalem. That draught was offered to Jesus when he reached Golgatha. But having tasted it, he would not drink it. Edersheim describes his inner struggle:

> No man could take his Life from him; he had power to lay it down and to take it up again. Nor would he here yield to the ordinary weakness of our human nature; nor suffer and die as if it had been a necessity, not a voluntary self-surrender. He would meet Death, even in his sternest and fiercest mood and conquer by submitting to the full. And so was he nailed to his Cross, which was placed between, probably somewhat higher than, those of the two criminals crucified with him.

One thing only still remained; to affix to his cross the so-called 'title' (*titulus*) on which was written the charge on which he had been condemned. It had evidently been drawn up under the direction of Pilate. It was trilingual: in Latin, Greek and Aramaic. It seems only natural that the fullest and, to the Jews, most offensive description should have been in Aramaic, which all could read.

We imagine that the Sanhedrists had originally no intention of doing anything so un-Jewish as not only to gaze at the sufferings of the crucified but to even mock him in his agony, or perhaps they had not intended going to Golgotha at all. But when they found that Pilate had organised the sign in Aramaic, some of them hastened to the place of crucifixion and mingling with the crowd, sought to incite their jeers, to prevent any deeper impression which the significant words of the inscription might have produced.

Before nailing him to the cross, the soldiers parted his clothes among themselves. There was, as John states, first a division into four parts – one to each of the soldiers – of such garments that were of nearly the same value. The headgear, the outer cloak, the girdle and the sandals, would differ little in cost. But the question of which of them was to belong to each of the soldiers would naturally be decided, as the Gospel writers inform us, by lot. But, besides these four articles of dress, there was the seamless woven inner garment, by far the most valuable of all and for which, as it could not be partitioned without being destroyed, they would specially cast lots.

It was when they nailed him to the cross and parted his garments that he spoke the first of the so-called Seven Words: 'Father, forgive them, for they know not what they do' (KJV). Even the reference in this prayer to 'what they do' (not in the past, nor future) points to the soldiers as the primary, though certainly not the sole object, of the Saviour's prayer. The first and the last of his utterances begin with 'Father', so does he show by the unbrokenness of his faith and fellowship the real spiritual victory which he has won. Has this prayer of Jesus been answered? We dare not doubt it; we perceive it in some measure in those blessings which have fallen upon Gentile unbelievers and have left also to Israel, even in its ignorance, 'a remnant according to the election of grace' (Romans 11:5, KJV).

And now began the real agonies of the cross – physical, mental and spiritual. It was the weary, unrelieved waiting, as thickening darkness gradually gathered around. Before sitting down to their melancholy watch over the crucified, the soldiers would refresh themselves with cheap wine after their exertion in nailing Jesus to the cross, then lifting it up and fixing it. As they swigged it, they drank to him in their coarse brutality and mockingly came to him, asking him to respond.

Edersheim is blunt in his condemnations:

> What is the most galling is the unutterable abasement of the
> Leaders of Israel – their moral suicide as regarded Israel's hope
> and spiritual existence. There, on that Cross, hung he, who at least
> embodied that grand hope of the nation; who, even on their own
> showing, suffered to the extreme for that idea, and yet renounced it
> not, but clung fast to it in unshaken confidence; One, to whose Life
> or even teaching no objection could be offered, save that of this
> grand idea. And yet, when it came to them in the ribald mockery
> of these heathen soldiers, it evoked no other or higher thoughts
> in them; and they had the indescribable baseness of joining in the
> jeer at Israel's great hope, and of leading the popular chorus in it!

'He saved others ... but he can't save himself! He's the king of Israel! Let
him now come down now from the cross, and we will believe in him.'
These are the words of the Sanhedrists, and they seem to respond to those
of the soldiers, as reported by Matthew, and to carry them further.

Now, at the close of his Messianic work, the tempter suggested, in the
challenge of the Sanhedrists, that Jesus had suffered absolute defeat and
that God had publicly disowned the trust which the Christ had put in
him. 'He trusts in God. Let God rescue him now if he wants him.'

Here, as in the temptation in the wilderness, the words misapplied
were those of Holy Scripture – in the present instance, those of Psalm
22:8. The derision of the Sanhedrists under the cross was not entirely
spontaneous but had a special motive. The place of crucifixion was close
to the great road which led from the north to Jerusalem. On that feast day,
many would pass in and out of the city and the crowd would naturally
be intrigued by the spectacle of the three crosses. Equally naturally they
would have been impressed by the title of Christ over the cross. The
words, describing the Sufferer as 'The King of the Jews' might, when

taken in connection with what was known of Jesus, have raised the most dangerous questions.

The Sanhedrists were keen to prevent this by turning the crowd's attention in a totally different direction, through their taunts. Their self-condemnation was building and building.

MATTHEW 27:44; MARK 15:32; LUKE 23:39-43

The thieves on the cross joined in the derision of the Sanhedrists and the people. Perhaps they felt that any sympathy or possible alleviation of their sufferings might best be achieved by joining in the scorn of the leaders? But Luke also records a vital difference between the two thieves on the cross. The impenitent thief takes up the jeer of the Sanhedrists: 'Aren't you the Messiah? Save yourself and us!' The utterance of the 'penitent' thief was to criticise his comrade. In that terrible hour, amid the tortures of slow death, did not the fear of God creep over him, at least so far as to prevent his joining in the vile jeers of those who insulted the dying agonies of the Sufferer?

This man did feel the 'fear' of God and now learned the new lesson in which the fear of God was truly the 'beginning of wisdom'.[79] And, once he gave place to this moral element and under the fear of God corrected his comrade, this new moral decision became to him, as so often, the beginning of spiritual life. Rapidly he now passed into the light, and onwards and upwards: 'Jesus, remember me when you come into your kingdom.' The response? 'Truly I tell you, today you will be with me in paradise.' This was the Second Utterance from the cross.

JOHN 19:25-27

Some hours – probably two – had passed since Jesus had been nailed to the cross. We now trace the movements of John. When the Saviour was nailed to the cross, he seems once more to have returned to the city, this time, to bring back with him those special women who we now

---

79. Psalm 111:10.

find standing close to the cross. A more delicate, tender, loving service could not have been rendered than this. Alone, of all the disciples, he is there, not afraid to be near Jesus, in the palace of the high priest, before Pilate and now under the cross. And alone he renders to Jesus this tender service of bringing the women and Mary to the cross and to them the protection of his guidance and company. He loved Jesus best and it was fitting that to his manliness and affection should be entrusted this unspeakable privilege. The narrative leaves the impression that with the beloved disciple these four women were standing close to the cross: the mother of Jesus, the sister of his mother, Mary the wife of Clopas and Mary Magdalene.

It seems as if John had fulfilled to the letter the Lord's command, 'Here is your mother' and literally from that very hour taken her to his own home. If we are right in this supposition, then, in the absence of John, who led Mary away from that scene of horror, the other three women would withdraw to a distance, where we find them at the end, 'beholding afar off' (Matthew 27:55, KJV) and now joined by others also, who had loved and followed Jesus.

MATTHEW 27:45-56; MARK 15:33-41; LUKE 23:44-49; JOHN 19:28-30

Now at last all that concerned the earthward aspect of his mission, so far as it had to be done on the cross, was ended. He had prayed for those who had nailed him to it, in ignorance of what they did; he had given the comfort of assurance to the penitent thief, who had owned his glory, and he had made the last provision of love for those nearest to him. In a sense that which touched his human nature had been fully met. He had done with the human aspect of his work and with earth.

For three hours had the Saviour hung on the cross. It was midday. And now the sun was covered in darkness from the sixth to the ninth hour. No purpose can be served by attempting to trace the source of this darkness. It could not have been an eclipse, since it was the time of the full moon; nor can we place reliance on the later reports on this subject by certain writers. It seems natural to regard the occurrence of the event as supernatural, while the event itself might have been brought about by natural causes; and among these, we must call special attention to the earthquake in which this darkness terminated.

The language seems to imply that this darkness extended, not only over the land of Israel but also over the inhabited earth. The expression must, of course, not be pressed to its full literality, but explained as meaning that it extended far beyond Judea and to other lands. The three hours' darkness was a time when Jesus, also, entered into darkness: body, soul and spirit. Into this fathomless depth of the mystery of his sufferings, we dare not enter. It was of the body; yet not of the body only, but of physical life. And it was of the soul and spirit; yet not of them alone, but in their conscious relation to humanity and to God. And it was not of the human only in Christ but also in its unbreakable connection with the divine.

We allow Edersheim to describe what happened next:

The increasing, nameless agonies of the Crucifixion were deepening into the bitterness of death. All nature shrinks from death and there is a physical horror of the separation between body and soul which, as a purely natural phenomenon, is in every instance only overcome and that only by a higher principle. In those dark hours there was the sense of forsakenness from man and his own isolation from man; so, also, had the intense silence of God, the withdrawal of God, the sense of his God-forsakenness and absolute loneliness.

We dare not here speak of punitive suffering, but of forsakenness and loneliness. Yet another element must be taken into account. Christ on the Cross suffered for man; he offered himself a sacrifice; he died for our sins, that, as death was the wages of sin, so he died as the Representative of man. He obtained for man 'eternal redemption', having given his Life 'a ransom for many.' For, men were redeemed with the precious Blood of Christ, as of a Lamb without blemish and without spot and Christ gave himself for us, that he might redeem us from all iniquity.

This sacrifice, vicarious, expiatory, and redemptive character of his Death, if it does not explain to us, yet helps us to understand, Christ's sense of God-forsakenness in the supreme moment of the Cross; if one might so word it, the passive character of his activeness through the active character of his passiveness. It was this combination of the Old Testament idea of sacrifice and of the Old Testament ideal of willing suffering as the Servant of Jehovah, now fulfilled in Christ, which found its fullest expression in the language of Psalm 22.

It was fitting that the willing suffering of the true Sacrifice should now find vent in its opening words; 'my God, my God, why hast Thou forsaken Me?' – Eli, Eli, lema sabachthanei? These words, cried with a loud voice at the close of the period of extreme agony, marked the climax and the end of this suffering of Christ, of which the utmost event was the withdrawal of God and the felt loneliness of the Sufferer.

It can scarcely have been a minute or two from the time that the cry from Psalm 22 marked the high point of his agony. The words 'I thirst' (KJV) emphasised the human aspect of the suffering, indicating that the other and more terrible aspect of sin-bearing and God-forsakenness had passed.

To us, therefore, this seems the beginning of the end. He now could and did yield himself to the mere physical wants of his body. One of the soldiers, moved by sympathy, now ran to offer some slight refreshment to the sufferer by filling a sponge with the rough wine of the soldiers and putting it to his lips, having first fastened it to the stem of the caper (*hyssop*), which is said to grow to the height of even 2 or 3ft.

The two last 'sayings' of the Saviour now followed in rapid succession; first, that with a loud voice, which expressed it, that the work given him to do, as far as concerned his Passion, was *finished* and then, that in the words of Psalm 31:5, in which he commended his Spirit into the hands of the Father.

Then 'he bowed the head and gave up his spirit'. And now a shudder ran through nature, as its Sun had set. As the first token, it records the rending of the Temple veil in two from the top down to the bottom; as the second, the quaking of the earth, the rending of the rocks and the opening of the graves. Although most writers have regarded this as indicating the strictly chronological succession, there is nothing in the text to bind us to such a conclusion. Thus, while the rending of the veil is recorded first, as being the most significant token to Israel, it may have been connected to the earthquake, although this alone might scarcely account for the tearing of so heavy a veil from the top to the bottom.

On those who stood under the cross and near it, did all that was witnessed make the deepest and most lasting impression. Among them, we specially mark the centurion under whose command the soldiers had been. Many a scene of horror must he have witnessed in those sad times of the crucifixion, but none like this. Only one conclusion could force itself on his mind. It was that which, we cannot doubt, had made its impression on his heart and conscience. Jesus was not what the Jews, his infuriated enemies, had described him. He was what he professed to be, what his bearing on the cross and his death marked him to be: 'righteous' and hence, 'the Son of God'. From this there was only a step to personal allegiance to him and we may possibly owe to him some of those details which the Gospels have preserved.

JOHN 19:31-37

The brief spring day was verging towards the evening of the Sabbath. In general, the Law ordered that the body of a criminal should not be left hanging unburied overnight. Perhaps in ordinary circumstances, the Jews might not have appealed so confidently to Pilate as actually to ask him to shorten the sufferings of those on the cross, since the punishment of crucifixion often lasted not only for hours but days, before death ensued. But here was a special occasion. The Sabbath about to open was a 'high day' – it was both a Sabbath and the second Passover Day, which was regarded as in every respect equally sacred with the first.

And what the Jews now proposed to Pilate was, indeed, a shortening, but not in any sense mitigation, of the punishment. Sometimes there was added to the punishment of crucifixion that of breaking the bones (*crurifragium*) using a club or hammer, making it difficult to raise themselves on their arms or legs to breathe. This would not itself bring immediate death, but the breaking of the bones was always followed by a *coup de grâce*, by the sword, lance, or stroke, which immediately put an end to what remained of life. Thus, the breaking of the bones was a sort of increase of punishment, by way of compensation for its shortening by the final stroke that followed.

Perhaps it was when John consulted with Joseph of Arimathea, with Nicodemus, or the two Marys, measures for the burying of Christ, that he learned of the Jewish deputation to Pilate, followed it to Praetorium, and then watched how it was all carried out on Golgotha. He records how Pilate agreed to the Jewish demand and gave directions for the *crurifragium* and permission for the removal of the dead bodies, which otherwise might have been left to hang, till putrescence or birds of prey had destroyed them.

When, in the *crurifragium*, the soldiers had broken the bones of the two thieves and then came to the cross of Jesus, they found that he was dead already, and so 'Not one of his bones will be broken'. Had it been otherwise, the Scripture concerning the Passover Lamb, as well as that concerning the righteous suffering servant of Jehovah,[80] would have been broken.

The prophecies of Zechariah foretold how, on the day of Israel's final deliverance and national conversion, God would pour out the spirit of grace and of supplication and as 'They shall look on him whom they

---

80. Isaiah 53:1-3.

pierced' (KJV). The soldiers, on finding Jesus dead, broke not one of his bones, yet, as it was necessary to make sure of his death, one of them, with a lance, 'pierced Jesus' side' with a wound so deep that Thomas would afterwards thrust his hand into his side.[81]

MATTHEW 27:57-61; MARK 15:42-47; LUKE 23:50-56; JOHN 19:38-42

One other scene remains to be recorded. A strange application came to Pilate. It was from one apparently well known, a man not only of wealth and standing, whose noble bearing corresponded to his social condition and who was known as a just and a good man. Joseph of Arimathea was a Sanhedrist, but he had not consented either to the decision or the deed of his colleagues. It must have been generally known that he was one of those who 'waited for the kingdom of God'.

But he had advanced beyond what that expression implies. 'Secretly for fear of the Jews' (KJV), he was a disciple of Jesus. He went to Pilate and asked for the body of Jesus. Joseph, now no longer a secret disciple, but bold in his reverent love, would show the greatest respect to the dead body of his Master. And the divinely ordered sequence of circumstances not only aided his purpose but invested all with deepest symbolic significance. It was Friday afternoon, and the Sabbath was drawing near. No time, therefore, was to be lost, if due honour were to be paid to the body.

Pilate gave it to Joseph of Arimathea. Such was within his power, and a favour not infrequently accorded in like circumstances. But two things must have powerfully impressed the Roman governor and deepened his former thoughts about Jesus: first, that the death on the cross had taken place so rapidly, a circumstance on which he personally questioned the centurion, and then the bold appearance and request of such a man as Joseph of Arimathea.

---

81. John 20:25.

The proximity of the holy Sabbath and the consequent need of haste may have suggested or determined the proposal of Joseph to lay the body of Jesus in his own unused rock-hewn tomb. Joseph, with those who attended him, wrapped the sacred body in a clean linen cloth and rapidly carried it to the rock-hewn tomb in the garden close by.

Such a tomb (*meartha*) had niches (*kukhin*), where the dead were laid. There was a 'court', 9ft square, where ordinarily the bier was deposited, and its bearers gathered to do the last offices for the dead. There we suppose Joseph to have carried the body and then the last scene to have taken place. For now, another had come. The same boldness which had brought Joseph to open confession, also motivated that other Sanhedrist, Nicodemus. He now came, bringing 'a mixture of myrrh and aloes', in the fragrant mixture well known to the Jews for the purposes of anointing or burying.

It was in the court of the tomb that the hasty embalmment took place. None of Jesus' former disciples seems to have taken part in the burial. John may have withdrawn to bring tidings to and to comfort Mary; the others also, that had stood afar off, beholding,[82] appear to have left. Only a few faithful ones, notably among them Mary Magdalene and the other Mary, the mother of Joses, stood over against the tomb, watching at some distance where and how the body of Jesus was laid. It would scarcely have been following Jewish manners if these women had mingled more closely with the two Sanhedrists and their attendants. From where they stood, they could only have had a dim view of what passed within the court and this may explain how, on their return, they 'prepared spices and ointments' (KJV) for honouring Jesus after the Sabbath was past.

For, it is of the greatest importance to remember that haste characterised all that was done. It seems as if the 'clean linen cloth' in which the body had been wrapped was now torn into swathes, into which the body, limb by limb, was now bound, no doubt, between layers of myrrh and aloes,

---

82. See Matthew 27:55, KJV.

with the head wrapped in a napkin. And so they laid him to rest in the niche of the rock-hewn new tomb.

And as they went out, they rolled, as was the custom, a 'great stone' (KJV) – the *golel* – to close the entrance to the tomb, probably leaning against it for support, as was the practice, a smaller stone, the so-called *dopheq*. It would be where the one stone was laid against the other that on the next day, Sabbath though it was, the Jewish authorities would have affixed the seal, so that the slightest disturbance might become apparent.

MATTHEW 27:62-66
We read:

> The next day, the one after Preparation Day, the chief priests and the Pharisees went to Pilate. 'Sir,' they said, 'we remember that while he was still alive that deceiver said, "After three days I will rise again." So give the order for the tomb to be made secure until the third day. Otherwise, his disciples may come and steal the body and tell the people that he has been raised from the dead. This last deception will be worse than the first.'
>
> 'Take a guard,' Pilate answered. 'Go, make the tomb as secure as you know how.' So they went and made the tomb secure by putting a seal on the stone and posting the guard.

But was there really a need for it? Did they, who had spent what remained of daylight to prepare spices to anoint the dead Christ, expect his body to be removed, or did they expect – perhaps in their sorrow even think of his word, 'I will rise again'?

Edersheim leaves us dangling with a question:

> But on that holy Sabbath, when the Sanhedrists were thinking of how to make sure of the dead Christ, what were the thoughts of Joseph of Arimathaea and Nicodemus, of Peter and John, of the

other disciples, and especially of the loving women who only waited for the first streak of Easter-light to do their last service of love? What were their thoughts of God – what of Christ – what of the Words he had spoken, the deeds he had wrought, the salvation he had come to bring, and the Kingdom of heaven which he was to open to all believers?

Chapter 54: Resurrection

(Book 5: Chapter 16)

The history of the life of Jesus closes with a miracle as great as that at its beginning. The one casts light upon the other. If he was what the Gospels claim him to be, he must have been born of a virgin, without sin, and he must have risen from the dead. If the story of his birth is true, we can believe that of his resurrection; if that of his resurrection be true, we can believe that of his birth. Although the latter was incapable of strict historical proof, his resurrection demanded and was capable of the fullest historical evidence.

The apostles and disciples grieved over the loss of Jesus because it seemed like the enemy had won! Yet his death could not have been totally unexpected if they were to remember the many predictions he had given earlier. Jesus had spoken of this ever since the Transfiguration, despite their resistance and reluctance to believe. He had also referred to his resurrection, but they had trouble grasping the concept of a literal resurrection of that crucified body in a glorified state.

Jesus had clearly taught them all this during his ministry on earth, but there was nothing more effective than 'show and tell'. It was the event itself that would soon teach them. It would have been impossible really to teach something as unprecedented as the resurrection, except by witnessing it!

Here is a question to be faced. Considering their previous state of mind and the absence of any motive, how are we to account for the change of mind on the part of the disciples about the resurrection? There was no doubt that they came to believe in the resurrection as a historical fact. It would form the basis of all their preaching of the kingdom, as it would be for the apostle Paul, a bitter enemy of Jesus until his dramatic conversion.

Indeed, the world would not have been converted to a dead Jewish Jesus, although his intimate disciples might have continued to love his memory. But they preached everywhere, first and foremost, the resurrection from the dead! In the language of Paul: 'If Christ be not risen, then is our preaching vain, and your faith is also vain. Yea, and we are found false witnesses of God ... ye are yet in your sins' (1 Corinthians 15:14-17, KJV).

Edersheim continues:

> A dead Christ might have been a teacher and wonder-worker and remembered and loved as such. But only a Risen and Living Christ could be the Saviour, the Life, and the Life-Giver, and as such preached to all men. And of this most blessed truth we have the fullest and most unquestionable evidence. We can, therefore, implicitly yield ourselves to the impression of these narratives, and, still more, to the realisation of that most sacred and blessed fact. This is the foundation of the Church, the inscription on the banner of her armies, the strength and comfort of every Christian heart, and the grand hope of humanity.

MATTHEW 28:1-10; MARK 16:1-11; LUKE 24:1-12; JOHN 20:1-18
(Book 5: Chapter 17)

The grey dawn was streaking the sky when they who had so lovingly watched his burial were making their lonely way to the rock-hewn tomb in the garden. It was the first day of the week; according to Jewish reckoning, the third day from his death. The narrative implies that the Sabbath's rest had delayed their visit to the tomb, but we can believe that the relatives and friends of the deceased were in the habit of going to the grave up to the fourth day (when presumably corruption was supposed to begin), to make sure that those laid there were *really dead*.

Whether or not there were two groups of women who started from different places to meet at the tomb, the most prominent figure among them was Mary Magdalene. She seems to have reached the grave and, seeing the great stone that had covered its entrance rolled away, hastily judged that the body of the Lord had been removed. Wasting no time, she ran back to inform Peter and John of the fact.

The Gospel writer here explains that there had been a great earthquake and that the angel of the Lord, appearing as 'lightning' and in a brilliant white garment, had 'rolled back the stone and sat on it'. Then the guards, frightened by what they heard and saw and especially by the heavenly presence and power of the angel, had been seized with mortal fear. They had remembered the events connected with the crucifixion and must have been on a knife-edge with various scenarios haunting their thoughts as they stood guard over that tomb that night.

We suppose the event itself to have taken place after the resurrection of Christ, in the early dawn, while the women were on their way to the tomb. The earthquake cannot have been one in the ordinary sense, but a shaking of the place, when the Lord of life reclaimed his glorified body and the lightning-like angel descended from heaven to roll away the stone.

While Mary rushed, probably by another road, to the house of Peter and John, the other women also had reached the tomb, either separately or together. They must have wondered about this huge stone blocking the tomb until it was shown to them that this difficulty *no longer existed*. They now entered the tomb. Here the appearance of the angel filled them with fear. But the heavenly Messenger calmed them; he told them that Jesus was not there, nor yet any longer dead, but risen, as indeed he had foretold in Galilee to his disciples. Finally, he urged them to tell the disciples the message that, as Jesus had already told them, they were to meet him in Galilee. This was a connection between these wonderfully unravelling events with the familiar past.

And when the women, dazed and confused, obeyed the command to go in and examine for themselves the now empty niche in the tomb, they saw two angels – probably as Mary Magdalene afterwards saw them – one at the head, the other at the feet, where the body of Jesus had lain. They waited no longer, but rushed away, without speaking to anyone, to tell the disciples of things of which they could not even yet grasp the full importance.

Meanwhile, Mary had run to the lodgings of Peter and to that of John. Her startling story encouraged them to go at once. John, as the younger, outran Peter. Reaching the tomb first and 'stooping down' (KJV), he saw the linen clothes. If reverence and awe prevented John from entering the tomb, his impulsive companion, who arrived immediately after him, thought of nothing else than the immediate and full clearing up of the mystery.

As he entered the tomb, Peter saw the linen swathes that had been bound around Jesus' head. There was no sign of hurry, but all was orderly, leaving the impression of one who had calmly removed all of what no longer was of use to him!

Peter now believed in his heart that the Master was risen, for until then they had not yet figured out from Holy Scripture the knowledge that he must rise again. And this also is most instructive. It was not the belief previously derived from Scripture that the Christ was to rise from the dead which led to expectancy of it, but the evidence that he had risen which led them to the knowledge of what Scripture taught on the subject.

The two apostles returned to their home, either feeling that nothing more could be learned at the tomb or to wait for further teaching and guidance. But the love of Mary Magdalene drove her on; she could not rest satisfied while there was doubt over the fate of his body. It must be remembered that she knew only of the empty tomb. For a time, she agonised, then, as she wiped away her tears, she stopped to take one more look into the tomb, which she thought empty. It was no longer empty.

At the head and feet, where the sacred body had lain, were seated two angels in white. Their question, so deeply true from their knowledge that Jesus had risen: 'Woman, why are you crying?' This seems to have come upon Mary with such overpowering suddenness that, without being able to realise – perhaps in the semi-gloom – who it was that had asked it, she spoke, only to declare, 'They have taken my Lord away ... and I don't know where they have put him.'

As she spoke, she became conscious of another presence close to her. Quickly turning around, she gazed on one whom she regarded as the gardener. A moment's pause and he spoke her name. She had not known his appearance, just as the others did not know at first, so unlike, and yet so like, was the glorified body to that which they had known. But she could not mistake the voice, especially when it spoke to her, and spoke her name.

As in her name, she recognised his name, the rush of old feeling came over her and with the familiar 'Rabboni!' – my master – she would have grasped him. Was it the unconscious impulse to take hold of the precious treasure which she had thought forever lost; the unconscious attempt to make sure that it was not merely an apparition of Jesus from heaven but the real Christ in his flesh on earth; or a gesture of veneration, the beginning of such acts of worship as her heart prompted? Probably all these, and yet in her state of happy confusion she was not at that moment distinctly conscious of either or of any of these feelings!

But to them all, there was one answer and that included a command: 'Touch me not; for I am not yet ascended to my Father' (KJV). Not the Jesus appearing from heaven – for he had not yet ascended to the Father.

MARK 16:12-13; LUKE 24:13-35

It was the early afternoon of that spring day perhaps soon after the early meal when two men from the group of disciples left the city. Their narrative allows us deeply interesting glimpses into the circle of the Church in those first days. The impression conveyed to us is of utter bewilderment, in which only some things stood out unshaken and firm; love for the Person of Jesus; love among the brethren; mutual confidence and fellowship together with a dim hope of something yet to come – if not Christ in his kingdom, yet some manifestation of it.

The 'apostolic circle' seems broken up into units. Even the two chief apostles, Peter and John, are only 'certain of them which were with us' (KJV). Jesus 'was a prophet, powerful in word and deed before God and all the people'. But their rulers had crucified him. What was to be their new relation to Jesus? What to their rulers? And what of the great hope of the kingdom, which they had connected with him?

Thus, they were unclear on that very resurrection day even as to his mission and work; unclear as to the past, the present and the future. What need for the resurrection and for the teaching which the Risen One alone could bring! These two people had on that very day been in communication with Peter and John. It seems that no one had really pieced the whole story together yet.

The women had come to tell of the empty tomb and of their 'vision of angels', who said that 'he was alive'. But as yet the apostles had no explanation to offer. Peter and John had gone to see for themselves. They had brought back confirmation of the report that the tomb was empty, but they had seen neither angels nor him whom they were said to have declared alive. And, although the two on the Emmaus Road had evidently left the circle of the disciples, if not Jerusalem before Mary came, yet we know that even her account did not carry conviction to the minds of those that heard it.

Of the two we know that one bore the name of Cleopas. The other, unnamed, could, for that very reason – and because the narrative of that work bears in its vividness the character of personal recollection – possibly be identified with Luke himself.

A mysterious stranger joined the two. For all these six or seven miles their conversation had been of him and even now their flushed faces bore the marks of sadness on account of those events of which they had been speaking. To the question from the stranger, they replied in language which shows that they were so absorbed by it themselves, they scarcely understood how a festive pilgrim and stranger in Jerusalem could have failed to know it, or understand its supreme importance.

Edersheim then unpacks the event:

Yet, strangely unsympathetic as from his question he might seem, there was that in his appearance which unlocked their inmost hearts. They told him their thoughts about this Jesus. Their words were almost childlike in their simplicity, deeply truthful, and with a pathos and earnest craving for guidance and comfort that goes straight to the heart. To such souls it was, that the Risen Saviour would give his first teaching.

He spoke it and fresh hope sprang up in their hearts, new thoughts rose in their minds. Their eager gaze was fastened on him as he now opened up, one by one, the Scriptures, from Moses and all the prophets and in each well-remembered passage interpreted to them the things concerning himself. Oh, that we had been there to hear – though in silence of our hearts also, if only we crave for it, and if we walk with him. The brief space was traversed and the Stranger seemed about to pass on from Emmaus. But they could not part with him. 'They constrained him.' Love made them ingenious. It was towards evening; the day was far spent; he must even abide with them. What rush of thought and feeling comes to us, as we think of it all, and try to realise time, scenes, circumstances in our experience, that are blessedly akin to it. The Master allowed himself to be constrained. He went in to be their guest, as they thought, for the night. The simple evening-meal was spread. He sat down with them to the frugal board.

And now he was no longer the Stranger; he was the Master. No one asked, or questioned, as he took the bread and spoke the words of blessing then, breaking, gave it to them. But that moment it was as if an unfelt Hand had been taken from their eyelids, as if suddenly the film had been cleared from their sight. And as they knew him. He vanished from their view – for that which he had come to do had been done. They were unspeakably rich and happy now. But, amidst it all, one thing forced itself ever anew upon them, that, even while their eyes had yet beholden, their hearts had burned within them, while he spoke to them and opened to them the Scriptures.

1 CORINTHIANS 15:5; MARK 16:14; LUKE 24:36-43; JOHN 20:19-25

That same afternoon the Lord had appeared to Peter, but we are not given any extra information here. These two in Emmaus could not have kept the good tidings to themselves. So they left the uneaten meal and hastened back along the road they had travelled with the now well-known stranger – but with what lighter hearts and steps! They met the apostles, though Thomas was not with the others on that evening of the first 'Lord's Day'.

When the two from Emmaus arrived they found the little band as sheep sheltering within the fold from the storm. Whether they expected persecution simply as disciples, or because the story of the empty tomb, which had reached the authorities, would stir the fears of the Sanhedrists, special precautions had been taken. The outer and inner doors were shut, both to conceal their gathering and to prevent surprise. But those assembled were now sure of at least one thing. *Christ has risen.* And when they from Emmaus told their wondrous story, the others could reply by relating how he had appeared, not only to Mary but also to Peter.

And still, they seemed not yet to have understood his resurrection. They were sitting at a meal, discussing, in their state of confusion, the real importance of these appearances of Jesus. But all at once, he 'stood in the midst of them' (KJV). Were they gazing on 'a ghost'? This was unmistakably Jesus, demonstrated by the marks of his sacred wounds and he readily joined their supper of broiled fish.

Once more he spoke the 'Peace be with you!' and now it was to them an emblem of faith, the well-known greeting of their old Lord and Master. It was followed by the regathering and constitution of the Church as that of Jesus Christ, the risen one. The apostles were commissioned to carry on Christ's work, and not to begin a new one.

And so it was that he made it a very real commission when he breathed on them, not individually but as an assembly and said, 'Receive the Holy Spirit' and this not in the absolute sense, since the Holy Spirit was not yet given, but as the connecting link with and the qualification for the authority bestowed on the Church.

JOHN 20:26-29

Thomas had been absent from the circle of disciples on that evening. Even when told of the marvellous events at that gathering, he refused to believe unless he had personal evidence of the truth of the report. It can scarcely have been that Thomas did not believe in the fact that Christ's body had left the tomb, or that he had really appeared. But until this apostle was also convinced of the resurrection it was impossible to reform the apostolic circle. This seems to be the reason why the apostles still remained in Jerusalem, instead of hastening, as directed, to meet the Master in Galilee.

MATTHEW 28:16; JOHN 21:1-24

The scene moves to the Lake of Galilee. The manifestation to Thomas and the restoration of unity in the apostolic circle had occurred. On that morning there were only seven apostles by the lake. Five of them only are named. They are those who most closely kept in company with him – perhaps also they who lived nearest the lake. The scene is introduced by Peter's proposal to go fishing. It seems as if the old habits had come back to them with the old associations. Peter's companions naturally proposed to join him. All that still, clear night they were on the lake but caught nothing. Then there stood the figure of one whom they did not recognise, not even when he spoke. Yet his words were intended to bring them this knowledge. The direction to cast the net to the right side of the ship brought them, as he had said, the haul for which they had toiled all night in vain.

They stepped onto the beach. They dared not even dispose of the netful of fishes which they had dragged on to the shore until he directed them what to do. And now Jesus directed them to bring the fish they had caught. When Peter dragged up the net, it was found full of great fish, not less than a 153 in number. There is no need to attach any symbolic importance to that number, as the Church Fathers and later writers have done. This, as John notes, was the third appearance of Christ to the disciples as a body.

And still, this morning of blessing was not ended. Attention moved to Peter. Had Peter not confessed, quite honestly yet, as the event proved, mistakenly, that his love for Christ would endure even an ordeal that would disperse all the others? And had he not, almost immediately afterwards and though prophetically warned of it, three times denied his Lord? It was to this that the three-fold question to the risen Lord now referred. Turning to Peter, with gentle irony mixed with personal affection, Jesus asked: 'Simon son of John, do you love me more than these?'

'Yes, Lord ... you know that I love you.' And even here the answer of Christ is characteristic. It was to set him first the humblest work, that which needed most tender care and patience: 'Feed my lambs.' Yet a second time came the same question, although now without the reference to the others and then a third time did Jesus repeat the same question. Peter was grieved at this three-fold repetition. It recalled only too bitterly his three-fold denial.

Yes, and Peter did love the Lord Jesus. He had loved him when he said it, only too confident in the strength of his feelings, that he would follow the Master even to death.[83] And Jesus saw it all.

MATTHEW 28:17-20; MARK 16:15-20

Beyond this narrative we have only the briefest of accounts: by Paul, of Jesus manifesting himself to James, the Lord's brother,[84] which probably finally convinced him to believe in him, and the Eleven meeting him at the mountain, where he had appointed them; by Luke, of the teaching in the Scriptures during the forty days of communication between the risen Christ and the disciples. But this two-fold testimony comes to us from Matthew and Mark, that then the worshipping disciples were once more formed into the apostolic circle – apostles, now, of the risen Christ.

And this was the warrant of their new commission: 'All authority in heaven and on earth has been given to me.' And this was their new

---

83. Matthew 26:33-35.

84. 1 Corinthians 15:7.

commission: 'Therefore go and make disciples of all nations, baptising them in the name of the Father and of the Son and of the Holy Spirit', and this was their work: 'teaching them to obey everything I have commanded you.' This is his final and sure promise: 'And surely I am with you always, to the very end of the age.'

1 CORINTHIANS 15:6; LUKE 24:44-53

We are once more in Jerusalem, where he had told them to go to tarry for the fulfilment of the great promise. Pentecost (*Shavuot*, to be specific) was drawing close. And on that last day – the day of his ascension – he led them on to Bethany. From here he had made his last triumphal entry into Jerusalem before his crucifixion; now would he make his triumphant entry visibly into heaven. Once more would they have asked him about that which seemed to them the final consummation – the restoration of the kingdom to Israel. But it wasn't the time for such questions. Theirs was to be work, not rest; suffering, not triumph. The great promise before them was of spiritual, not outward, power of the Holy Spirit – and their call not yet to reign with him, but to bear witness for him.

MARK 16:19-20; ACTS 1:3-12

And, as he so spoke, he lifted his hands in blessing upon them and, as he was visibly taken up, a cloud received him. And still they gazed, with upturned faces, on that luminous cloud which had received him and two angels spoke to them this last message from him, that he should 'so come in like manner' (KJV) as they had beheld him going into heaven.

Reverently they worshipped him; then, with great joy, returned to Jerusalem. So it was all true, all real and Christ 'sat at the right hand of God'. Henceforth, neither doubting, ashamed, nor yet afraid, they were 'continually at the temple, praising God', 'And they went forth, and preached every where, the Lord working with them, and confirming the word with signs following. Amen' (KJV).

The last words belong, quite rightly, to Alfred Edersheim, that incredible servant of God who has blessed us all with his astute, Godly observations and conclusions:

Amen! It is so. Ring out the bells of heaven; sing forth the Angelic welcome of worship; carry it to the utmost bound of earth! Shine forth from Bethany, Thou Sun of Righteousness, and chase away earth's mist and darkness, for heaven's golden day has broken! This Easter Morning, our task is ended and we also worship and look up. And we go back from this sight into a hostile world, to love, and to live, and to work for Risen Christ. But as earth's day is growing dim, and, with earth's gathering darkness, breaks over it heaven's storm, we ring out – as of old they were wont, from church-tower, to the mariners that hugged a rock-bound coast – our Easter-bells to guide them who are belated, over the storm-tossed sea, beyond the breakers, into the desired haven. Ring out, earth, all thy Easter-chimes; bring you offerings, all ye people; worship in faith, for – 'This Jesus, When was received up from you into heaven, shall so come, in like manner as ye beheld him going into heaven.'
'Even so, Lord Jesus, come quickly!'

Epilogue

What a ride this has been! Alfred Edersheim's book has blessed me more than any other and taught me so much about the real world of Jesus as he struggled against those who wished to muzzle him. I just hope that I have done it justice, bearing in mind that I had to jettison 80 per cent of the original material to shoehorn the epic story of *The Life and Times of Jesus the Messiah* into this shorter volume, as well as being tied up in knots by some of his convoluted nineteenth-century sentence structures!

It amazed me, when reading his Preface to the second and third edition of his book, that he had to counter some charges placed against him for being – believe it or not – anti-Semitic in his presented material. It was felt that perhaps he was being a little too harsh on his 'co-religionists', the Jewish religious authorities at the time of Jesus. This hurt him deeply and he felt he had to refute these incorrect objections, which he did clearly, methodically and effectively.

His perceived harshness on the scribes and Pharisees was well-founded because it was clear that once Satan had failed to deflect Jesus from his moral purpose in the wilderness, Plan B was to set up the Jewish religious authorities with their skewed and ungodly traditions as his representatives in the *conflict of kingdoms*. They failed because Jesus was always in control of the narrative, right up to the end, and ensured the *triumph of mercy* in this 'Greatest Story ever told'.

There's an important point to make on this. Bearing in mind that as we read the Gospels now, we enter the world of first-century Israel and get sucked into the story to various degrees. This can have a negative effect if unconsciously (or perhaps even consciously) we follow the narrative as if it literally equates to our modern world. The conflict of kingdoms may have been between Jesus and the Rabbinical Judaism of his day, but it isn't the case now. Satan has found many representatives these days to act on his behalf, from other religions to philosophies and lifestyles, in the *kingdom of the world*. The Jewish people of today are not the enemy, though there may still be many in the Church who perhaps believe otherwise. Rabbinical Judaism sadly obscures the light of the gospel from its own people, but it has no effect on the world at large. It is my hope that this book may help to perhaps spur some of you on to greater efforts to present Jesus to any Jewish people God may place on your path.

May the Lord bless you as you mull over anything new he may have taught you through reading this re-telling of Edersheim's classic. It certainly gave me a new perspective, particularly on the inner struggles that Jesus had to face and the wonderful ways that he dealt with them, turning them to the advantage of his moral purpose in the kingdom of God. This cannot fail to impress, along with the great sacrifice he made for us. How can someone not be touched by such love?

'But God demonstrates his own love for us in this: while we were still sinners, Christ died for us' (Romans 5:8).

Appendix: The Life and Times of Alfred Edersheim

———

(The following is adapted mainly from *Alfred Edersheim*, by Marianna Edwards Richardson)[85]

The great man was born on 7 March 1825, the youngest of four children in a Jewish family living in Vienna, Austria. His father was a Dutch banker and his mother was from a wealthy German family. He was brought up to appreciate the arts and intellectual pursuits and also to be fluent in three languages, including English.

He was a clever and lively lad and did well in his studies, attending a private school as well as a Jewish school attached to the local synagogue, where he learned Hebrew, Jewish culture and history as well as the Jewish Scriptures.

In 1841 he enrolled at the University of Vienna to study philosophy but left before the end of his course, owing to his father's financial reversal. Instead, he moved to Pest in Hungary and continued his studies there, self-financed. He met a Scottish chaplain, John Duncan, who was attempting to set up a mission to Jews, and took a job with him as a German tutor and translator. They became friends and Alfred was introduced to the New Testament. His eyes were opened by the Sermon on the Mount and the teachings of Jesus and he happily entered the kingdom of God!

The Hebrew Scriptures now came alive for him, as he re-evaluated the Old Testament as a follower of Jesus. He remarked on the unity and continuity in the teaching of the Old Testament and how all of it speaks of Christ. His life was turned around and refocused and he dedicated the rest of his days to strengthening his brethren by becoming

---

85. Marianna Edwards Richardson, *Alfred Edersheim: Jewish Scholar for the Mormon Prophets* (Springville, UT: Cedar Fort, 2008).

a preacher, a missionary and a writer of spiritual insights on the Old and New Testament.

His studies were now focused on theology and he was also baptised into the Church of Scotland. He moved to Edinburgh and in 1843 began his studies there under the watchful eye of John Duncan, who was the chair of oriental languages. The following year he went to the University of Berlin to conduct research and became acquainted with a fellow Jewish believer, Professor Johann Neander, who took him under his wing.

In 1846 he gained a theological degree and was ordained to the ministry, now the Free Church of Scotland, where he preached in four small parishes in Edinburgh. He was a good, effective and popular preacher and people loved to hear him speak, with his love of life and Jewish humour. Later that year he felt the call to work with his fellow Jews as a missionary and took a year out to travel to Moldavia, to work with the Russian Jewish population there. It was there that he met his future wife, Mary, a fellow missionary to the Jews and also from Scotland. They married in 1848.

They settled in Aberdeen and he ministered in the Old Aberdeen parish until 1860, also teaching in the local university. It was there that his writing career started to take off. In 1860 his health took a downturn, so the family moved to Torquay in Devon, with its warmer climate. He founded a thriving church there and they stayed in the area for another ten years. His writing career was on hold at this time because of his ministry and it was in this period that their beloved daughter, Ella, was born. In 1868 his brother, Julius, accepted Christ and joined his congregation. But it was also a sad time. His wife, Mary, died, leaving Alfred with eight daughters and a son to bring up. He remarried quickly within a year. His new wife was Sophia, the youngest daughter of a local admiral.

In 1870 his health problems necessitated a trip to warmer parts of Europe, but they persisted and he was forced to resign his position in Torquay. This was a troubling time for him, emotionally as well as physically, having to leave the church that he had founded. The family then moved to Bournemouth.

Alfred was responsible for many insightful and valuable books, (such as *The Temple: Its Ministry and Services at the time of Jesus Christ, Sketches of Jewish Social Life in the Days of Christ* and *Bible History: Old Testament*) but none more so than *The Life and Times of Jesus the Messiah*. It was published in 1883 and in his Preface he stated, 'All my previous studies were really in preparation for this.' It took him seven years of solitude in a remote village to accomplish this, his *magnum opus* and he was greatly helped by his daughter Ella.

Alfred Edersheim died on 18 March 1889 at the age of sixty-four in Mentone on the Italian Riviera. He was living there to help with his ailing health, and he loved the place because it reminded him of the Holy Land. His death was totally unexpected and his last written words were unfinished: 'We are reproached that we treat not the historical documents of the Bible in exactly the same manner as the ordinary history of those times in which the miraculous and the legendary are accepted. Now there are two points of view ...'

He leaves us hanging here but not so in the rest of his writings, which have blessed so many of us and provided us not just with points of view, but absolute clarity and direction. His legacy remains undiminished and long may it be so.

May his memory be a blessing.